Additional Praise for
Fiscal Hangover

"As a historical account of what went so badly wrong, *Fiscal Hangover* is an excellent read. Keith Fitz-Gerald, however, goes a lot further and lays out a road map showing you how to profit from the greatest industrialization program the world has ever seen. China is booming and is no longer content simply being the factory to the world. Keith Fitz-Gerald makes it possible for even the smallest retail investor to take advantage of this secular, once-in-a-lifetime growth story. If you're serious about taking charge of your own financial destiny, you need to read this book."
> —Kishore K. Sakhrani, Director, ICS Trust (Asia) Ltd.

"The wheels are in motion. There is no turning back. In his book *Fiscal Hangover*, Keith Fitz-Gerald not only makes the case for the coming financial catastrophe that we are all facing in the West, but also provides the solutions that we can implement today to deflect the inevitable. This is a must read if you are serious about your money . . . and more serious about keeping it!"
> —Karim Rahemtulla, Investment Director,
> Mt. Vernon Research

"*Fiscal Hangover* is easy to read and even easier to understand. Any investor serious about not only recovering his money but growing it in the years ahead will find *Fiscal Hangover* worth reading. A must read, actually."
> —John Casti, Senior Research Scholar, IIASA;
> Cofounder, The Kenos Circle, Vienna

"Keith Fitz-Gerald is my go-to guy when it comes to investing in Asia. Keith lays out the future in terms you can understand and, more importantly, use to profit. You would be well served to read Keith's new book."
> —Doug Fabian, President, Fabian Wealth Strategies;
> Editor, *Making Money Alert*

"This is a terrific book. Keith combines the skills of persuasive big picture analyst, finger firmly on the pulse of today's global megatrends, with the technical discipline of an in-the-trenches trader with over two decades of experience making money in the financial markets. 'Those who can, do teach,' after all."
> —Nicholas Vardy, President, Hayek Capital;
> Executive Director, London Junto;
> Editor, *Global Stock Investor*

"In this insightful book, Keith shows readers why it is more important than ever for American investors to invest in high-growth economies such as China. I highly recommend it!"
> —Robert Hsu, Editor, *China Strategy* and *Asia Edge*;
> Managing Director, Absolute Return Capital Advisors;
> Author, *China Fireworks*

"In my 30 years of monitoring the financial newsletter industry, there is no advisor I would recommend more strongly for his integrity, track record, research skills, and investment insights than Keith Fitz-Gerald. Anyone looking to create a portfolio designed to meet the challenges of the future, prepare against risk, and be positioned to benefit from the opportunities offered in emerging markets will find no better guide for success."
> —Steven Halpern, TheStockAdvisors.com

"A fascinating book that will help investors see the world through the lens of the future. A must read for those who want to profit from the next era of wealth creation."
> —Ted Haberfield, Executive Vice President,
> HC International, Inc.

The Readers Speak

Instead of loading up with celebrity comments, we thought you'd enjoy hearing from a few of Keith's long-time readers—people just like you. So, here you go.

"I've been reading Keith Fitz-Gerald's sage and clever writings for years. It's rare to find someone who presents complex, global market concepts with such approachability and wit, and his insights are always well-considered, well-informed, and a pleasure to read. I continue to follow his lead, as he's made me a more thoughtful, profitable investor. He's undoubtedly well on his way to becoming one of the luminaries in the industry."

—Matthew Coble

"The combination of talent and discipline makes a hero. Keith is a hero in his profession and in life. He applies these virtues diligently and continuously. The result? An exceptional human being and brilliant work! Outstanding investment analysis; track record of profitable picks; amazingly accurate economic prediction; and sometimes jokes about the market. . . . Why do I continue to subscribe? I need to have the confidence of investment, knowing I pick the right ones. I love the lively inspiration that Keith brings to life: the drive to excel in everything you are into."

—Hairong Karen Gui

"Keith is like a light in the darkness of the current investing world morass. He is the Rogue Warrior™ of investment professionals, blazing his own trail, and defying conventional wisdom. Why do I continue to subscribe? Well, what better testament to Keith than the fact that as my friends got hammered when the markets fell, my portfolio didn't fall very far, and on top of that, it has already returned to pre-fall levels and beyond as it continues to grow! I want someone I can trust and Keith is the man. He's honest and not afraid to tell it like it is. You can't ask for more than that."

—Doug O'Connor

FISCAL HANGOVER

FISCAL HANGOVER

*How to Profit from the
New Global Economy*

KEITH FITZ-GERALD

WILEY

John Wiley & Sons, Inc.

For general information on our other products and services or for technical
support, please contact our Customer Care Department within the
United States at (800) 762-2974, outside the United States at (317) 572-3993
or fax (317) 572-4002.

Wiley also publishes its books in a variety of electronic formats. Some content
that appears in print may not be available in electronic books. For more
information about Wiley products, visit our web site at www.wiley.com.

ISBN 978-0-470-28914-3

Printed in the United States of America

10 9 8 7 6 5 4 3 2 1

*This book is for
the millions of disillusioned investors
around the world who,
despite being taken on a white-knuckle ride
they didn't deserve,
know that the way forward is through
a better understanding of how we got here
and what it will take to get ahead in the new global economy—
if only someone would show them the way.*

Never fear shadows. They simply mean there is a light shining somewhere nearby.

—*Ruth E. Renkel*

CONTENTS

ACKNOWLEDGMENTS

As a writer, this book is clearly an extension of me. But without others, it simply wouldn't have been possible.

When I sat down with my publisher, Mike Ward, in a little Thai restaurant tucked off Monument Square in Baltimore a few years back, and we shared the vision that has become the Money Map Press of today, it sounded fantastic. Almost too good to be true. Yet, here we are now, with 500,000 readers each day in 30 countries around the world. I have Mike to thank for that—not only for his professional judgment as my executive publisher, but for his friendship, his integrity, and his wisdom. All are increasingly rare qualities in today's world.

I also have to thank my wife, Noriko, and my boys, Kunihiko and Kazuhiko. Without their support and constant encouragement, this simply would not have been possible. Then there's my assistant, Sid Riggs, who has gone to great lengths to understand my voice and my madness, as has Larry D. Spears, for whom the pen truly is mightier than any sword (or derivative investment) will ever be.

Thanks also go to the entire team at Agora Publishing and Money Map Press. All the long hours we've spent together analyzing markets, ferreting out the truth about money, crafting stories, and then getting them into the hands of investors who deserve that truth are somehow worth more than ever. I am eternally grateful for the excellence you bring to the table each day, as well as the friendships we enjoy.

And to my friends in the business; you know who you are. The years of wisdom and experience you poured into me have not gone unnoticed—or unappreciated.

Finally, to the hundreds of thousands of Money Map Press "family" members across the world who regularly read my work and who take time out of your busy schedules to see me at conferences around the globe, this book is as much yours as it is mine. I am honored and humbled by the trust you place in me.

Keith Fitz-Gerald

FISCAL HANGOVER

INTRODUCTION

A REFRESHER COURSE IN GRANNY'S WISDOM

Never forget, the world is bigger than your backyard.

—Virginia Gruner

It was 1980 and, though I didn't know it at the time, the seeds of my financial career were being planted in my head during an afternoon discussion with my grandmother, Virginia Gruner. We were sitting in her den over ham sandwiches and milk—her favorite.

Because I wanted to travel the world as she had done, and because I was precociously interested in anything that had to do with money, she had seen to it that I was always fed a diet of *Forbes* magazine and *The Wall Street Journal*. I even managed, at the tender age of 15, to make quick work of *Barron's* each Saturday, and to read my annual *Value Line* binder from cover to cover almost as soon as I received it.

Every time I wanted to make an investment using money I had saved up from summer jobs (I was quite the neighborhood lawn baron), I got the whole nine yards from Mimi, which was my pet name for her.

"Do you really understand what you're buying? How does it fit with what you already own, and what purpose is it serving in your portfolio?" she would ask.

Of course, being young and headstrong, I really didn't understand her overbearing concerns. But, boy, did I learn quickly.

My grandmother had been widowed early, and her husband left her with only a small sum of money to raise both my aunt and my mother. By her own admission, she knew nothing about the markets when she first began investing. But, by virtue of necessity, she set out to learn everything she could about finances and how to make her money grow. She became so skilled at investing that, in effect, she became a financial planner before there *were* financial planners. She also understood modern portfolio theory before it was modern.

For years, I thought she was simply better at picking stocks than everybody else. It was only much later in my life, once I formally began my career at Wilshire Associates, that I came to realize what she really understood better than anybody is something that's only beginning to be understood now by most investors.

"Keith," she used to say, "it's not the way you diversify your money that matters, but the way you concentrate it that leads to bigger, more consistent returns—particularly when it comes to capturing the best the *world* has to offer."

And that's why I've written this book—the one I could never have imagined writing all those years ago.

A PERFECT TIME FOR MIMI'S LESSONS

The way I see it, we've arrived at a unique time and place in history in which the lessons I learned from Mimi—lessons that have been reinforced over my last 20-something years in the markets—couldn't be more relevant. Yet sadly, these lessons are very poorly understood by most investors.

Thanks to a series of boom-and-bust cycles brought on by the greatest credit inflation of all time, the world has recently borne witness to the single largest spree of wealth destruction in recorded market history. Over $30 trillion in value was essentially vaporized—in less than a year! And, though a modest market rebound has taken place, many investors are understandably still frightened out of their wits and beset with feelings of helplessness. Still others feel shafted by the system and are very, very angry.

I don't blame them one bit.

Not only did relatively few people make huge piles of money with borderline fraudulent—if not outright illegal—financial manipulation, but virtually the entire establishment, which was supposed to prevent such things from happening, was asleep at the switch. Adding insult to injury, the powers-that-be ignored a constant stream of warning signs and displayed a callous disregard for reality, as well as repeated suggestions from those few folks like me who dared to contend that these fiscal emperors had no clothes.

Thanks to the Establishment and the millions of people who blindly bought into it, Americans are likely to pull in their fiscal horns for at least a generation. I think the United States will be fortunate to see its economy grow 2 percent year over year—and that kind of slow growth could be around for decades. As profit margins crumble—and as government bailouts of the private sector go on for much longer than people expected—there is clearly a new *normal* in the financial markets, one most investors are ill-equipped to grapple with.

Still, as bad as it sounds, there is a flip side to the slow-growth coin. It's the side that, thankfully, speaks to how much we have to gain as investors once we recognize what the new normal looks like. This new reality—this realization that we're now groping with what is essentially a "fiscal hangover"—has me more excited than I've ever been before about the markets.

You see, history shows that periods of great turmoil are inevitably followed by a time of tremendous wealth creation. To be fair, I don't know precisely when our economy will fully recover from this hangover. Nobody does. But a quick review of the data suggests it *will* happen, just as sure as the sun will come up tomorrow—and, ironically enough, the recovery will likely come when most people least expect it.

KEY QUESTIONS TO ADDRESS NOW

Therefore, the most important questions in my mind, and in the minds of savvy investors the world over, are: What do we do now to protect and grow our assets, and how do we make sure our money is prepared for maximum profitability when we do come out of this mess?

Fortunately, accomplishing this feat is not as tall an order as you might think. Contrary to what most people believe, the credit crisis we've experienced is not entirely different from other periods in history. It just feels different to most of us now because what has taken place recently is unique to the vast majority of today's investors.

This time around, the market participants haven't changed. Nor is there some new technology that's caused market realignment. Instead, the very rules of money itself have changed, and so has everything that drives those rules. Investors who hope to preserve and even grow their wealth in the years ahead must adapt to these new rules of money.

As I tell the hundreds of thousands of readers of my weekly columns, and the thousands of investors who sit in on my presentations around the world each year, the risks of success have never been higher than they are today. Unfortunately, neither have the opportunities for failure.

You might think I mean the "opportunities for success" and the "risks of failure"—but I don't. We have reached a point at which the upside we want to achieve *must* take a backseat to the risks we want to avoid.

Part of adapting to the world's new money rules begins with the recognition that events taking place thousands of miles from America's borders will more likely than not dictate all we know about investing for years to come. These events will affect every asset class on the planet.

This is why the investors who are most successful in the next few years will be those who come to terms soonest with the fact that the credit crisis aftermath is likely to produce positive, profitable changes away from the so-called "modern" industrialized nations and their large-scale fiscal imbalances. It will instead drive newly emerging economies to increasing roles of importance and relevance in the global marketplace.

People have paid lip service to this for years, so I'll just be blunt. Nearly 75 percent of the world's economic activity now takes place *outside* the United States. And it's only going to get *more* unbalanced, for one simple reason: Worldwide investments are expected to double to more than $300 trillion in the next 5 to 10 years—and better than half of that is likely to come from outside mature markets like the United States and Japan.

A PREVIEW OF YOUR ROAD MAP TO SUCCESS: *GO GLOBAL OR GO HOME*

This new reality means you've got to make a vitally important decision right now. You must either go global, or go home.

In Part I of this book, we take a brief journey through history, examining how the United States grew to be the dominant economic force in the world and how American consumerism created a model for spenders around the globe. We then look at some of the crucial things that began to go wrong amid a drunken economic binge that ultimately set the credit, real estate, and financial markets reeling, resulting in the fiscal hangover we're now living through.

Then we move on to Part II, where you'll learn that the recent period of turmoil is hardly the world's first era of catastrophic change. You'll see why the current crisis is nothing more than a replay of similar transformational events in history, albeit with different causal factors. And, you'll discover that virtually every other great crisis has been followed by a period of dramatic "redeployment," in which substantial amounts of wealth were created—a fact that should help melt away much of your anxiety.

Then, we turn to Part III, where you'll learn why global markets truly do follow the money, and why the odds are very high that global investing is the way out of the financial mess so many investors are in.

And, finally, I show you how to structure a simple, internationally concentrated portfolio with built-in safety brakes that you can maintain with very little time and just a little bit of effort. If you're nearing retirement, or if you are already retired, I show you how to find stable, income-producing investments without taking on more risk than you can handle. I also share a few of my favorite battle-tested tactics. After reading this section, you'll be unlikely to buy any stock the same way ever again.

By the time we're done, you will have everything you need to know to successfully manage your own money using a simple, consistent framework that increases your returns, reduces your risk, and gives you the potential to outperform most other investors.

In my mind, it doesn't matter whether you're in your early 20s, late 60s, or well beyond. It also doesn't matter whether you're a novice investor or consider yourself an expert. The way I see it, we're all in this together.

That's why I've chosen this time to write this book. I firmly believe that, as bad as things seem, there is never a wrong time to do the right thing, both in my personal life and in my investing activity. To that end, I can assure you that the recommendations in this book are, with only a rare exception, the exact actions I am now taking or will take at the appropriate time.

But let me warn you right up front . . . these recommendations will require you to do something that *always* makes Wall Street cringe—which is to *think for yourself.*

I'll consider this book a success if you do three things when you're done reading it:

1. Understand what I am saying (because you're sure as heck not going to get the truth about money from traditional Wall Street sources).
2. Develop new knowledge or reconsider subjects about which you thought you already knew a lot.
3. Use that information to build a more prosperous and successful future. After all, if you can't build more wealth—and then keep it—what's the point?

I have absolutely no doubt that the current financial crisis has rewritten the rules of money and investing. But it is also generating a whole host of new profit plays—plays that literally represent the beginnings of a new Golden Age of Wealth Creation.

Investors who ignore this new reality will get left behind—but if you have the courage and conviction to press ahead, using the strategies you'll find in the pages ahead, you could well find this to be *the greatest profit opportunity of your lifetime.*

The world, as Mimi would say, truly will be "our oyster."

PART ONE

AMERICA'S FISCAL HANGOVER AND THE BINGE THAT GOT US HERE

Shhhhhhhhhh!!

Don't turn those pages so loudly!!

Can't you see we've got a splitting headache? Look at how our hands are shaking. We ache all over, our stomach's upset, and we keep getting nauseated at the mere thought of investing again.

We've tried to figure out what happened, but our brain is clouded, our eyes are blurry, and the whole picture is fuzzy . . . kind of out of focus.

One minute, we were cruising along in our big, secure financial SUV. The economic engine was purring smoothly, the road ahead appeared clear and the GPS indicated we were on course toward future prosperity. Then, in what seemed like a matter of minutes, the road got very bumpy, peppered with potholes to dodge. We slowed down, then stopped, and when we looked around, it was like we'd plowed straight into the world's biggest fraternity party on a Saturday night.

The house we entered was full of bankers and brokers, who had gotten drunk with greed and were now staggering around a floor littered with foreclosed mortgages and worthless stock certificates. They were being chased by whole committees of politicians and regulators, some confused after being roused from prolonged complacency, others still drunk with power, and all now frantically looking for a way out.

Cries for designated drivers to take us safely home went unanswered as a whole string of Presidents, past and present, were accused of drunken and reckless driving, while both Federal Reserve and Treasury officials were facing multiple counts of drunk and disorderly behavior.

It was utter chaos.

Overcome by fear and uncertainty, we scrambled back out to our car. (Fortunately, it was a Toyota Prius since the Chevrolets, Cadillacs, Chryslers, and Jeeps had all stopped running and the Fords were sputtering on dwindling drops of $5.00-a-gallon gas.) We threw it into reverse and hauled our shrinking assets back to where we'd come from—and far, far beyond.

Now, it's the morning of a new day and we're sitting here, aching heads in shaky hands, suffering from this dreadful Fiscal Hangover—a painful reminder of last night's binge, a hangover that's afflicting not just us, but most of the rest of the world as well. We're searching for a cure, trying to figure out how we can regain fiscal sobriety and once again start moving back toward financial health—and future wealth.

But our prognosis remains uncertain. The only thing that's absolutely, 100 percent clear is that we *don't* need more of the hair of the dog that bit us. We need a different medicine, something new, something that's both safe *and* highly effective. But where do we find one?

Perhaps if we turn the page . . . (quietly, please).

CHAPTER 1

HISTORY 101

From 13 Colonies to Global Economic Power

Histories make men wise.

—Sir Francis Bacon

To fully understand where America's economy is going in the future—and how you can best profit from that journey—you really need to know how it got to where it is today. However, since I'm sure you didn't intend to sign on for a history degree when you picked up this book, I'll do my best to keep it brief.

Boil the economic development of the United States down to 25 words or less, and it comes to this: Adversity happens. People adapt. Innovation pops. Wealth results.

That's it—with 17 words to spare.

Wise men say there's no better teacher than experience, and U.S. history assures me, time and again, that no matter how bad things get, they *will* get better, leaving us with even more chances to achieve even greater wealth than we ever had before.

To prove it—and begin getting you back on the road to personal financial recovery—I want to start back at the country's beginnings, track the emergence of U.S. economic power over the last 300 years, and review the actions earlier investors took to overcome their challenges and reach the next level of prosperity. (Unbeknownst to most modern investors—and the majority of Wall Street "pros"—U.S. hegemony actually dates back to pre-Colonial days.)

Then, we can strategize proactively on how to catch the next monster-wealth wave—moving on to Parts II and III of this book, where I detail some of my preferred investment strategies, share some of the "dirty little tricks of the trade" I regularly employ, and offer some specific recommendations to help you more wisely and successfully navigate your way in today's perilous financial waters.

IN THE BEGINNING, THERE WAS . . .

The modern American economy traces its roots to the quest of European settlers for economic gain—not just religious freedom—in the sixteenth, seventeenth, and eighteenth centuries. Actually, Vikings were the first Europeans to "discover" North America, in the year A.D. 998. A Norse sailor named Bjarni stumbled on Greenland after being blown off course on his way to Iceland. But, since the Viking livelihood, like most of Europe's, was then centered primarily on agriculture, land ownership, and the occasional pillaging and plundering, the possibility of expanding Scandinavian trade really wasn't foremost in their minds. Land-grabbing and settlements were—but, in the end, they abandoned even that.

Fast forward about 500 years to 1492, when Christopher Columbus—an Italian sailing under a Spanish flag (investors were thinking multinational even then)—chucked the idea that the world must be flat and sailed forth to find a southwest route to the spicy-priced goods of Asia.

Surprise! Columbus bumped into a "New World" instead—igniting a 100-year "place race" of exploration by the English, Spanish, Portuguese, Dutch, and French, all trying to beat one another out in their pursuit of gold, silver, and untold other riches.

Unfortunately, early explorers found little more in North America than some crazy weather, what today is prime beachfront property, and tribes of indigenous peoples, whom they mistakenly called "Indians," thinking they had actually reached India instead of a strange New World. These indigenous Americans enjoyed simple lives, engaging in hunting, gathering, and growing. They traded among themselves and had virtually no contact with the rest of the world before their economies were profoundly and forever altered by the arrival of their "discoverers" and the ensuing influx of European fur traders, firearms, and other wares.

Early colonists had scores of reasons for coming to the Americas—led by the Pilgrims, who famously sought to escape religious persecution. But it was the opportunity for economic advancement that brought most European colonists to the New World. In fact, colonies such as Virginia, founded primarily as business ventures, capitalized nicely on the dovetailing of piety and prosperity.

Governor William Bradford of Plymouth Rock fame, operating in survival mode in the midst of a killer first year, decided to embrace the idea of "individual initiative"—the forebear (or underlying principle, if you prefer) of true capitalism. He harnessed the power of the Puritan work ethic and granted each family its own plot to farm, a seismic shift in economic thinking for 1620. Changing the economic rules from communal to private farming allowed everyone—religious zealot to adventurer to indentured servant—equal opportunity to reap the rewards of their own hard labor (or lack thereof) instead of settling for a proportionate share of the whole. And it worked!

Later, England's brilliant use of charter companies to settle the New World gave each group of stockholders—usually merchants and wealthy landowners—a vested interest in making its colony a thriving economic success. They also got political and judicial powers—and the undying gratitude of their King for furthering his own expansionist agenda.

The system experienced a hiccup when many of the monied investors, quickly tiring of life in a luxury-free wilderness, withdrew back to England, abandoning their charters to settlers, who basically had to figure out how to build something out of nothing—or starve.

Once again, individual initiative grabbed hold and marginally successful farms became hugely profitable by raising highly addictive crops like sugar and tobacco. British demand for colonial crops skyrocketed, "American entrepreneurialism" soared and a brave, new middle-class America emerged.

BIRTH OF A CONSUMER NATION

Soon, specialized mills, shipyards, and iron forges developed to support growing trade. By the eighteenth century, standards of living in the 13 colonies (except for slaves) outstripped those in England. New World prosperity fueled a fierce desire for greater autonomy. As Bradford had recognized 150 years earlier, the people who did all the heavy lifting wanted to enjoy the fruits of their labor—and have a say in how those fruits were spent.

However, that was impossible under the Navigation Acts imposed by Britain in the mid-1600s. The laws, based on the economic system of mercantilism (colonies exist only to serve the Mother Country), decreed that only British ships could carry colonial goods and all exports and imports had to be sold or purchased through Great Britain. Adding insult to injury, colonial manufacturers were forbidden to compete directly with British manufacturers.

The colonists chafed at their wallets. Mother England was increasingly perceived as corrupt and hostile to American economic interests. By 1770, colonial "consumer politics" erupted into open protest against "taxation without representation." Boycotts were creatively staged (think Boston Tea Party) and trade parity was demanded.★

When England refused to be moved, the Revolution was on. The "sovereign United States of America" proclaimed independence on July 4, 1776, in a Declaration that its chief composer, Thomas Jefferson, penned as a singular "expression of the American mind."

The rest, as they say, is history.

★History shows that it was actually Chinese tea that American revolutionaries threw into Boston Harbor in 1773. Daniel Burstein and Arne de Keijzer, *Big Dragon* (Simon & Schuster, 1998), 29.

LIKE THE ECONOMY, FEWER CELEBRATIONS SPARKLE

The roots of America's recent financial problems may not reach all the way back to the founding of our country in 1776, but those troubles have certainly affected our commemoration of that historic event. The skies were quite a bit darker on the evening of July 4, 2009, as budget short-falls forced nearly 50 communities around the country to cancel their public fireworks displays, and many more had to turn to private dona-tions to fund their celebrations. Still other communities chose to show their patriotism in a way more appropriate to the hard times. Montebello, California, canceled its fireworks display and donated the $40,000 the show would have cost to groups distributing food to the needy.

THE INDUSTRIAL REVOLUTION—GO WEST, BY TRAIN, SAY BUY!

The Industrial Revolution arrived almost simultaneously with the end of the American Revolution in 1783, pulling the new nation away from its agrarian roots and pushing it toward industrial domina-tion. But first, after eight years of tortuous warfare, the Founding Fathers needed a prosperity plan.

A national bank was established to assume the public debts incurred (mostly to France) during the war. The Constitution, adopted in 1787, empowered our government to ban taxes on interstate commerce, regulate foreign and domestic trade, create money and set its value, fix standards of weights and measures, and grant patents and copyrights. These new national powers—conceived by the Constitution's primary author, James Madison—were designed to tell the world that America was now one big unified and rapidly growing market.

The advent of industrial machines revolutionized the U.S. econ-omy (and the world) in the late 1700s and early 1800s. It brought major changes to agriculture, manufacturing, mining, printing, and transportation—and major wealth to industrialists and middle-class entrepreneurs who quickly adapted the new technologies. Steam-powered manufacturing made water-powered plants obsolete, freeing up industries previously fettered to the rivers of New England to relocate anywhere they pleased.

Even ordinary laborers benefited on the mass production lines of transformed urban centers. Granted, they suffered under harsh working conditions, and protections against child labor were virtually nil, but concentrating workers into sweatshops and factories soon spawned trade unions, which were organized to improve working conditions and wages through collective bargaining.

Eli Whitney's invention in 1793 of the cotton gin turned a chump-change Southern crop into a booming international market. Wealthy planters bought up land from scratch farmers who, in turn, chose to head west. There, they joined thousands of Yankees who yearned for more fertile Midwestern farmlands rather than rocky Nor'eastern hills.

To facilitate migration and underwrite emerging new agricultural markets, the federal government paid for new national roads and waterways such as the Cumberland Pike (1818) and the Erie Canal (1825)—adding an additional stimulus to the young nation's economy. As new territories were acquired—from Texas to California—technology developed to support expanding domestic trade.

Railroads, in particular, rocked the status quo, opening up vast new American vistas for development. Between 1850 and 1890, rail mileage increased a whopping 1,300 percent (from 9,021 miles to 129,774), transitioning the United States from an agrarian society into an urbanized industrial nation—and turning the men who owned those rails into millionaires. Consequently, railroads attracted huge domestic and European private investment, as well as large government subsidies in the form of land grants. Train barons, by necessity, had to reinvent how to run large-scale enterprises and deal with managerial complexities, labor unions, and competition—in effect creating the blueprint for modern-day corporations.

THE CIVIL WAR AND RECONSTRUCTION

Despite the changing landscape, urban industry still defined the Northeast and rural farms the South. The South depended on the North for capital and manufactured goods; the North relied on the South for cotton for textile manufacturing, but little else. So, to maintain some semblance of trade balance, Southern economic interests required cheap labor. Unfortunately, slavery was the only economic option that fit the bill. Thus, when President Abraham Lincoln called for ending the expansion of slavery and instead expanding industry, commerce, and business, the South rose up and the American Civil War ensued (1861–1865).

War is tragic, but it's also profitable—especially for diversified, industrialized states. The North had the advantage in terms of industrial strength and resources, and could easily convert commercial manufacturing to military production. The South, more isolated and dependent on a single cash crop, had no real war-ready reserves to draw upon.

The North won, the slaves were freed, plantation-driven economics were destroyed, and Northern industry, which had expanded exponentially thanks to wartime demands, surged ahead. Reconstruction followed, with a host of new (and highly controversial) policies designed to restore the American (not just Northern) Union, rebuild the South, and "fix" the Constitution. The latter required formally abolishing slavery and electoral discrimination, and instituting provisions to educate former slaves.

FISCAL FLASHPOINT

The Civil War foreshadowed how important the "military-industrial complex" would eventually prove to be to America's modern economy, even though that term wouldn't actually exist for nearly a century. It was ultimately coined by President Dwight D. Eisenhower, a five-star general and Supreme Allied Commander during World War II, to describe the infrastructure needed to engage in the Cold War.

THE GILDED AGE OF INVENTION, DEVELOPMENT, AND TYCOONS—1865 TO 1900

America returned to the gold standard in 1879, creating an acceleration in money growth as a direct result of the flow of new gold. The Gilded Age sparked a period of deflation, an explosion of inventions (cars, telephones, radios, and airplanes), and the rise of the *tycoon,* when every man could be a potential Andrew Carnegie.

Discoveries of massive coal deposits in the Appalachian Mountains and fields of "black gold" and iron across the Midwest stoked the fires of the nation's industrial infrastructure. Men who were quick to see the inherent potential for new services or products—men like John D. Rockefeller in oil, Jay Gould in railroads, J. Pierpont Morgan in banking and, yes, Carnegie in steel—amassed vast financial empires.

The new Americans—hardy individualists and unsophisticated risk takers who had flocked to the New World to create their own destinies—enthusiastically embraced money-making. They were also quick to flaunt their flamboyant lifestyles—much to the chagrin of the more rigidly class-conscious Europeans. "Diamonds may be a girl's best friend," British nobility would sniff, "but they don't belong around the neck of Mrs. Stuyvesant Fish's pet pooch." But when, by the late 1880s, the United States surpassed Great Britain as the globe's most powerful economy by more than two-to-one, the world had no choice but to take notice.

In spite of its growing economic power, the United States didn't engage in any territorial empire building in the final days of the nineteenth century, mostly because imperial rule seemed inconsistent with America's democratic principles. It did, however, pick up several new territories—annexing Hawaii in 1898, then getting Puerto Rico, Guam, the Philippines, and Cuba from Spain following the Spanish-American War (though Cuba was quickly granted independence in 1902).

And, as the new century dawned, it also began to show increasing foreign-policy assertiveness around the world.

GROWTH, GOVERNMENT INTERVENTION,
AND THE GREAT WAR: THE PROGRESSIVE ERA—
1890 TO 1920

Before 1900, most American politicians were reluctant to intervene in the private sector, except when it came to transportation. *Laissez-faire*—a government-hands-off-the-economy doctrine—generally guided policy making. However, as the developmental pace of industrial technology steadily increased, middle-class entrepreneurs— weary of fighting corrupt officials, cutthroat tycoons, radicalized farmers, and labor movements—pressed for government regulation to protect competition and free enterprise.

They found sympathetic ears in Presidents Theodore Roosevelt (1901–1909) and Woodrow Wilson (1913–1921). Before they came to power, Congressional laws regulating railroads (Interstate Commerce Act of 1887) and monopolies (Sherman Antitrust Act of 1890) went rigorously *unenforced*. Roosevelt put new teeth into those laws, and also established the Food and Drug Administration (FDA). Wilson followed with creation of the Federal Trade Commission (FTC), and also contributed to two other acts destined to foster our eternal regret:

1. The Sixteenth Amendment to the Constitution, ratified by Congress in 1913, instituted the first federal income tax.
2. The Federal Reserve Act, also passed in 1913, created the Federal Reserve System, or simply the Fed, a quasi-public, quasi-private central banking system intended to deal proactively with bank panics—though its influence since has extended far beyond those original parameters.

The practice of doing business in America was definitely maturing. However, the event having the greatest impact on the U.S. economy arrived in 1914, when imperial European politics spawned World War I. The major European nations, chafing from a prolonged loss of colonial power, had for years been embroiled in a scramble for control of 10 million square miles of Africa (roughly one-fifth the world's land mass). When the conflict finally returned home, it ultimately pulled most of the world's powers into one of two opposing alliances: The Triple Entente (Allies) and the Central Powers (Germany & Co.).

Some 70 million troops were activated in this "war to end all wars," and combatant countries pumped the full scope and range of their scientific and industrial capabilities into the war effort. More than 15 million people died, making this first technology-heavy global conflict the deadliest in history.

It was also one of the most economically devastating. To pay for essential war materials, Great Britain cashed in its massive investments in U.S. railroads and began borrowing heavily on Wall Street. President Wilson—who managed to delay America's entry into the war until 1917—had been parceling out aid to Europe in the early days, but in 1916 allowed for a huge increase in government lending to the Allies, most of which came back to the United States for war purchases. Gross Domestic Product (GDP) soared. All told, America lent the Allies $7 billion during the war—mostly for military equipment, food, and medical needs—and another $3 billion shortly after the war ended.

Once the United States declared war on Germany, a radical expansion of governmental powers ensued. New federal departments, Cabinet posts, and executive powers were created, new taxes levied, and new laws enacted—all designed to bolster the war effort. The nature of the economy also shifted dramatically. With the prime of America's mostly male workforce drafted into military service, an unprecedented number of women took their places—setting the stage for a more modern view of women's role in society and underscoring the postwar case for granting women the right to vote.

THE ROARING TWENTIES AND THE CRASH—
1920 TO 1929

With peace restored and Armageddon put to bed, America returned to the business of doing business, this time as a world power tied to other countries by trade, politics, and joint interests. The United States also began to extend its economic reach into the rest of the world. Before the war, foreigners had invested more money in the United States than Americans had invested in other countries—about $3 billion more. World War I reversed that trend.

Increased foreign investment was not the only sign of America's growing financial influence. By the end of World War I, the United States produced and consumed more goods and services than any other country, both in terms of total Gross National Product (GNP) and GNP per person. By 1920, the U.S. national income outstripped the combined incomes of Britain, France, Germany, Japan, Canada, and 17 others. Quite simply, in a few short years, America had become the world's greatest economic power.

Cultural and societal upheaval and an influx of new wealth swept over the United States—and spread to the rest of the world. People swapped out "everything old" for "everything modern." Jazz defined *hot,* flappers defined "the new woman," and excess defined everything else. The Roaring Twenties were on!

Unprecedented industrial growth, inventiveness, and ample credit accelerated consumer demand and significant changes in lifestyle. The slogan "Anything goes!" fit perfectly because anything *did* seem possible with modern technology. When mass production made luxury affordable to most middle-class Americans, cars proliferated, movie attendance skyrocketed, and a newfangled entertainment medium called radio swept the country.

Rapid growth of the auto industry stimulated oil drilling, gas production, and road building. Tourism soared. Consumers traveled farther for shopping. Small cities, big cities—everybody prospered— creating a boom in construction. Electrification transformed business, farming, and everyday life. Telephones became commonplace rather than rarities. And, for the first time, millions of families moved into their own houses and began investing heavily in stocks, borrowing money to do both—simply because they could. (Sounds vaguely familiar, no?)

Of course, all that came to a screeching halt in October 1929 when Wall Street fell apart. In terms of duration and fallout, the

1929 Crash (which was more than a one-day affair) was the most devastating economic event in our nation's history to that point. The catastrophic downturn triggered widespread panic and the failure of banks all across the country, followed by the onset of an unprecedented and devastatingly long Great Depression. Notably, given current events, the Crash came on the heels of a sharp decline in real estate values, which had peaked in late 1925.

THE GREAT DEPRESSION AND THE NEW DEAL— 1929 TO 1941

"Experts" still disagree on the precise cause of the Crash, but not its effects. For the next decade, economic contraction gripped the world. It was "fear mixed with . . . disorientation . . . cauterized with denial, both official and mass-delusional," wrote Steve Fraser, author of *Wall Street: A Cultural History*. The Roaring Twenties were roaring no more.

There was absolutely nothing selective about the Great Depression, the impact of which lingered until 1940 and affected everyone, rich and poor—and with devastating global effects. The worldwide impact was doubly painful to the United States because a revolving system of German reparations collapsed in 1931 and most of the $10 billion the United States had lent to Europe for World War I was never repaid.

International trade plunged by one-half to two-thirds, as did U.S. personal income, tax revenue, commodity prices, and corporate profits—if the companies even managed to stay in business. Cities that depended on heavy industry were hard hit. Construction came to a virtual standstill. Crop prices fell by roughly 60 percent, forcing many farmers to abandon their fields. With consumer demand plummeting, total unemployment hit 23.6 percent by 1932—with even worse numbers in heavy industry, lumber, agricultural exports, and mining.

Desperate times called for innovative thinking, and Franklin D. Roosevelt brought that to the Presidency in 1933. He balanced the regular budget, but increased the emergency budget (funded by debt) from 33.6 percent of GNP to 40.9 percent. A patchwork of new public-sector programs—known collectively as the New Deal—was instituted in an effort to alleviate the crisis. One of those was the radical—some would say socialist—Work Projects Administration (WPA), which put millions of unemployed Americans to work.

The New Deal also extended federal authority over banking, farming, and welfare; set minimum wage-and-hours standards for private employers; set up the Securities and Exchange Commission (SEC) to regulate the stock market; established the Federal Deposit Insurance Corporation (FDIC) to guarantee bank deposits, and created the Social Security Administration (SSA) to provide assistance for the elderly.

Innovation also grew in the private sector, where companies like Procter & Gamble survived by pursuing new advertising avenues, such as sponsoring radio shows. Movie theaters kept their doors open and seats filled by installing air conditioning, using giveaways, and offering cash door prizes. Breweries—still suffering the morning-after effects of Prohibition—diversified into dairy production and other agricultural enterprises.

The upshot? America began to show early signs of renewed economic health by late 1934, matched many pre-Crash numbers by 1936, and was almost fully recovered by 1940. (GNP was 34 percent higher in 1936 than in 1932, and 58 percent higher in 1940.) Then, to complete the recovery, along came World War II.

STRICT CONTROLS AND A WARTIME BOOM—1941 TO 1945

With no small amount of foresight, the New Deal also created power-sharing departments among three key economic players—the government, the military, and business—to better coordinate on matters of national security. As a result, when World War II broke out, America was prepared—just as a world power should be.

The War Production Board coordinated national productivity to meet military needs—for example, converting auto manufacturing plants to wartime production of tanks and aircraft. Similarly, the

Office of Price Administration set rents and rationed scarce products like sugar and gas to prevent rampant inflation.

With massive spending, strict price controls, War Bond sales campaigns, rationing, raw materials management, prohibitions on new housing and new automobiles, guaranteed cost-plus profits, subsidized wages, and the draft of 12 million soldiers, the United States quickly turned into the "Arsenal of Democracy" that Roosevelt had envisioned—one that could stand against the Axis powers of Germany, Italy, and Japan.

Given those efforts, it's not surprising that prices remained comparatively lower during World War II than they had during World War I, helping the economy grow another 56 percent between 1940 and 1945.

Anyone, anywhere, with a company and a plan for converting to wartime production made money during that time—though, in a preview of some of the more recent complaints about poor business ethics, there were more than a few charges of war profiteering.

POSTWAR PROSPERITY—1945 TO 1963

From the end of World War II to the early 1970s, American capitalism enjoyed a golden era. Many Americans had feared that the drop in military spending after World War II might revive the Great Depression. However, pent-up consumer demand fueled exceptionally strong economic growth in the postwar period. The auto industry successfully converted back to producing cars, and new industries such as commercial aviation and electronics grew by leaps and bounds.

A housing boom, stimulated in part by easily affordable mortgages for military veterans, added to the expansion. Gross Domestic Product (GDP) rose from about $97 billion in 1940 to $273 billion in 1950 and close to $520 billion in 1960. (And, as Figure 1.1 illustrates, that rapid growth continued to accelerate all the way to the twenty-first century.) The simultaneous jump in postwar births— the so-called "Baby Boom"—increased the number of consumers and ballooned the ranks of middle-class Americans.

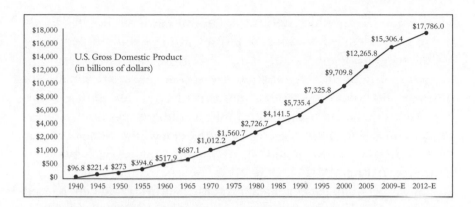

FIGURE 1.1   The Growth of American GDP—1940 to 2012

Sources: White House Office of Management and Budget; Budget for Fiscal Year 2008, Historical Tables.

The need to produce war supplies had given rise to the aforementioned military-industrial complex, and the ties between business and the military did not disappear with the war's end, due in large part to the descent of the Iron Curtain across Eastern Europe. Despite intense "guns or butter" debates, the U.S. government—embroiled in a new Cold War with the Soviet Union—chose to maintain a substantial fighting capacity (also needed to support the Korean Conflict) and invest in advanced weapons, such as the hydrogen bomb.

As President Dwight Eisenhower took office in 1953, ushering in a decade of peace, American business entered a period of consolidation, with smaller companies merging to create large, diversified conglomerates. The U.S. workforce also changed significantly. In the mid-1950s, the number of U.S. service providers surpassed the number of manufacturing workers and, by 1956, a majority of U.S. workers held white- rather than blue-collar jobs. In spite of the move by workers out of factories, though, labor unions continued to gain strength.

Farmers, by contrast, faced tough times. Gains in productivity led to agricultural overproduction and lower crop prices. Farming transformed into a big business enterprise, making it increasingly difficult for small family farms to compete. More and more farmers left the land—and, as a result, the number of people employed in the agricultural sector, which stood at 7.9 million in 1947, began a steady decline. By 1998, U.S. farms employed just 3.4 million people—a 56.9 percent decrease.

Other Americans were also on the move. Growing demand for single-family homes and ever-increasing car ownership led to a migration from central cities to suburbs. Technological innovations— effective and affordable air conditioning being a major one—also spurred surges of development in Sun Belt cities like Phoenix, Houston, Atlanta, Miami, and other Southern and Southwestern locales. As new four-lane highways and interstates created better access to the suburbs, business patterns began to change as well. Shopping centers multiplied, growing from just eight at the end of World War II to 3,840 in 1960. Many industries soon followed, leaving decaying inner cities for newer and less-crowded suburban "business parks."

REVOLUTION, ACTIVISM, AND TURMOIL— THE SIXTIES AND BEYOND

Civil rights. Women's rights. Anti-war. Cold War. Iron Curtain. Counterculture. Che Guevara. Hari Krishna. IRA. SLA. Space race. Human race. Black Power. Flower Power. Cultural evolution. Sexual revolution.

Welcome to the Sixties—when the only thing that changed was everything.

Globally, the tumultuous, wrenching, and yet strangely prosperous 1960s kept replaying the same three scenarios over and over: Heavy-duty militarization provoking economic change, violent street protests agitating for political change, and revolutionary thinking activating social change. President John F. Kennedy even ushered in a more activist approach to governing when he entered the Oval Office in 1961. Asking his fellow countrymen to meet the challenges of a "New Frontier . . . of unfulfilled hopes and dreams, a frontier of unknown opportunities and beliefs in peril," he metaphorically launched the United States into outer space and passed the largest tax cut in history to accelerate economic growth.

On Wall Street, stocks overcame the shock of JFK's 1963 assassination and made a bull run from 1962 to 1968, with the Dow Jones Industrial Average hitting 1,000 for the first time in 1966. Productivity and Gross Domestic Product (or purchasing power parity) swelled, as did the ranks of the middle class and consumer demand. The U.S. government even financed some private sector research and development, most notably ARPANET (precursor to the Internet).

But the heavy build-up of the military because of the Cold War and escalating involvement in Vietnam required a monetary policy that conformed to the needs of foreign policy. (More about the increasing ties between U.S. monetary and foreign policy in Chapters 3 and 4.) In short, with Lyndon Johnson now at the helm, the United States elected to finance 70 percent of its military spending with public debt.

Then, under President Richard Nixon, the United States unilaterally withdrew from the gold standard so as to retain flexibility in domestic economic policy. Little did he know that this would be one of the most historically significant and questionable decisions of our lifetimes, as evidenced by the current crisis. But I'll have more on that later.

During Johnson's tenure, from 1963 to 1969, federal spending increased dramatically as he introduced the Great Society, launching new programs such as Medicare (health care for the elderly), Food Stamps (food assistance for the poor), and numerous education initiatives. Vietnam also mushroomed into a major military conflict but, ironically, spending for the two wars—on poverty at home and on Communism in Vietnam—brought prosperity in the short term.

That changed under Nixon. *Stagflation,* an epic combination of continuing inflation and stagnant business activity, coupled with rising unemployment, gripped the nation—and the government experimented with wage-and-price controls. America's growing dependence on foreign oil also became shockingly clear during the 1973–1974 oil embargo by Arab members of the Organization of Petroleum Exporting Countries (OPEC). Ugly gasoline shortages ensued, and energy prices shot sky-high (at least by 1970s standards, if not by today's). Even after the embargo ended, energy prices remained high, adding to inflation and rising unemployment.

Federal budget deficits grew, foreign competition intensified, and the stock market sagged. Productivity growth was pitiful, if not negative. Interest rates remained high, with the prime rate hitting 20 percent in January 1981. (Newspaper columnist Art Buchwald quipped that 1980 would go down as the year when it was cheaper to borrow money from the Mafia than from your local bank.)

In desperation, President Jimmy Carter tried to combat the persistent economic weakness and unemployment by increasing government spending while also establishing voluntary wage-and-price guidelines to control inflation. Both efforts were largely unsuccessful.

A sea change in economic theory arrived with President Ronald Reagan's 1980 election. His fiscal agenda centered on his belief that the federal government had become too big and intrusive. In 1981, he introduced "Reaganomics," which was based on supply-side economic theory. His plan advocated reducing tax rates so people could keep more of what they earned, thus inducing them to work harder and longer, which would lead to more savings and investment, resulting in more production. That, in turn, would lead to higher reinvestment in business, which would lead to new job opportunities and higher wages—stimulating overall economic growth.

Reagan cut marginal federal income tax rates by 25 percent, and while he was at it, also slowed the growth in funding for social programs and reduced or eliminated government regulations affecting the consumer, the workplace, and the environment. Fearing that the United States had neglected its military in the wake of the highly unpopular Vietnam War, Reagan also successfully pushed for big increases in defense spending. The budget deficit ballooned, the Fed further cut the money supply, and the economy continued to wallow in recession. U.S. trade deficits, coming off seven bad years in the 1970s, swelled to even bigger negativity in the 1980s, and rapidly expanding economies in Asia—Japan in particular—challenged America for economic power.

Focus on the economy eased in Reagan's second term as he and his successor, George H. W. Bush, presided over the fall of the Berlin Wall, the disintegration of the Soviet Union, and the collapse of communist regimes across Eastern Europe. The focus also shifted somewhat on Wall Street, where "corporate raiders" made mergers and acquisitions (M&A) an art form, buying companies with depressed stock prices and then either restructuring them or dismantling them piece by piece.

Although President Bill Clinton brought Democratic ideology back to the White House in 1993, he took a cue from Reagan, declared that the era of "big government" was over, and reduced the size of the federal workforce. After a brief initial slump in 1993–1994, the economy once again got healthier and people once again got wealthier, in part thanks to greatly expanded trade opportunities after the fall of the Iron Curtain. Technological developments brought a wide range of sophisticated new electronic products. Innovations in telecommunications and computer networking spawned vast hardware, software, and Internet enterprises, precipitating the eventual "dot-com bubble," but also revolutionizing forever the way many industries operate.

The economy—and corporate earnings—rose rapidly. The U.S. economy grew more closely intertwined with the global economy than ever before and Clinton, like his predecessors, continued to push for the elimination of trade barriers. U.S. GDP in 1998 exceeded $8.62 trillion and accounted for more than 25 percent of the world's economic output.

Entering the twenty-first century, the U.S. economy was bigger than ever. Prices remained stable, unemployment dropped to historically low levels, Washington posted a budget surplus, and the stock market gained by leaps and bounds.

Everyone, it seemed, had it made—*but the worst was yet to come.*

CHAPTER 2

GROWTH OF THE AMERICAN CONSUMER

Role Model for World Spending

America is back.

—President Ronald Reagan

One of the biggest factors in America's rise to global economic dominance has been the strength of its citizens—as consumers. Indeed, over the past 250 years, American consumers have arguably been the single greatest economic force in the history of the world.

So, how did the U.S. consumer revolutionize our economy and make it so strong? How did American products come to symbolize quality and unparalleled desirability worldwide? After all, the United States started some 230-odd years ago with limited commerce, virtually no industry, and a governmental system conceived and implemented by what was basically a tattered collection of colonial farmers breaking soil out on the edge of global nowhere. By contrast, current problems notwithstanding, today's America is a slick, well-oiled, highly lucrative commercial machine that makes up more than a quarter of the world's economy.

Welcome to free-market capitalism!

SECRETS OF THE STONE AGE OF U.S. CONSUMERISM

The original settlers in the New World had a simple economy—they bartered or traded for what they couldn't hunt, fish, reap, hew, or forage for on their own. But, as colonial industry developed and producers of goods grew increasingly prosperous, the still-fledgling Americans decided it was time to eliminate the restrictive trade regulations and tax levies imposed on them by the British Navigation Acts.

It took a revolution, but they got their way—plus a new country. They inked the ultimate expression of their entrepreneurial aspirations into the Declaration of Independence, which states that all citizens "are endowed . . . with certain unalienable Rights, that among these are Life, Liberty and the pursuit of Happiness."

And now, thanks to those foresighted Founding Fathers, Americans can park their $80,000 SUVs out in the heat and rain, next to their J/35 sailboats, in front of their 5,600-square-foot, single-family McMansions—a necessity because their three-car garages are filled with all the ATVs, motorcycles, sports gear, toys, and, let's face it, downright junk, that U.S. and foreign manufacturers can produce.

In fact, consumerism is even responsible for one of the Top 10 U.S. growth industries over the past 20 years—offsite storage facilities. Americans have bought so much stuff, it won't even fit in their homes anymore! Talk about a great economic success story!

But back to the subject at hand. The first great hit out of the ballpark for consumers came sandwiched between American independence and the first Industrial Revolution. Throughout the country's youth, scarcity of resources had been the norm, but then this unusual situation arose: For the first time, products were available in unbelievable numbers, at unbelievably low prices, to practically everyone.

Suddenly, you had this situation in which there were more goods than buyers—meaning merchants had to start pitching their wares to the working class, not just to the upper crust and the Fancy Dans. It became necessary to create more demand—in a deliberate and coordinated way, on a very large scale—through mass-marketing techniques. Thus were born the rather deeply intertwined concepts of "mass consumption" and "consumer capitalism."

Those phrases suggest a certain degree of coercion—if not outright manipulation—of consumer demand. Almost un-American, you might say. Well, yes—and no. Department stores in the 1850s— such as Wanamaker's in Philadelphia—were the first to employ advertising and marketing techniques that sought to change consumer habits. They wanted customers to stop walking into a store and thinking *needs,* and instead start walking into a store and thinking *wants.*

You can witness the success of Wanamaker's psychological gamble every time you walk into your local geek store and your kid points excitedly at the newest generation PlayStation video game console and shouts, "I want that PS3, Daddy!" Just try to say no. See? It worked!

THE ADVENT OF THE AD MEN

The first Industrial Revolution changed how Americans viewed goods, whereas the second Industrial Revolution (post-1890) changed the way people *bought* and *consumed* goods. Production in the United States exploded 14 times over, while the population increased only threefold. With more discretionary income than ever—especially among the working class—consumption took off.

To intensify consumer demand for their products, businesses began embracing new styles of merchandising, display, packaging, and advertising. An army of mail-order houses, door-to-door sales companies, chain stores, and department stores appeared. Think Sears and Roebuck (the original low-tech Amazon.com), Avon and Fuller Brush, the good ol' A&P and Macy's, respectively. In concert, they helped transform the mass-consumption landscape by bringing an array of goods directly to the consumer.

But it was the ad agencies—those "merchants of desire"—that changed shopping from a necessity and a chore into a combination leisure activity, competitive sport, and full-time religion. Social status had once depended on a person's family name. Now, consumerism provided social mobility through a display of one's wealth—or, at least, the perception thereof.

Economist and sociologist Thorstein Veblen called it "conspicuous consumption." New York comic strips called it "keeping up with the Joneses." But, essentially, it meant the same thing: an obsession to impress friends and influence enemies by flaunting what you had.

Today, status symbols no longer carry any social stigma—courtesy of those early public relations artists. As consumerism grew, they continually found new ways to equate personal happiness with consumption and the purchase of their respective clients' products. Women love showing off their Chanel handbags, young men strut their Nikes on the basketball court, and CEOs proudly schedule their lives on their iPhones. And the Houses of Chanel (purses retail for $2,000 to $118,000 per), Nike ($18.6 billion in sales), and Apple (123 percent growth, with more than 21 million iPhones sold in just two years; 500,000 in just one day) are thrilled.

THE ART OF CONSUMER SEDUCTION

By the 1920s, consumer seduction became an art form practiced by salesmen promoting the pleasures of looking and touching via showy display windows, glass cabinetry, and mirrors throughout the store. Pioneering companies provided a range of services intended to appeal directly to women—newly viewed then, as they are now, as the primary purchasers for the family. Stores offered everything from restrooms to restaurants, from package delivery to charge accounts—all with the intent of "enhancing" the shopping experience for their "very special" customers. (Alas, this sometimes backfired when department stores found themselves battling women shoplifters—diagnosed with a new medical term, dubbed *kleptomania*.)

New technology also improved the channels of mass-market communication—and, with it, the medium's manipulative power. Wide

---

FISCAL FLASHPOINT

In 1914, Western Union offered its customers the very first "charge card" as a means of obtaining very short-term loans (usually 30 days) to make purchases. Cardholders were required to pay each month's charges in full. Since there was no loan, per se, there was no interest and no minimum payment option. However, a partial payment (or no payment) resulted in the cardholder getting slapped with a severe late fee (as much as 5 percent of the balance) and possible restricted use or cancellation of the card. The initial charge cards were printed on paper; it wasn't until 1959 that embossed plastic cards came into use.

---

circulation magazines such as *Ladies' Home Journal, McCall's,* and *Good Housekeeping* helped foster consumption by linking "womanly duties" and "respectability" to the emerging consumer culture. Editorials then urged women to purchase brand-name products or encouraged buying vacuum sweepers to replace their brooms.

Then came radio. The first commercial radio station went on the air in Pittsburgh in 1920—and, within two years, three million U.S. households had radios. Sales of receivers—most packaged in large wooden furniture pieces—increased 2,500 percent, and manufacturers tallied annual sales of $850 million by 1929.

"Commercial" radio—with programs sponsored by specific products or brands—cashed in by having the program's stars hawk the sponsor's wares during commercial breaks (a technique wholeheartedly adopted by television when it came into vogue). Sponsors also began enticing consumers by linking popular movie stars and public personalities to their products. Thus celebrity endorsements were born, adding another layer of emotional desire into the marketing mix.

However, the precise results of such testimonials and endorsements can be hard to quantify. As an example, celebrity endorsements were hugely popular in China, which now has the most rapid rate of consumerism growth on the planet. Then the government, in a bid to protect citizens against questionable medical practices, passed a law in

2007 banning health care professionals, pop stars, actors, and musicians from endorsing drugs or nutritional supplements. "A celebrity . . . is more likely to mislead consumers," Beijing rationalized.

This changed the style of much advertising, but apparently did little to suppress consumerism as China's GDP exploded from $3.3 trillion in 2007 to $4.4 trillion in 2008.

THE BIRTH OF INSTALLMENT FINANCING

America's consumer confidence and spending were at all-time highs in the mid-1920s, but product producers, in their never-ending quest to expand consumer demand, still needed a way to enable more people to buy big-ticket items and high-priced luxury goods. The introduction of extended automobile-purchase plans provided a foundation for the transformation to "installment financing," and consumer spending again ramped up to new heights. By 1929, ads reflected how broadly acceptable installment buying had become as a way to finance your purchases—and the GDP (in current U.S. dollars) hit $103.6 billion!

Also around the mid-1920s, Alfred P. Sloan revolutionized the auto industry—and consumer demand for General Motors cars—by instituting the first annual model-year change. As a merchandizing tactic, it was brilliant. Really. With this one simple idea, Sloan succeeded in shifting the world away from a focus on technological innovation and toward satisfying market expectations. He also tapped into the "upgrading urge" people naturally feel with regard to improving themselves and their position in life.

By 1925, people at every income level had come to consider the automobile a necessity rather than a luxury. People were willing to sacrifice food, clothing, and their savings in order to own a car. Annual auto production rose from just over 2.0 million vehicles in 1921 to 5.5 million vehicles in 1929. There was one automobile for every five Americans—theoretically allowing for every person in the United States to be on the road at the same time. (Okay, they might have had to squeeze a little.)

FISCAL FLASHPOINT

In most of the world, car ownership continues to be considered a necessity—and auto demand has grown steadily since the 1920s. In 2007, there were 806 million cars and light trucks on the road—about 250 million of those in the United States alone. That same year, 71.9 million new cars were sold worldwide: 22.9 million in Europe, 21.4 million in Asia-Pacific, 19.4 million in the United States and Canada, 4.4 million in Latin America, 2.4 million in the Middle East, and 1.4 million in Africa. Of the major markets, Russia, Brazil, India, and China saw the most rapid growth. Given the problems with GM, Chrysler, and others, growth numbers for 2008 and 2009 will no doubt decline—but that will almost certainly be temporary.

THE "AMERICANIZATION" OF THE WORLD

The next verse in the economic "gospel of consumption" arose during World War II. Consumer spending in the United States dropped by about 50 percent during the war because of large expenditures by the government and the conversion of consumer-product manufacturing to wartime production. However, advertisers explicitly sought to counterbalance the trend by encouraging U.S. citizens to view consumption as the ultimate patriotic act—both as a defining principle of freedom and as a promise for postwar life. One 1944 *Life* magazine advertisement for Revere Copper and Brass Incorporated read, "After total war . . . total living!"

Retail analyst Victor Lebow proposed the ambitious plan: "Our enormously productive economy demands that we make consumption our way of life; that we convert the buying and the use of goods into rituals; that we seek our spiritual satisfaction, our ego satisfaction, in consumption. We need things consumed, burned up, replaced and discarded at an ever-accelerating rate."

After the war, the federal government carefully (and some would say, covertly) orchestrated institution of a "disposable, fast-food society"

PAYING IN FULL

While the initial charge card didn't appear until 1914, the concept was actually first described (11 times) by Edward Bellamy in his 1887 utopian novel *Looking Backward*. However, the modern credit card's DNA came from a variety of merchant credit schemes. The first card that offered customers the option of paying different merchants using the same card was created in 1950 by Ralph Schneider and Frank X. McNamara, founders of Diners Club. This first "general purpose" credit card required the *entire* bill to be paid with each statement. What a concept!

as a means to revitalize the economy. With the United States carrying the burden of rebuilding Europe—and engendering lots of "good will" for its efforts—"Americanizing" both our Allies and enemies (especially Germany) as we helped rekindle their economies made great commercial sense.

It enabled U.S. producers who'd lost business during the war to immediately tap entire new markets full of grateful consumers who had nothing and were located in countries that had no immediate capacity to produce anything. They were eager to forge a new community, shared with the world, and a new lifestyle based on modern tastes and habits that reflected America—and came almost exclusively packaged in American-made products like Levi's jeans, Buicks, and Buster Brown Shoes. It was an enormous opportunity.

Proposals for postwar economic reform were rooted in the "Ford model" which was based on the automaker's vertically integrated manufacturing system, but applied to consumption instead of production. Mass appeal was key, and marketing focused on popular culture, such as American cinema and music—areas where the United States could trade on the promise of prosperity for all, could speed establishment of a peacetime social order overseas and, perhaps most important, could create a homogenous global market for U.S.-made goods.

CONSUMERISM AS WE KNOW IT TODAY

After its huge growth spurt both here and abroad in the 20 years following World War II, rampant consumerism took some time off as the country wrestled with more idealistic issues such as civil rights, women's rights, student unrest, and the Vietnam War.

Given this environment, it's no surprise that, when President Ronald Reagan celebrated his 1981 inauguration with an $11 million night of balls and pageantry, and First Lady Nancy Reagan quickly ordered a new $200,000 set of china for the White House, the First Family was roundly criticized for ostentatious displays of wealth—even though private funds, not public, paid the bills.

However, Reagan could not have found a more effective way to put the world on notice that a new uptick in American "shop-till-you-drop-ism" was on the way. "America is back," the President told reporters who hinted the actions were inappropriate in light of the lingering 1970s recession.

And America *was* back. After Reagan took office, consumer spending as a percentage of the total U.S. economy exploded—so much so that 72 percent of U.S. Gross Domestic Product (GDP) now comes from personal consumption.

The early upsurge was so dramatic that a 1986 survey found the percentage of Americans who believed "having lots of money" was "extremely important" had gone up to roughly 65 percent from less than 50 percent in 1977. It ranked higher than any other goal in life. A later U.S. study found the most frequent reason given for attending college had changed to "making a lot of money"—outranking such reasons as becoming an authority in a field or helping others in difficulty.

As the new century approached, it seemed that American culture really had become obsessed with the emerging force Benjamin Barber dubbed "McWorld"—a culture of "fast music, fast computers and fast food, with MTV, Macintosh and McDonald's pressing nations into one commercially homogenous global network."

By 2007, luxury goods accounted for a $157 billion industry, and electronics innovations had further mushroomed consumer demand.

Personal and notebook computers, smartphones, MP3 players, digital media, and a host of other devices had quickly integrated themselves into not just the affluent world, but also the average American's everyday lifestyle.

As a reflection of that, the U.S. personal savings rate had been in a prolonged decline heading toward a 2005 bottom of just below zero. In other words, everyone was spending. No one was saving. And, as the attitudes of Americans changed, so, too, did the distinction between what we need and what we want. Americans increasingly came to want more—and, as you'll see in Chapter 4, they became more and more willing to go into debt to get it.

IS A MAJOR CHANGE COMING?

As I noted at the beginning of this chapter, U.S. consumers have arguably been the single greatest economic force in world history for two centuries, and many economists assure the world that these consumers remain integral to international monetary flows—particularly when it comes to building personal wealth.

Investors blindly assume economists are right—but what if they're not?

Current indications are that America's prolific spending habits are reversing. After a three-year bottom just above zero, the U.S. savings rate actually rose in 2008—the first net gain in more than a decade. It was actually negative from the first quarter of 2005 to late 2006—the first full-year savings deficit since 1932–1933. Then, in May 2008, when the first government stimulus checks hit mailboxes, the U.S. savings rate jumped to 4.9 percent. And, with the dour news on the employment front and the sorry state of the auto and retail industries in the first half of 2009, savings accounts were continuing to get pumped with cash as Americans put their dollars away for the future at a rate of 6.9 percent.

That's bad news for the economy of what has come to be known as the world's foremost "consumer nation"—the nation whose citizens, on average, spent $49,638 in 2007 (latest figure).

Of course, even with the recent contraction, America can hardly be described as a pauper state. GDP actually increased 1.3 percent in 2008 to $14.3 trillion, and was running at a $14.1 trillion pace for the first quarter of 2009, keeping the United States firmly in place as both the world's largest economy and the world's biggest spender.

That could change, however—and I personally think it will, in fairly short order—as China, the Red Dragon, moves to a dominant world position in both consumer spending and overall economic power (both of which I discuss in more detail in later chapters).

No doubt, in the short term, the American consumer and U.S. government will continue to provide the rest of the world with liquidity in the form of low-cost capital and abundant debt. But, as an astute investor, you must ask these two questions:

1. "How much longer can the United States hold its lead?"
2. "What do I do now so I'll be ready when the rules of the game change within the next five years?"

For what I believe to be the correct answers, just keep on reading.

CHAPTER 3

THE BEGINNINGS OF AMERICA'S UNDOING

The fall of a great nation is always a suicide.

—Arnold Toynbee

When things are bright and sunny and warm summer breezes drift across the land, there's no question that baseball is America's national pastime. But, when the clouds roll in and trouble erupts, the focus in the United States turns to a different sport—the "blame game."

This sport is certainly not unique to the United States, but we're undoubtedly the masters at it—thanks in large part to the need of our national politicians to get re-elected at regular intervals and our free media's insatiable appetite for scandal and controversy. Add in a public that's rarely willing to take personal responsibility for any mistake, then give them the right to scream for "justice" by any means from snail mail to Twitter, and you've got all the ingredients needed for a witch hunt.

That's why, in the period since the fiscal mess that began in late 2007 became evident, we've seen far more outrage expressed over "who" might be at fault than we've seen energy expended on how to actually fix the problems America now faces.

The most popular of the perceived villains, at least among those of a liberal mind-set, has been former President George W. Bush. Not alone, of course. His free-market economic advisers, enmeshed in a conspiracy with Vice-President Dick Cheney and his oil industry cronies, also assisted—abetted by a host of greedy bankers and Wall Street tycoons.

Those with a more conservative and anti-regulatory bent have preferred to identify the bulk of the problem as a legacy of President Bill Clinton's administration and the changes it made in housing and mortgage-lending policies, as well as assorted social issues. Still others, blessed with longer memories, have found seeds of our current destruction way back in the actions of Presidents Ronald Reagan and Jimmy Carter.

Personally, I really don't care "whodunit"—preferring to look forward at how to recover and profit from the situation rather than back at who might have caused it. Still, in the interests of clarity— and possibly helping to recognize future potential meltdowns a little more quickly—it's probably not a bad idea to review what I believe are some of the key factors that led to America's economic undoing.

FROM GOOD MONEY TO BAD—THE EROSION OF MONETARY STANDARDS

For starters, let me say that there's almost certainly enough blame to spread among all of them. Like all good urban legends, each scenario is based on at least a few actual facts—like it happened on a Tuesday, or they were all wearing underwear.

Obviously, the current crisis wasn't sparked by any one event—or by any one administration. Rather, it was the cumulative outcome of an extended series of actions taken and policies instituted over a prolonged period of time. Also, being an optimistic sort and generally believing the best of people, I doubt much of the "evil intent" implied by some of the more vocal blame-sayers cited. I figure that's more politics than economics, so we won't waste a lot of time on it.

I will say that the critics who looked all the way back to Reagan and Carter made one mistake—they were too shortsighted. Actually, I think the true roots of America's economic problems extend back almost two decades *before* Carter's election, to the early 1960s. That's when the Bretton Woods system of monetary management, which had been in place since the waning days of World War II, first began to break down, starting a slow erosion of the U.S. dollar's role as the world's dominant currency.

For those of you who've slept since your last history class (or slept *in* your last history class), the Bretton Woods Agreements were signed in late July of 1944 after a three-week meeting of delegates from the 44 Allied nations at Bretton Woods, New Hampshire. Though World War II was still raging, the Allied countries could sense victory and recognized the need to rebuild the international economic system.

The main goal of the negotiations was to establish a system of rules, procedures, and institutions to govern monetary relations among the independent countries of the world. To that end, the planners established the International Monetary Fund (IMF) and the International Bank for Reconstruction and Development (IBRD), known today as the World Bank, both of which became operational in 1945. They also created a system of guaranteed international exchange wherein each country that adopted the accord promised to maintain a fixed exchange rate for its currency. The fixed rate was pegged to the price of gold in a given currency, with an allowed variation of plus or minus 1 percent, and the IMF was charged with ensuring convertibility of one currency into another by bridging temporary imbalances in payments due among the various countries.

THE DOLLAR TAKES THE DOMINANT ROLE

The U.S. dollar, then carrying a value of $35 per ounce of gold, was designated the world's primary currency against which all others would be pegged, though this action was not without some controversy, particularly in Britain. At the time the accord was signed, one Bank of England official called it "the greatest blow to Britain next to the war" because it formalized the shift in global financial power from the United Kingdom to the United States.*

Despite that resistance, there was little any other nation could do to alter the terms because the United States was clearly the most

MONEY—A DILEMMA OF HISTORICAL PROPORTIONS

From the earliest days of human mobility and commerce, the issue of money has been a contentious one. Lacking any formal system of exchange or agency of intertribal oversight, the first money used by traders of goods and services was "commodity money." This meant it had intrinsic value based on the material from which it was made—examples over the years being gold and silver coins, shells, bushels of grain, and so forth.

By contrast, most modern money is so-called "fiat money." Fiat money has no intrinsic value based on a real underlying asset, but is instead declared by the government that issues it to be "legal tender"—meaning it must be accepted by that government's citizens as payment "for all debts, public and private."

As such, fiat money can be acceptable for international trade and commerce only if its value is acknowledged by other countries based on an agreement like Bretton Woods or established by an international trading system such as the foreign exchange (FOREX) markets (or pacts like the so-called "swap agreements" China is now signing with other countries around the world).

---

*As the end of the war neared, U.S. officials were determined to increase access to the British empire. At the time, British and U.S. commerce accounted for well over half the world's trade in goods. But, while Britain had economically dominated the nineteenth century, the United States intended for the second half of the twentieth century to be under U.S. hegemony. To achieve that, the United States first had to split up the British trade empire—and Bretton Woods helped do that. One unnamed commentator said the agreement worked only because the United States was clearly "the most powerful country at the table" and thus ultimately able to impose its will on the others, including an often-dismayed Britain. Discussed in Lundestad, Geir, "Empire by Invitation? The United States and Western Europe, 1945–1952," *Journal of Peace Research* 23 (3) (Sept. 1986), Sage Publications, Ltd., www.jstor.org/stable/.

powerful country at the time, as well as the dominant economic force in the world. In fact, when the accord went into force in 1945, the United States was producing half of the world's manufactured goods and holding half of its gold-backed monetary reserves.

Because of America's power and economic dominance, the Bretton Woods system worked well—for a while. Then, however, the burdens of helping the postwar reconstruction of both allies and enemies began to weigh on the U.S. Marshall Plan, the organization and funding of NATO in 1949, and countless other loans and aid plans— coupled with the growing expenses of the expanding Cold War with the Soviet Union—forced the United States to run a balance of payments deficit throughout the Eisenhower administration. That pressured the dollar, drawing complaints about overvaluation from some nations, but the United States was able to hold the line until the early 1960s.

THE SYSTEM BEGINS TO SELF-DESTRUCT

At that point, a variety of events conspired to break down America's ability to sustain the Bretton Woods monetary system and support the value of the dollar. Motivated by the Cuban missile crisis, President John F. Kennedy launched the largest military build up since World War II, which President Lyndon B. Johnson expanded as the Vietnam War escalated. Johnson also instituted a variety of new Great Society social programs and resisted all efforts to raise taxes to pay for them and cover the burgeoning war costs.

The result was a steady deterioration in the U.S. balance-of-trade position, rampant domestic inflation, and increasing international dis- satisfaction with the dollar's role as the world's primary currency for international trade.

The pressure for change was particularly intense from the European Economic Community (EEC), led by West Germany, and Japan, both of which had rapidly rebounded from wartime devastation to become global economic powers. By 1965, Europe and Japan held more monetary reserves than the United States (which then held under

20 percent of the world's total, down from more than 50 percent in 1945), had a faster rate of growth, and were enjoying per capita incomes almost equal to that in the United States.

Aiding the assault by our ex-Axis foes on the dollar's dominance was the return to full convertibility of the Western European currencies, including Germany's deutsche mark, and the Japanese yen (in 1958 and 1964, respectively). Because their use had been restricted for so long, the D-mark and yen were both undervalued, and the Germans and Japanese had no desire to revalue, which would have increased the cost of their products in foreign markets.

The United States could have remedied this situation by officially devaluing the dollar, but refused to do so. Treasury officials said America had to maintain its commitment to fixed exchange rates and honor its on-demand obligation to convert dollars into gold at the stated price in order to preserve its credibility in the international markets.

THE BIRTH OF THE FOREIGN EXCHANGE MARKETS

About the time the United States was losing control of the Bretton Woods system, two other events were taking place that contributed to the change in world monetary activities.

The first was the coming of age of truly functional business computers, ones that could be routinely used in day-to-day commerce rather than restricted to the government and universities. This hugely accelerated the flow of money around the globe, with settlement times for financial transactions being reduced from several days to a few hours (minutes and seconds were still a couple of decades away).

The second was the formation, in 1964, of the first international banking consortium and the concurrent development of an organized international foreign-exchange market. By 1970, almost 80 percent of the world's largest banks had become members of such syndicates and were using the foreign-exchange market to transfer huge sums of

(continued)

money, both for investment purposes and trade payments, as well as to hedge risks and speculate on exchange-rate fluctuations.

This made it much more difficult for governments, including the United States, to hold to official exchange-rate levels, even when pressured to do so for domestic business or political reasons. When they tried, the stated exchange rates would quickly be recognized as unrealistic, based on actual market conditions, and speculators would rush in to take advantage of what was an essentially risk-free proposition. They would move from a weak currency to a strong one, hoping for a revaluation to bring official rates in line with the market. If one came, they'd score major profits—and if it didn't, they could shift back to other weaker currencies with no loss.

These speculations—especially when conducted by international banks with huge sums of available cash—helped destabilize the monetary system and lead to the ultimate abandonment of Bretton Woods. If you're a James Bond fan, this is largely the premise of the 1964 film *Goldfinger*, wherein the villain hopes to throw the Western world into economic chaos.

THE REBELLION AGAINST BRETTON WOODS GAINS RECRUITS

America's resolve on the subject of fixed exchange rates eroded steadily through the rest of the 1960s, and then dissolved completely in 1970 and 1971. To meet the Vietnam War costs and deal with its first trade deficit of the twentieth century, the United States steadily printed more money—without the gold to back it up. By the end of 1970, Treasury figures indicated that the United States had only enough gold to cover the value of 22 percent of the paper dollars in circulation, down from 55 percent in 1968. At home, this caused the inflationary spiral that was already rotating to spin even faster. Abroad, those who were holding dollars—or were owed them—grew more and more reluctant to accord them the value Bretton Woods specified.

A rebellion was under way, with West Germany leading the march. Fearful the United States would export its rising inflation rate and unwilling to devalue the D-mark to prop up the dollar, the Germans opted out of Bretton Woods in May 1971, telling no one in advance so they could prevent a run on the deutsche mark. Many of the other members protested, but they couldn't argue with the results—by July, the German economy was booming and the dollar had fallen 7.5 percent versus the mark.

Other European nations began attacking the dollar's excess valuation by demanding that America fulfill its obligation to redeem the currency for gold. France made a series of midsummer demands, cashing in a reported $191 million in dollars. Switzerland followed suit, trading $50 million in paper for gold in late July, then following West Germany's lead in early August and withdrawing the Swiss franc from the Bretton Woods system.

THE "NIXON SHOCK" ENDS IT ALL

Alarmed by the Bretton Woods defections and seeking to protect the dollar against gold-grabbing foreign nations, Congress issued a report in early August proposing the U.S. currency be officially devalued. However, President Richard M. Nixon went the lawmakers one better.

On August 15, 1971, in an announcement that was later labeled the "Nixon Shock" by foreign monetary officials, the President unilaterally ended the convertibility of gold into dollars, except on the open market. In an effort to stabilize the economy and put the brakes to runaway inflation, Nixon also imposed a 90-day freeze on wages and prices and instituted a 10 percent surcharge on imports, designed to protect U.S. consumers from foreign price gougers.

The American public generally supported the action, but international monetary officials—who had been neither consulted nor warned—were stunned by the changes. Nixon offered to retract the import surcharge in exchange for a general revaluation of the major world currencies and a provision allowing for larger variations (2.25 percent) from the specified exchange rates. That was accomplished

THE SECOND "NIXON SHOCK"

The term *Nixon Shock* got used again in February 1972 when Richard Nixon startled the world by becoming the first U.S. President to visit China. In a surprising twist of Cold War diplomacy, the once ardently anti-communist Nixon visited Beijing, Shanghai, and the Great Wall, met with Chairman Mao Zedong and held several sessions with Chinese Premier Zhou Enlai. Results of those talks were published at the end of the trip in the *Shanghai Communiqué*, a document that first opened a crack in the door that now allows Westerners to enjoy many of the Chinese opportunities detailed later in this book.

by the end of 1971 and, although Bretton Woods wasn't officially dead, its control of exchange rates as a tool of international monetary policy steadily dwindled. By March of 1976, all of the world's major currency values were "floating," meaning exchange rates were determined solely by market forces.

ENTER THE ERA OF PETRODOLLARS

In spite of the loss of economic clout it had suffered since the end of World War II, the United States remained the world's foremost superpower in the early 1970s. Thus, although Nixon ended the convertibility of the U.S. dollar into gold, it made perfect sense that the dollar would become the "reserve currency" for the rest of the world.

Just in case you haven't had lunch with Ben Bernanke lately, a reserve currency is one that is held by governments, banks, and other financial institutions as part of their foreign-exchange reserves, which are primarily used as a guarantee of settlement on international trade and debt obligations. In its role as a reserve currency, the dollar also typically serves as the pricing currency for many products traded on global markets, including oil and gold.

That latter role for the dollar contributed to one of the negative effects of the move away from a system of fixed exchange rates. With rates floating, open market currency traders quickly pushed the value

According to the International Monetary Fund, the U.S. dollar (64.0%) and the euro (26.5%) accounted for more than 90 percent of world currency reserves at the end of 2008.

of the dollar down in global markets. Initially, that cut sharply into the profits of members of the Organization of Petroleum Exporting Countries (OPEC), who were locked into fixed-price, dollar-denominated supply contracts, mostly with the major international oil companies—the so-called "Seven Sisters." OPEC tried several strategies to restore its "real" profits to pre-devaluation levels, including pegging the price of oil to the price of gold, but nothing worked very well and profits continued to lag.

Then, in late 1973, two things happened that altered that situation dramatically. The first was the failure of negotiations between OPEC and the Seven Sisters for new supply contracts. That essentially left the 13 member nations of OPEC free to sell oil to anyone and set their price at whatever level the market would bear. The second was the October 6 attack by Syria and Egypt on Israel, starting the Yom Kippur War, and triggering the subsequent U.S. decision to side with the Israelis and resupply their military.

In response to that U.S. decision, the seven Arab members of OPEC, as well as Egypt and Syria, decided to punish America. On October 16, they announced a 70 percent increase in the price of crude—to $5.11 a barrel. (Don't laugh; that may seem like a bargain in relation to the $140-a-barrel oil we've seen recently, but $5.11 was big money back then.)

The following day, Libya announced it would impose an embargo on oil shipments to the United States, and the other Arab countries quickly followed suit, later expanding the embargo to include Europe and Japan. The Arab oil ministers also voted to immediately cut crude production by 5 percent and continue to reduce output in 5 percent increments until OPEC's political and economic goals were achieved.

The Shah of Iran, at the time the United States's closest ally in the Middle East, outlined those objectives in an interview with *The New York Times,* saying the West would no longer be allowed to increase energy consumption by 5 percent a year, pay low oil prices, and then pass inflation back to the oil producers by selling them high-priced goods and food supplies.

"You increased the price of wheat you sell us by three hundred percent," the Shah told the *Times.* "It's only fair that, from now on, you should pay more for oil. Let's say ten times more."

The OPEC actions were a success—at least in Arab eyes—enormously increasing their position of power in the world and pushing the already reeling global financial system into an alternating series of recessions and inflationary surges that carried into the early 1980s.

FISCAL FLASHPOINT

The sharp 1973 oil price hikes were made all the more painful because the West was accustomed to extreme stability in the oil markets. From 1947 through 1967, oil prices had risen an average of just 2 percent per year.

PETRODOLLAR SURPLUSES QUICKLY PILE UP

American consumers, waiting in long lines at the pumps to buy $1.25-a-gallon gas (again, we should be so lucky today), were outraged at this turn of events, but there was little they could do. Oil demand in industrialized countries normally remains steady, regardless of prices, so the market price of oil had to rise sharply to reduce demand enough to match the drastically lower supply—and it did. Crude continued to climb, soaring to $12 a barrel by early 1974, then moving relentlessly upward to peak at near $40 a barrel in 1986.

The oil crisis had a major impact in a number of areas, both short and long term. The 1973 stock market crash intensified and carried through all of 1974, new U.S. energy policies were adopted, promoting increased oil exploration and greater conservation, and the United States and other Western nations adopted more restrictive monetary policies to better combat inflation.

However, the most significant result of the events of 1973 and 1974—and one that still reverberates through the financial markets today—was the massive transfer of wealth from the industrialized West to the Middle East in the form of so-called "petrodollars."

Actually, the term *petrodollar*—meaning a U.S. dollar earned by another country through the sale of petroleum—was itself a result of the 1973 oil crisis. It was coined by Georgetown University economics professor Ibrahim Oweiss, who felt there was a need for a word to describe the huge sums of money, in dollars, OPEC countries were earning as a result of the spike in oil prices.

Whether the term was actually needed or not, the number of petrodollars being amassed by the Middle Eastern oil producers was staggering—far more than they could possibly invest in their own countries, most of which had small populations and minimal industrial activity. To put that in numerical terms, the IMF reported that, from 1974 to the end of 1981, the current-account surpluses for all OPEC nations totaled more than $450 billion, with 90 percent of that amassed by the Arab countries. Of course, the flip side of that coin was the woe of oil-importing nations. The IMF said the 100 largest oil users saw their foreign debts increase by 150 percent from 1973 to 1977 alone.

With all those extra dollars on hand, the Middle East cash barons had little choice but to pour most of it back into investments in the West—something they're still doing today.*

This "recycling" of petrodollars was a double-edged sword. On the plus side, it helped soften the blow of higher oil prices on the world economy, which would have undoubtedly contracted to a far greater degree had the money merely been tucked away in Mideast mattresses. On the negative side, the return of petrodollars to the West added to the inflation problem, pushing up the prices of anything the Arabs wanted to buy. With so much money in your pocket, why

---

*Which is why I continually remind people that, even though high oil prices don't feel good, there is actually a stabilizing effect on our markets as a result.

negotiate—just keep raising the offer price till you get what you desire. Right?

WHY THIS MATTERS IN THE CURRENT CRISIS

An entire book or two could be written—and several actually have been—about the longer-term implications of the petrodollar phenomenon, so I won't over-analyze them here. What's important are the factors that contributed to the economic crisis of 2008–2009—which, in very brief terms, include:

- *The use of oil as a weapon in world affairs.* OPEC learned the lesson of the 1970s well and has often used oil-price hikes and production cuts in the years since to pressure the United States, Japan, and other oil-dependent nations into making adjustments in international policies. Few can argue that the 2008 explosion in oil prices—which nearly everyone scoffed at when I predicted it a few years earlier—was a major contributing factor in intensifying our economic woes, eating up available credit, forcing cash-drained companies to cut production and jobs, and essentially leading to the downfall of the U.S. auto industry.
- *The decline in the value of the dollar.* With the price of oil denominated in dollars, any rise in the quotes for crude amounts to a de facto devaluation of the dollar, something we've seen several times since the 1970s, culminating in the crushing 2008 value adjustment.
- *The impact of oil on U.S. foreign and domestic policies.* There's substantial debate about this, but most agree that America's oil dependence has been a hidden force in determining U.S. foreign policy for several decades, and was a key consideration in many domestic policies, particularly during the administration of President George W. Bush. In fact, his sharpest critics say oil favoritism contributed to many of Bush's most damaging economic decisions, helping trigger the meltdown.

- *The steady worsening of U.S. trade deficits.* Higher import costs for oil; lower export profits from a declining manufacturing base for nearly everything else. 'Nuff said.
- *Increased Third World debt and dependence on credit.* OPEC turned to the big international banks to help them invest their petrodollar surpluses in the 1970s and early 1980s, but the weak economic conditions at the time made many investments undesirable. So, the bankers lent the money to developing nations in South and Central America, Africa, and to Middle East countries without oil of their own. Many of these nations became dependent on such loans for things they otherwise couldn't have afforded, and have since had trouble repaying these debts, disrupting their own economies and creating recurring tensions with developed nations and world monetary authorities.
- *A pattern of pricing bubbles.* The concept of *bubbles* is far from new, stretching back several centuries and involving assets ranging from tulips to nonexistent South Seas properties. However, the excess liquidity created by the surplus of petrodollars has sparked recurring bubbles since the mid-1970s. Some of these were limited, primarily involving luxury items like yachts, private jets, and other items the oil barons wanted to buy. Others were bigger, such as stocks in the mid-1980s, major U.S., European, and Far Eastern office buildings and other "trophy" properties in the 1990s, and dot-com companies approaching the turn of the century. Add in even more liquidity created by lax Federal Reserve policies and unreasonable expectations about both credit terms and housing prices, and you have the huge burst bubbles we're struggling with now—and will be for years to come. (More on this in Chapter 4.)

"PHANTOM MONEY"—HOW CREDIT REPLACED CURRENCY

It may seem strange since I've just spent several pages talking about problems caused by the devaluation of the U.S. dollar and the excesses brought on by an excess of petrodollars, but I must now tell you that the most important factor contributing to America's fiscal undoing wasn't money at all—at least not "real" money.

If all we'd had to deal with was actual physical dollars—or even bank deposits and debt instruments backed 100 percent by real money—I have no doubt the United States could have avoided (or at least handled fairly easily) the majority of the problems we're now facing. Unfortunately, the money that has caused us so much trouble is *phantom money.*

When I say phantom money, I'm talking primarily about money created by easy credit, granted at artificially low interest rates based on unrealistically accommodating federal monetary policy and available to almost anyone because of ultraflexible loan requirements set by bankers more concerned with fee income than with fiduciary responsibility. (Again, more on that in Chapter 4.) However, there are other forms of phantom money as well.

One, also linked to government policy and banking rules, is the massive pool of lendable funds created by the United States' fractional-reserve banking system. The term *fractional reserve* simply means that banks are required to keep only a small portion of their deposits on hand to meet any demands by depositors for the return of that money. The rest they can lend out.

At first glance, that seems perfectly rational. After all, how are banks supposed to make a profit if they can't lend out the money you deposit with them? The problem arises when you look at how big a percentage of the money you give them they're allowed to lend— and how many times they can lend it.

For starters, only so-called "demand" accounts even carry a reserve requirement. That includes checking accounts, money market accounts, and banknotes, which are essentially loans the bank makes to itself to finance investments. Savings accounts, certificates of deposit, and other fixed-term deposits aren't subject to reserves, so a bank can immediately turn around and lend out 100 percent of the money it receives in such accounts.

As for the amount of the reserve requirement itself, the required ratios recently ranged from zero for small banks holding less than $10.3 million in demand accounts to a maximum of 10 percent for those holding more than $44 million. Banks in between had to maintain reserves of 3 percent of on-demand deposits.

What that means is best explained by an example. If you put $100 in your checking account at a bank with a required reserve ratio of 3 percent, the bank can lend out $97 of that, holding just $3 in reserve against the possibility you'll demand your money back. If the person who borrows the $97 then pays that money to someone else, and that person deposits the cash into the same bank, the bank can

---

FISCAL FLASHPOINT

A bank's required reserve is usually held in the form of actual paper currency stored in its own vault—known as "vault cash"—or as a deposit with a Federal Reserve bank. (Strategy Point: Savvy bank robbers should *always* go for the vault cash, not just what's in the tellers' drawers.)

---

immediately make a new loan in the amount of $94.06. Repeat the payment-and-deposit cycle, and the bank can make another new loan in the amount of $91.23—and so on and so on and so on.

When money is free, the rational lender will keep on lending until there is no one else to lend to.

—*George Soros*

Theoretically, the bank can make up to $3,333 in loans—secured only by your original $100 deposit ($100/0.03 = $3,333.33)—before there's not enough reserve left for another loan. And if that extra $3,233.33 isn't phantom money, I don't know what is!

The government can, of course, reduce the amount of phantom money creation by increasing bank reserve requirements. For example, with a 10 percent reserve ratio, the bank could expand the initial $100 deposit to only $1,000, and a 20 percent requirement would cut it to just $500. But that didn't happen at any time during the lending frenzy that precipitated the current problems.

ARTIFICIAL EQUITY—ANOTHER FORM OF PHANTOM MONEY

No one will dispute the role the collapse of housing prices played in the meltdown, but the tremendous buildup of home values before the reversal did almost as much damage. Inspired by the easy money available in the mortgage markets, more people than ever before bought houses. When this surge in demand sent real estate prices rapidly and sharply higher, a few sensible homeowners said, "Wow, that's nice," then contentedly sat on their equity cushion and enjoyed their houses. Sadly, far too many others slipped into a state of irrational exuberance and, believing prices would continue rising at the same frantic pace, did one of two things—both bad.

The consumers among the nouveau equity-riche crowd cashed in every penny of their gains, which was really just phantom money because it was created by artificial demand—demand born of easy money rather than truly "earned" buying power. They then bought cars, boats, recreational vehicles, big-screen TVs, $700 cell phones, you name it, skewing all sorts of other economic numbers, from durable goods orders and retail sales to payroll and job-creation numbers. This bonanza of happy statistics cheered government officials, who felt reassured their policies were working and thus continued them, until they didn't—work anymore, that is.

The investors in the group also cashed in, but with different objectives. Some used the funds to buy other assets, such as stocks, helping sustain that market to overvalued levels. Others opted to play real estate tiddlywinks, selling rather than refinancing, then pressing their profits by flipping them into new properties, confident prices would keep rising so they could do it again. And they did, until they didn't—rise anymore, that is.

Obviously, that's an enormously simplified account of what actually went on as the real estate bubble built, but you get the idea. There was an enormous amount of buying and selling and lending and borrowing going on, all of it based on *money that wasn't really there.*

DOES ANYONE *REALLY* UNDERSTAND DERIVATIVES?

Let's be honest here. I use a lot of options in my stock trading activities—in fact, you'll even learn a couple of strategies employing them later in this book. I've also traded a few futures or forward contracts over the years. As such, I always thought I had a pretty good handle on exactly what "derivatives" are and how they work.

I'll tell you, though, some of the things I've seen floated in the derivatives markets the past few years are *way beyond* my comprehension—especially those constructed in over-the-counter transactions. And I'm not alone. Even Warren Buffett called them "weapons of financial mass destruction" and correctly said they posed a "mega-catastrophic risk" for the economy.

Even worse, I'd wager that maybe 90 percent of the people buying and selling the most complicated ones—credit default swaps, interest rate swaps, and the like—didn't understand them, either.

As evidence of this, I'm going to temporarily abandon my vow against using financial jargon and print, verbatim (and with typos), the definition of a credit default swap as supplied on the web site of the International Swaps and Derivatives Association, Inc. (www.isda.org).

> *Product description: Credit default swaps*—A credit default swap is a credit derivative contract in which one party (*protection buyer*) pays an periodic fee to another party (*protection seller*) in return for compensation for default (or similar *credit event*) by a *reference entity*. The reference entity is not a party to the credit default swap. It is not necessary for the protection buyer to suffer an actual loss to be eligible for compensation if a credit event occurs.

Yeah, right! I don't know what that means, and I'm not going to hold my breath while I hunt for someone who can explain it in English.

What I do know is that instruments like that were used to create literally billions in phantom money by taking pools of ordinary mortgages—both prime and subprime—rerating them, repackaging them, splitting them again, selling new packages, insuring them, and then selling the insurance policies. Such unregulated manipulations were used to create billion-dollar bundles of *negotiable agreements*—they can't be called securities—some backed by pools of mortgages with face values of as little as $10 million.

What I also know—and talk about in greater detail in Chapter 4— is that when the defaults actually started to mount, bursting the credit and housing bubbles, all that phantom money quickly disappeared. And when it did, showing up as losses on balance sheets across the land, it took down such financial giants as Bear Stearns, Lehman Brothers, and AIG—and, simultaneously, in conspiracy with other events chronicled in this chapter, the entire economy.

Adding insult to injury, it took millions of investors on a white-knuckle ride they didn't sign up for—and still haven't recovered from.

CHAPTER 4

———

"BUBBLE" GUM

How We All Finally Got Stuck

Banking should not be exciting. If banking is exciting, there is something wrong with it.

—Clay Ewing, president of an Indiana community bank, in early 2008

In the financial world, a *bubble* is generally defined as the "trading of products or assets in high volumes at prices that are considerably above their intrinsic value." A shorter definition—or maybe a synonym—is "speculative mania." Typically, the word *bubble* also carries a modifier—examples being *market bubble, stock bubble, price bubble, housing bubble,* or just the more generic *economic bubble.*

Whatever you choose to call it, though, one thing is certain: Financial bubbles are almost always just as messy as their pink Bazooka counterparts when they blow up in our faces—and far, far more expensive (there are no penny gumball machines for financial bubbles).

As noted earlier, bubbles are certainly not unique to the modern financial era. They date back several hundred years—and probably beyond, had historians been around to note them. If the first decade is any indicator, however, the twenty-first century could be heading for a record, with three massive ones already on the books—the "dot-com bubble," the "housing bubble" and the "credit bubble."

THE DOT-COM BUBBLE

The first of these—the *dot-com bubble*—actually began to inflate around 1995 and didn't pop until March 10, 2000. (I know; purists would say that wasn't *really* in the twenty-first century, which didn't technically start until January 1, 2001, but let's not quibble here.)

That's when the technology-heavy NASDAQ Composite Index hit its intraday peak of 5132.52 before pulling back to close at 5048.62, still more than double its value of a year earlier. Full deflation didn't come until late September of 2002, when the Composite bottomed at 1139.90—though, in fairness, some of that collapse must be attributed to 9/11 and other non-tech-specific factors.

Why This Bubble Even Matters

Essentially, the dot-com bubble was built on all things Internet—and success was easy. All you had to do was start a company, give it a nice technical-sounding name, say you wanted to engage in the business of "e-anything," ask some irrationally exuberant venture capitalist to put up four or five times as much start-up capital as any "normal" business could get, and then watch your IPO stock shoot up 10-fold in price.

As such, I'm not going to devote a lot of time to this particular bubble because, relative to our current *e-conomic* mess, it's only truly relevant for about three reasons.

First, it gave both investors and analysts a very large dose of *unreality* with respect to such fundamental financial concepts as unique business models, market share, sustained growth, actual revenues, and real bottom-line profits—items the huge majority of dot-com companies had none of.

Second, it provided an enduring primer on how easy it can be to attract good money to really bad ideas when interest rates are too low and credit is too easy.

FISCAL FLASHPOINT

There was one other unusual factor besides Internet mania that helped drive the huge run-up in technology stocks, particularly those of information technology (IT) companies—the Y2K scare. Most twentieth-century computers were built to operate with just two-digit date codes—in other words, 95, 96, 97, instead of 1995, 1996, 1997. As such, no one knew for sure what would happen when the world's computers had to deal with dates beginning *20,* as in 2000, 2001, 2002. Would they think it was 1900, 1901, 1902—and crash? Billions of dollars were spent on patches, new software, and even entirely new computers as a precaution, all of which added to the 1995–1999 buying frenzy for tech stocks.

Finally, by erasing an estimated $5 trillion in technology sector market value in about 30 months, it convinced a lot of investors that stocks in general weren't really safe and they should put their money into vehicles with more tangible underlying value. You know, things like California, Nevada, and Florida real estate and collateralized mortgage obligations.

Which brings us to the more recent credit and real estate bubbles—the two events that most intelligent observers believe precipitated the 2007–2009 global economic meltdown. (When I say "intelligent" observers, I'm talking about those looking for actual *causes,* not those just looking for someone to blame.) These two bubbles are almost as inextricably intertwined as the proverbial chicken and egg, but I'll try to separate them for the sake of clarity.

THE HOUSING BUBBLE—BORN OF THE AMERICAN DREAM

Slogans have always been a major factor in American political campaigns, and one of the most memorable came back in 1928 when Herbert Hoover got elected with a promise to fulfill the American Dream by putting "two chickens in every pot and a car in every

garage." Of course, the Hoover version of the Dream ended somewhat poorly with the onset of the Great Depression, but FDR's New
Deal programs kept the concept alive. Like everything else, though,
the Dream was beset by inflation and, by the 1950s, the major feature
for most Americans was home ownership.

Presidents from Ike to LBJ paid lip service to making home ownership more attainable, but it wasn't until Carter and Congress teamed
up to adopt the Community Reinvestment Act (CRA) in 1977 that
the federal government got fully invested in promoting the notion (in
my opinion, always a bad turn of events). According to the Federal
Reserve Board's web site, the original CRA was "intended to encourage depository institutions to help meet the credit needs of the communities in which they operate, including low- and moderate-income
neighborhoods, consistent with safe and sound operations."

Sounds good at first reading, but critics have persistently claimed it
didn't "encourage," but rather "forced" banks to lend to less-than-
creditworthy borrowers, primarily in minority areas. They also dispute the "safe and sound operations" part, saying the new CRA rules
threw accepted standards of banking prudence right out the window.

As it has turned out, the critics were probably right, but no major
damage resulted for the next 15 years or so. Then, in 1992, under

---

FISCAL FLASHPOINT

Fannie Mae is short for the Federal National Mortgage Association
(FNMA), and Freddie Mac short for the Federal Home Loan Mortgage
Corporation. Fannie Mae was founded in 1938, during the Great
Depression, then chartered by Congress as a "government-sponsored
enterprise" (GSE) in 1968. The government created Freddie Mac, also a
GSE, in 1970 to compete with Fannie Mae and thus "facilitate a more
robust and efficient secondary mortgage market." Both corporations
are owned by public shareholders (and now partially by the government
under the "bailout" program). Neither lends money directly to home
buyers. Rather, they purchase loans made by banks, pool them, and sell
them to investors on the open market as "mortgage-backed securities."

pressure from big-city community groups and then–candidate Bill Clinton, Congress pushed through legislation that ramped up the CRA lending guidelines, actually mandating that Fannie Mae and Freddie Mac devote 30 percent of their loan purchases to mortgages for moderate- and low-income borrowers.

Following Clinton's election, that pressure intensified even more. Shortly after the January inauguration, Housing Secretary Henry Cisneros unveiled new rules to allow no-down-payment loans, expand the size and type of loans the government would insure against losses, and use Fannie Mae and Freddie Mac to direct still more money into low-income CRA programs. Related federal rule changes were also made to increase leverage for Fannie and Freddie, which were required to hold just 2.5 percent of capital to back their mortgage investments, as opposed to 10 percent for banks.

To meet their revised goals, the two corporations had to adopt new, looser guidelines for home mortgages. For example, Freddie Mac began approving low-income buyers with bad or no credit, as

---

FISCAL FLASHPOINT

During the 1980s and early 1990s, many non-bank lenders had been accused of redlining—the practice of drawing red lines on city maps of poorer areas and then refusing to make loans to anyone living inside those boundaries. In Congress, Rep. Maxine Waters (D-California) called financial companies not covered by the CRA "among the most egregious redliners," and Clinton administration officials warned if they didn't make more loans to poor minorities, CRA regulations would be extended to *all* mortgage lenders.

In response to that criticism, the Mortgage Bankers Association (MBA) took a surprise step in 1994. It signed an agreement with the Department of Housing and Urban Development (HUD), vowing to make more loans to minorities and join in efforts to loosen lending standards. The first MBA member to sign up? Countrywide Financial, the mortgage company that would eventually be at the heart of the subprime meltdown.

long as they were current on rent and utility payments. They also started counting money from seasonal jobs and welfare toward the income minimums for loan approval. After all, why let facts get in the way of political gain?!

Fannie and Freddie also requested help from large lenders— including nonbanks, which weren't covered by the CRA—in setting up "alternative qualifying" programs. One of these, the Sears Mortgage Corporation, let borrowers qualify for loans with monthly payments equal to 50 percent of their income, as opposed to the 33 percent maximum on standard mortgages.

Although the new Clinton housing rules weren't formally adopted until January 1995, their effect was felt immediately. From 1993 through 1998, the number of CRA mortgage loans increased by 39 percent versus a rise of only 17 percent for other loans.

"Fannie Mae has expanded home ownership for millions of families in the 1990s by reducing down-payment requirements," boasted Franklin D. Raines, Fannie Mae's chairman and CEO at the time. "Yet there remain too many borrowers whose credit is just a notch below what our underwriting has required who have been relegated to paying significantly higher mortgage rates in the so-called subprime market."

"Dubya" Adds His Contribution

In a bid to deal with Raines' complaint, federal housing rules got a further tweaking once President George W. Bush took office. Bush promoted increased home ownership, particularly among minority groups, as part of his plan to bring the nation out of its post–9/11 slump and win liberal support for other programs, including the war on Iraq. In a speech delivered in October 2002, Bush said, "We can put light where there's darkness and hope where there's despondency in this country. And part of it is working . . . to encourage folks to own their own home."

To that end, he eased regulations controlling lenders, urged the Federal Reserve, under then-Chairman Alan Greenspan, to keep interest rates low, pushed for an increase in low-income loans, and persuaded Congress to pass a bill to spend up to $200 million a year to help first-time home buyers with down payments and closing costs. As a result, U.S. home ownership hit record numbers and housing prices moved steadily higher—to levels well beyond what Americans could actually afford, given the limited growth in personal incomes in the same period.

Bush does get credit for requiring mortgage lenders to better explain loan terms—which buyers, eager to get into their new dream homes at all costs, still routinely ignored—and asking Congress to impose tougher regulations on Fannie Mae and Freddie Mac, something Congress resolutely refused to do. Instead, aiming to increase the number of minority homeowners by up to 5.5 million, Congress imposed more new affordable-housing goals on Fannie and Freddie. In response, over the next three years, the two mortgage giants purchased more than $1 trillion in new loans to low- and moderate-income borrowers—and, by the end of 2007, either owned or guaranteed almost 50 percent of the $12 trillion U.S. home mortgage market.

The program was such a success that, by mid-2008, both corporations were on the verge of collapse because of massive loan losses. They were, as they say in Texas, "all hat and no cattle."

At a press conference on September 7, 2008, Treasury Secretary Henry Paulson announced that both the GSEs would be placed under the conservatorship of the Federal Housing Finance Agency (FHFA). Paulson's statement said the move was made to achieve

FISCAL FLASHPOINT

Conservatorship is a legal term denoting establishment of outside supervision—by an independent conservator—over an organization or institution. It's similar to "guardianship" for individuals. With respect to government control over private corporations, as in the case of Fannie Mae and Freddie Mac, it implies a looser, more temporary control than *nationalization,* a term more commonly used in foreign countries.

A LESSON IN HOUSING HYPOCRISY

As already noted, housing has been a major component of the American Dream since World War II—and, as such, has long been an emotionally charged political issue, one both candidates and incumbents can use to reach out and touch voters at all economic levels. It has also proven to be a fertile breeding ground for political hypocrisy, especially now that the real estate bubble and mortgage crisis have forced a severe rethinking of past policies. Two prime practitioners who have been "outed" by the current crisis are Rep. Maxine Waters (D-California) and Rep. Barney Frank (D-Massachusetts), Chairman of the House Committee on Financial Services.

As cited earlier, Waters was one of the most outspoken proponents of expanding the CRA and mandating that lenders lower standards to include poor and minority borrowers. Once that happened, her praise of the "good job" Fannie Mae and Freddie Mac were doing was widely and frequently quoted. In 2004, when Bush and Republicans in Congress tried to push through stronger regulation of the GSEs, she said, "We do not have a crisis at Freddie Mac, and in particular at Fannie Mae, under the outstanding leadership of Frank Raines." (If you'd like to watch her actual speech and find links to dozens of others Waters made on the subject, go to www.youtube.com/watch?v=_MGT_cSi7Rs.) Later, when Raines suggested that, just maybe, Fannie might actually need more regulation, Waters firmly rejected the idea.

She also was among the first to reverse fields and criticize nearly everybody when those same poor and minority borrowers—and many others—began to default on their loans and lose their homes to foreclosure. "Everybody wants tough oversight," she said in a 2007 interview with Fox News. "[W]e need to restructure the loans so people can afford them." Then, in February 2009, speaking for a House plan to help families save homes, she said, "[I]t would ensure that predatory lending entities are not allowed to participate ... because they've been ripping off our homeowners." (Both speeches are also on YouTube.) Finally, to top

(continued)

it off, she bit into the whole bailout idea, setting up a meeting between Treasury officials and OneUnited Bank, the nation's largest black-owned bank (on whose board her husband formerly sat) so OneUnited could request $50 million in special TARP funding. They got $12 million.

Frank (who also has a lengthy roster of contradictory speeches on YouTube) had an even more prolonged relationship with Fannie, Freddie, and high-risk, low-income mortgages. First elected to Congress in 1980, he helped implement the initial CRA-linked housing rules. In 1991, he lobbied to have Fannie Mae ease lending guidelines for multifamily properties despite high default rates. He outspokenly backed the Clinton efforts to expand loan access and, in 2003, helped block the Bush plan to set up an agency to supervise Fannie and Freddie.

Frank opposed any oversight, fearing it might limit low-income and minority loans. He said, "These two entities, Fannie Mae and Freddie Mac, are *not* facing any kind of crisis. The more people exaggerate these problems, the more pressure there is on these companies, the less we will see in terms of affordable housing." He repeated his confidence in their "soundness" in 2004.

But, come September 2008, after both had incurred massive losses and been placed under control of the FHFA, Frank said, "Relative to Freddie and Fannie and the conservatorship, (it) was probably an appropriate, a necessary step. I think it was a good thing for both of them . . ."

Thus, it appears that—when it comes to housing, mortgage lending, and politics—expediency easily outweighs long-term commitment, and hypocrisy reigns supreme.

"three critical objectives: providing stability to financial markets, supporting the availability of mortgage finance, and protecting taxpayers—both by minimizing the near-term costs to the taxpayer and by setting policy makers on a course to resolve the systemic risk created by the inherent conflict in the GSE structure."

When I wrote this, it still hadn't worked.

A Closer Look at the Actual Housing Market

Since you're most likely wondering exactly how Fannie Mae and Freddie Mac (and a lot of other folks in the housing finance industry) got into so much trouble so quickly, I should probably give you at least a brief review of what had happened in the housing market itself.

The basic problem in the housing market—and, really, in the entire economy—was that almost everyone confused reckless consumption with legitimate economic growth, and asset inflation with genuine wealth creation. Flush with home equity and emboldened by rock-bottom teaser rates, U.S. homeowners acted as if they had won the lottery. They made rash decisions and spent lavishly, based on ridiculous assumptions, the consequences of which many are only now beginning to comprehend.

I'm generally not a big fan of overpowering people with statistics, but citing a few is most likely the quickest and easiest way to show exactly what the housing bubble was all about. The following numbers are from the Federal Reserve's Statistical Release on "Annual Flow of Funds Accounts," which came out June 11, 2009:

- In 2000, the total value of U.S. homes was $11.84 trillion. It rose to $16.18 trillion by the end of 2003, peaked at $21.89 trillion in 2006, and had plunged back to $18.33 trillion by the end of 2008.
- In 2000, the median price of a *new* home in the United States was $200,500 and the average price for a new home was $163,400. The median new home price rose to $252,000 in 2003 and peaked at $328,000 in March 2007; the average new home price hit $197,000 in 2003, peaking in 2007 at $267,000. By the end of 2008, those prices had fallen to $248,000 and $207,500, respectively.
- In 2000, homeowner equity was $6.583 trillion versus $4.817 trillion in mortgage debt. In percentage terms, that meant homeowner equity was 57.7 percent of total home values (which doesn't sound bad until you realize equity had fallen from 84 percent in 1945). By 2006, total equity had risen to

$10.945 trillion, but had fallen to 53.0 percent of total value, with $9.675 trillion in debt making up the rest. By the end of 2008, homeowner equity had plunged to just $7.916 trillion (estimated), just 43.1 percent of total value, with debt of $10.476 trillion (estimated) making up the other 56.9 percent.

Further emphasizing how rapidly the housing bubble deflated, the National Association of Realtors reported the median resale price of *existing* U.S. homes was $207,100 at the end of 2007 (already well off the peak), but then fell by 15.3 percent to end 2008 at just $175,400.

Obviously, all of these numbers are averages and some areas fared much better. But many metropolitan areas that had seen the biggest appreciation—including Los Angeles, San Diego, and Las Vegas, where prices skyrocketed by 80 percent from 2000 to 2006—saw much sharper declines as well.

Was Alan Greenspan Really the Culprit?

In late 2007, now former Federal Reserve Chairman Alan Greenspan admitted that the United States had indeed experienced a housing bubble and Fed officials, including himself, had been late to recognize it (an understatement, if ever I heard one). He further explained that the mortgage and credit crises were "caused by the inability of a large number of homeowners to pay their mortgages as their low introductory-rate mortgages reverted to regular interest rates."

Actually, many critics took an alternative view. They said the housing bubble, subprime mortgage crisis, and credit collapse were all caused by . . . you guessed it, Alan Greenspan!

And, quite frankly, I agree with that assessment. I believe that Greenspan and the Federal Reserve, through irresponsible monetary policies, not only caused the housing bubble that led to the mortgage crisis, but also gutted the value of the dollar and fueled the staggering price increases in commodities and energy in 2007 and 2008.

As for the credit crisis, I also question the contention by Greenspan and his successor Fed chairman, Ben Bernanke, that it was primarily the result of a lack of liquidity in the market.

DO YOU REALLY KNOW THE FED?

Most people think the Federal Reserve System is a government agency and the chairman of its board is a government official. Neither notion is strictly correct. The Fed, as it's commonly known, is actually a quasi-public banking system (a private entity with government components). And its chairman, while appointed by the President and confirmed by the Senate, is actually an independent banking official.

Created in 1913 by the Federal Reserve Act, the Fed is located in Washington, D.C., and serves as America's central banking authority. It is run by a seven-member Board of Governors and features 12 regional Federal Reserve Districts (with bank headquarters in 12 major U.S. cities), as well as the 12-member Federal Open Market Committee (FOMC), the Federal Advisory Council, and a Consumer Advisory Council. The 12 regional Federal Banks are privately held corporations with their own nine-member boards.

The Fed's duties are to supervise and regulate U.S. banks, maintain the stability of the banking system, and provide services such as clearing checks and acting as a center for foreign exchange. Its most important function, however, is to control the nation's monetary supply, which directly affects the U.S. economy.

The Fed has two primary tools it can use for this. The first is the ability to change the reserve ratio—the amount of money U.S. banks must keep on deposit in the Federal Reserve banks. Lower reserve requirements increase the amount of money banks have available to lend. More important is the Fed's control of interest rates, which are set by the FOMC. Chief among these is the so-called Fed funds rate—the rate banks charge each other for the use of Federal funds. When this rate is down, credit is cheaper, which lowers interest rates for all consumer, corporate, and bank loans. This makes doing business less expensive and stimulates economic activity. By contrast, higher rates make credit more costly, typically slowing down the economy and preventing inflation.

Members of the Board of Governors are appointed by the President to a single 14-year term, though a member named to complete an unexpired term may be reappointed to a full term. Two members of the

(continued)

board are designated by the President as chairman and vice-chairman for four-year terms, again confirmed by the Senate, and can serve multiple terms in their posts. As such, the post of chairman has been even more enduring than the U.S. Presidency—there have been only 15 Fed chairmen since William G. McAdoo was sworn in as the first in August 1914. Alan Greenspan had the second-longest tenure, taking over the post on August 11, 1987, and serving until January 31, 2006.

Greenspan also lifted the Fed chairman's position to near-celebrity status. Now, every word the chairman or board members utter is scrutinized by the press for clues as to how the economy is performing and whether the Fed will raise or lower rates at its next meeting.

For one thing, credit liquidity was actually worse well into the first quarter of 2009 than it had been when the crisis kicked in late in 2007. Interest-rate imbalances also persist among so-called "policy rates," such as the benchmark London Interbank Offered Rate (LIBOR) and U.S. Treasury offerings of comparable maturity.

This suggests banks still don't trust each other. They all know they've still got junk hidden in their closets and are thus keeping so-called Interbank borrowing rates high so as to reflect what they perceive to be the added risk of doing business. Many lending institutions are also still hoarding cash—something you wouldn't expect to see had a lack of liquidity really been the main credit problem.

Three Primary Factors in the Collapse

I'm more inclined to believe three other things were the primary underlying factors in the credit collapse:

1. Too *much* liquidity, which freed up too much money for too many people to use for really stupid things, such as investing in already overvalued assets, flipping already overpriced houses, and trading in long-term equity for short-term pleasures—and added debt.

2. Fundamental structural problems in the credit industry, including the almost-total lack of regulation, as well as the ability to create credit out of thin air. Consider, for example, all those credit-card offers we receive in the mail. Those aren't backed up by anything other than the good faith of the company issuing them. There's no vault, no gold, no assets in the government's ledgers that accounts for them. The credit-card companies have simply created money out of thin air.

3. The lack of transparency in complex financial instruments, such as collateralized mortgage obligations and credit default swaps, for which there is no public market, making them tough to value and nearly impossible to trade.

Because of these three factors, it has now become clear that a great deal of money was made fraudulently, if not outright illegally, in both the credit and derivatives markets, something made possible largely by Greenspan's lax monetary policy and refusal to raise interest rates.

My opinion on Greenspan is hardly stuck out there alone in the wilderness. Peter D. Schiff, the controversial columnist and frequent thorn in the side of Wall Street, wrote an online article in May 2009 titled, "History Will Show Alan Greenspan Played a Key Role in Creating the U.S. Housing Bubble." In it, he reviewed Greenspan's speech to the National Association of Realtors several days earlier in which the ex-Fed boss denied that he had *any* responsibility for the subprime mortgage crisis.

FISCAL FLASHPOINT

Alan Greenspan coined the phrase "irrational exuberance," using it in a December 1996 speech on monetary policy to warn investors that the stock market was overvalued. We'd all be in much better shape had he revived it when he was insisting on low interest rates and analyzing the 2005–2006 housing market.

After refuting all of Greenspan's contentions, Peter concluded he made "colossal errors on interest-rate policy that blew air into the real estate bubble." Peter also criticized Greenspan's earlier lack of understanding of the housing situation, recalling a 2004 speech in which the Fed chairman actively encouraged adjustable rate mortgages and praised homeowners for extracting home equity, saying it was an "innovative way" to promote economic growth.

Even the mainstream financial media have gone after Greenspan— at least in retrospect. In an April 3, 2009, post on its web site, *Forbes* gave feature play to an article it headlined, "It Really Is All Greenspan's Fault."

And, perhaps most telling, a true industry insider—the former CEO of a publicly traded West Coast financial company, who asked to remain anonymous—points the finger squarely at Greenspan:

> "Things started to go bad all the way back in 2001 when Federal Reserve Chairman Alan Greenspan lowered interest rates, then didn't raise them back up fast enough," he lamented. "And that bad interest-rate policy continued until it triggered the total collapse of the subprime mortgage market and an economic meltdown of near-apocalyptic proportions."

No doubt where he stands on the former Fed boss.

A Consistent Foe of Regulation

Actually, though, I'd extend Greenspan's culpability in the credit bubble back even further. In 1993, Congress attempted to rein in the Federal Reserve, making it more accountable and transparent. Greenspan spoke vehemently against the move, saying, "A central bank, with unlimited power to create money, is a necessity." And, with both Clinton and the Treasury also opposing any new restraints on the Fed, that bill died (as did a proposal by the Securities and Exchange Commission that would have extended capital reserve requirements to securitized mortgages and other kinds of derivatives).

About the same time, there was a downturn in housing prices (much smaller than the recent one) that hit particularly hard in

---

FISCAL FLASHPOINT

The "unlimited power to create money" is one of my longest-standing problems with the Federal Reserve—one I expressed quite forcefully in my "Open Letter to Ben Bernanke," which was published in March 2008 and has gone viral on the Internet. Printing money is presumed to stimulate demand, but it doesn't always work—and, when it doesn't, as was the case this time around, it can actually make things worse. That's because every dollar the Fed prints devalues every other dollar in circulation, and also stokes inflation—which was why Americans were pinched so hard in 2008.

California, as well as in fast-growing metropolitan areas elsewhere in the country, triggering numerous mortgage defaults. Fearful the pattern would spread, Congress again tried to impose its will on the Fed, but Greenspan resisted and argued the Fed needed unrestricted power to prevent such events. In his response to Congress, he wrote, "Only a central bank with unlimited power . . . can guarantee that such a process [a cascading sequence of defaults] will be thwarted before it becomes destructive." (Wait a minute! Isn't a "cascading sequence of defaults" exactly what we've just seen—probably *caused* rather than *prevented* by our central bank?)

Congress again failed to limit the Fed's powers, but did pass the Home Ownership and Equity Protection Act of 1994, which charged the Federal Reserve System with "issuing regulations defining unfair and deceptive lending practices" beginning in 1995. Had Greenspan done so, he could have nipped many of the fraudulent and predatory lending practices that caused our present mess in the bud—but he specifically refused to do so, never issuing the requested regulations.

Greenspan was criticized from several fronts regarding the lack of action—including from within the Fed itself. In 2000, Edward M. Gramlich, a Federal Reserve governor (who died in 2007), warned that "a fast-growing new breed of new mortgage lenders" was luring many people into "risky mortgages they could not afford." But,

> **FISCAL FLASHPOINT**
>
> With no regulatory restraints on lending coming from Fed boss
> Greenspan, the Treasury decided to try a different tack. In 2001, Sheila
> C. Bair, a senior Treasury official, tried to coax subprime lenders into
> adopting a code of "best practices" and to let outside monitors verify
> their compliance. Surprise! None of the lenders would agree to monitors,
> many rejected the code entirely—and, Bair later recalled, those who *did*
> adopt the practices soon abandoned them.

when Gramlich privately asked Fed examiners to investigate, he was
quickly shut down by Greenspan.

THE CREDIT BUBBLE—WHERE SUBPRIME MORTGAGES WENT WRONG

Given the push to get unqualified people into homes, the prolonged
low-interest-rate environment, and the rapid ballooning of housing
prices to unsustainable levels, it's really not that hard to see how the
subprime mortgage business went bad—especially when you factor
in the greed and irresponsibility of the subprime lenders themselves.

It was a situation that literally fed on itself—right up to the point
when it threw up.

Thanks to the Fed policy, there was tons of liquidity in the market,
all of it looking for assets. Plus the big investment banks were
leveraging it to the hilt—holding assets "off the books" at ratios of up
to 50-to-1 versus the usual 10- or 12-to-1. There were also SpIVs—
Special Investment Vehicles—which most people didn't really understand, but which allowed the banks to move even more questionable
assets off book.

Finally, you had these "baby analysts"—30-year-olds who'd never
seen a full economic cycle and didn't understand the inherent fallacy
underlying the steady rise in the price of houses. They assumed the

housing market was *always* going to go up, so you didn't need to rely on what customers could pay now because they could always refinance later based on the higher values.

Lending restrictions became looser and looser, luring more and more new home buyers into the market using subprime loans based on this theory of ever-increasing housing values. This led to lots of new loan products, including the now infamous "stated-income loans"—aka, "liar loans." Applicants for these didn't have to show proof of income—they only had to state what their income was. This let a lot of bottom-income-rung, blue-collar workers—and even illegal immigrants—into the market. They simply *stated* their income was $175,000 annually when, in fact, they were really only making maybe $20,000 to $25,000, if that much.

It was fraud—and everyone *knew* it was fraud—but nobody stopped it. Instead, the subprime mortgage issuers merely assumed higher losses would occur and set higher interest rates to kick in after a come-on period of "no money down, no interest for X-years." So-called "2/28" loans were hot: For two years, you paid a low interest rate; then, for the next 28 years, you paid a *much higher* interest rate based on the lie you'd told about your income.

But, of course, people *couldn't* pay that higher rate—and, when house prices quit rising, they couldn't refinance, either.

Next stop, Default City!

The Crisis Moves to the Lenders

Because of the risk, these loans were quickly packaged as "mortgage-backed securities" by mortgage bankers and outfits like Fannie Mae and Freddie Mac, then sold off to investment banks, pension funds, hedge funds, and even private investors—all of whom were eager to buy because of the excess liquidity. The market was huge—and nobody looked too closely at the true merit of the securities because of the big fees that came from selling them.

According to the Securities Industry and Financial Markets Association, an estimated $8.99 trillion in these securities was

EXACTLY WHAT ARE MORTGAGE-BACKED SECURITIES?

Mortgage-backed securities are similar to bonds in that they represent debt and promise to pay a fixed amount of interest for a set period of time. They are created when a broker, bank, or a GSE like Fannie Mae buys a bundle of mortgages from a primary lender—that is, from the company that actually gave borrowers their mortgages—and then uses the monthly payments from the homeowners as a revenue stream to pay investors who bought portions of the offering.

In addition to creating these securities, big Wall Street firms (like Bear Stearns and Lehman Brothers) also trade them. By selling the mortgages they make, lenders replenish their capital accounts, allowing them to lend again. In theory, buyers of mortgage-backed securities feel more secure because their holdings don't rely on the financial strength of just one borrower, but on the collective creditworthiness of many.

In practice, that proved to be a highly misleading assumption over the past few years.

outstanding at the peak in early 2008, with roughly a quarter of the underlying mortgages rated as subprime. That's out of a total of about $14.6 trillion in outstanding U.S. mortgages (this includes other properties besides homes).

That's a lot of money, but what's really scary is that it doesn't even include mortgage-based derivatives, such as credit default swaps and other synthetic securities—ones with no mortgages backing them whatsoever, created because somebody was willing to guarantee them and the fees for selling them were so high.

According to a release from the Depository Trust & Clearing Corporation, which facilitates trading in OTC derivatives, "as of October 9, 2008, credit default swap contracts registered in the Warehouse totaled approximately *$34.8 trillion*. This is down significantly from the approximately $44 trillion that were registered in the Warehouse at the end of April this year."

A MAJOR FAILURE OF THE CREDIT-RATING SYSTEM

Another culprit in the crisis was the credit-rating system—which failed to rate the subprime mortgage-backed securities properly—not that the rating agencies were all that objective to begin with. Wall Street and the ratings agencies have been in bed together for years, and they operate on what's essentially a "pay to play" model. If you want the ratings for new securities, you pay to get them.

Besides, the first derivatives were so complicated it took a super-computer to value them and 72 hours to do it—and those had just three *traunches.* Some of the derivatives that blew up in the recent meltdown had 20 or more traunches, which could take a supercomputer two weeks to analyze. (A *traunch* is the segment of an income-investment vehicle that gets a particular inflow of cash; for example, return of principal on a mortgage derivative might go to the first traunch and interest to the second, with the third getting paid only when the first two have collected $1 million each. As such, different traunches have different risk levels.)

That meant there was absolutely no way the ratings agencies could even understand the offering memoranda, much less the true risks. (The same could obviously be said for the buyers—and, truth be known, most likely for the top executives of the companies selling them. My bet is they did it for pure greed—and, if they actually did grasp the risks, chose to ignore them.)

Anyway, rating agencies—S&P, Moody's, and the like—didn't have a clue, but they did have long-standing relationships with the issuers; outfits like Lehman, Bear Stearns, and Fannie and Freddie. So they took their word that the securities were safe and started rating them AAA, just like regular asset-backed securities. Based on that, money market, retirement, and all sorts of other funds felt secure buying in—and ultimately got badly burned.

Wow—$8.99 trillion, $14.6 trillion, $34.8 trillion! The whole U.S. annual GNP in 2007 was *only $14.1 trillion.* So, it's no wonder everyone from Wall Street and the Fed to Congress and the President started quaking in their boots when the whole thing began to unravel—which it did in June 2007. (Actually, the unraveling started well before then, but that's when everybody first started to pay attention.)

THE BITTER END BEGINS

The summer of 2007 was when the foreclosure rate began to climb significantly for the first time. Concurrently, home prices started flattening out—or, in some places like California and Florida, actually going down. That quickly slammed the house "flippers"—the people who were really speculating—and their rush to sell and save themselves accelerated the reversal.

The first shock to reach Wall Street came on June 19, 2007, when two Bear Stearns hedge funds were forced into bankruptcy. They'd invested heavily in AAA-rated mortgage-backed securities, which plummeted in value when they essentially turned out to be junk. The actual money lost was $1.6 billion—which now seems like chump change given the losses we've seen since. But the fact that it had happened at Bear Stearns, a company known specifically for risk management, was a clear sign of how vulnerable the mortgage-backed security markets were—and how anyone involved in those markets could be vulnerable, too.

Joe Nocera of *The New York Times* summed up the situation when he wrote that the death of the two hedge funds wasn't the big news. "The world generally doesn't come to an end when that happens. But, in this case, the fact that these hedge funds are going under while holding mortgage-backed securities that were rated AAA . . . is a really scary thing."

By August, the level of fear was rising, not just on Wall Street, but around the globe—as evidenced by a sharp spike in the London Interbank Offered Rate (LIBOR), which is the rate the top international banks charge to lend money to other top banks. Normally, it runs about 20 basis points higher than the rate on three-month U.S. government-issued Treasury bills, but suddenly the difference (known as the *TED spread*) spiked to three times that—and stayed there.

I'm not going to bore you with every little detail of what happened from then on, mostly because it's been reported ad infinitum in the press, on TV, and all over the Internet, so you can't have missed it—and you're probably sick of it. Suffice it to say, things continued to deteriorate until mid-March of 2008, when—after two weeks of panicked negotiations—the government forced through a deal in which JPMorgan Chase & Co. bought Bear Stearns, which by now was at the brink of bankruptcy. Morgan initially offered just $2 a share for Bear's stock—which had traded as high as $171 in 2007—but ultimately raised the bid to $10 to make the deal work. (Note: That was *after* the Fed came up with $30 billion to guarantee Bear's toxic loans, and some vociferous behind-the-scenes whining that the stock really was worth more than "that.")

By then, it was obvious that the mortgage crisis was affecting everyone in the business, impacting all forms of credit—and steadily getting worse. On July 2, 2008, in a London speech, U.S. Treasury Secretary Henry Paulson called for improvements in regulatory structures for world capital markets. "For market discipline to be effective, it is imperative that market participants not have the expectation that lending from the Fed, or any other government support, is readily available," he warned—and then uttered his now-infamous statement: "For market discipline to constrain risk effectively, financial institutions must be allowed to fail."

Which they did!

Less than two weeks later, Paulson asked Congress for the authority to take over Fannie Mae and Freddie Mac, both wallowing in worthless mortgages. That happened on September 7, with the Federal Housing Finance Agency taking over as conservator and the government taking 80 percent ownership of each, giving them access to $200 billion in new capital.

THE GOVERNMENT GETS ONE RIGHT—BUT EVEN DOES THAT WRONG

The government then did the one thing I'd been loudly advocating they do since the very beginning: They let one of the big investment banks fail. But, in typical government fashion, they did it badly.

In speeches around the world since the crisis began, I've been very clear about this from the very start. The whole notion that something is "too big to fail" or "too much a part of American life to fail" is utter nonsense! Pure myth.

Now I'll be clear about it here, too.

Plenty of big companies have failed in the past—huge companies. And, yes, it hurt—sometimes a lot—but we *always* recovered. And, painful as it might have been, we would have recovered this time, too. So, no matter how big they were, the companies that failed this time around in the business world—from Fannie and Freddie through the banks and brokerages down to GM and Chrysler—should have been allowed to fail in real life. To fade out of existence, just like small companies that fail.

History will show that, if there was one really catastrophic mistake in this whole affair, it was approving the initial bailouts, and then allowing them to proceed on an ever-expanding scale under the new administration. Looking back, we'll see that the politicians and bureaucrats made things far worse with their meddling, and Americans will suffer for it—probably for generations.

We grew up in a world in which we were taught that, if we work hard and be careful with our money, we will reap the rewards. Now we are learning that we can do those things and, instead of being rewarded, have to involuntarily take care of the other guy—the guy who *didn't* work hard and *wasn't* careful with money.

The government's "bailout bonanza" is doing nothing but reinforcing the notion that bad boys get away with it, while responsible individuals get clobbered—and I'm mad as hell about it! What's worse, there are serious questions being raised about the constitutionality of what's been done.

Even former Fed Chairman Paul Volcker (among others) is on record as saying he's not sure that what's been done is legal. "The Federal Reserve has judged it necessary to take actions that extend to the very edge of its lawful and implied powers, transcending in the process certain long-embedded banking principles and practices," Volcker said in a speech to the Economic Club of New York. He also said it amounted to "an implied promise" of future bailouts, which the Fed lacks the legal authority to make.

I've actually read the 1913 Federal Reserve Act—the one that created the entire System—and nowhere in there does it say *anything* about the Fed having the power, or even the right, to bail out private companies. Nowhere! You can read it online at www.federalreserve. gov/aboutthefed/fract.htm. I think you'll be startled by what it says. I sure was.

Of course, this has become an academic argument since the Fed has already embarked on the bailout path, and the Obama administration has endorsed the whole thing. Now, as investors, all we can do is plan ahead so we can deal with it as painlessly and profitably as possible.

What They Did Wrong with Lehman

Enough of the rant—back to the Lehman deal. The problem wasn't that the government let Lehman fail. It was that they let it happen too quickly, without understanding the implications or making provisions to deal with the consequences.

Lehman, which had made billions in the now-toxic high-risk real estate market, needed extra financing, but it couldn't get a dime. It tried to make deals with Warren Buffett, Barclays, Bank of America, Morgan Stanley, HSBC, and sovereign wealth funds from the Middle East and China—all with no success. It finally resorted to a plea to a South Korean bank—and, when that failed, it was literally broke, with no collateral to cover its outstanding loans.

After the markets closed on Friday, September 12, Paulson and Fed Chairman Ben Bernanke summoned the heads of Wall Street's largest firms to the Federal Reserve Bank in New York. Paulson made it clear there would be no bailout for Lehman, and urged the banks and brokerage firms to find a buyer among their ranks. That process consumed the weekend, but no fish was found to take the hook and, on Monday, Lehman was forced to file for bankruptcy protection.

The reason that quick and unplanned action by Paulson and the government was such a major mistake was that they didn't understand just how heavily Lehman was into every aspect of the credit markets. Lehman's collapse resulted in a global loss of confidence in the markets—spawning an apocalyptic panic that saw investors "break the buck" of the Reserve Fund, a major money market fund.

Money funds had pledged to—and always before managed to—keep the value of their shares at $1.00, just adding or redeeming shares as fund values changed. However, investors pulled $50 billion out of the Reserve Fund overnight, draining the account down to zero. The Reserve Fund couldn't pay and had to let share values drop below a dollar. In the ensuing panic, investors drained *a quarter of a trillion dollars* out of all money market funds—in just three days. Had the government analyzed the potential impact in advance and taken some precautions, that panic could almost certainly have been prevented.

Lehman was also so heavily invested in the market for credit default swaps that swap rates jackknifed. Where it had previously been possible to insure $100 million in mortgage bonds for 75 basis points ($75,000), it was now costing 500 basis points, or $500,000. Nobody could, or would, pay that, and trillions of dollars worth of bonds were left uninsured. Overnight, the entire economy was so de-leveraged that no one could borrow money anywhere. Even corporate giants like General Electric were unable to get the short-term money needed to make payroll, and the government essentially had to nationalize insurance giant AIG so policy claims could be paid.

The result was the first of the financial bailouts we now so know and love. To prevent financial Armageddon, the government, based on a three-page bill Paulson sent to Congress on September 20,

---

FISCAL FLASHPOINT

Senator Christopher Dodd, the Connecticut Democrat who headed the Senate Banking Committee, later summed up the Congressional reaction: "The idea that they send you up a bill at 1:30 in the morning on a Saturday—a three-page bill saying, 'Give me $700 billion and, by the way, no agency can intervene and no court can intervene'—is really rather remarkable. A simple subprime mortgage is four pages long, and here he was, asking for $700 billion—twice the cost of the Iraq war—in three pages, and nobody can ask any questions."

stepped in and guaranteed everything—from retail bank accounts to corporate bonds and mortgage securities—everywhere across America.

It took Congress until October 3 to finally pass the bailout bill, but they did—since they really had no choice. Because Paulson, Bernanke and crew had plunged in so blindly to begin with, there was simply no longer a secondary market for any type of credit, and the global economy couldn't survive without one.

In fact, the outlook at the time was so bleak that former Bear Stearns CEO Alan "Ace" Greenberg said, "There is no Wall Street. It's a street just like Broadway or Madison Avenue now. There are no firms on it. The model of the investment banking firm is gone for-ever. It will never come back, in my opinion. There are no invest-ment banks."

Sounds terrible, and it was—and, for many folks, it still is.

But, as you'll see in Part II, it wasn't America's first catastrophic financial crisis—and *there are plenty of reasons to look ahead to a bright and even more rewarding future.*

PART TWO

THE GREAT DECOUPLING

In Chapters 1 and 2, you got a fairly thorough overview of how the American economy developed over the past 250 years, and how the economies of most of the world's other free-market nations became inextricably intertwined with that of the United States. That link was verified by the series of bubbles and busts, detailed in Chapter 4, that rocked the United States in recent years—events that had an equal, if not greater impact on much of the rest of the world.

However, as you saw in Chapter 3, the ties that once linked global economic and monetary systems are not nearly as strong as they once were, having steadily loosened over the last 40 years, beginning with the abandonment of the Bretton Woods agreements. And now, thanks largely to a startling shift in both production and consumption growth to emerging areas of the globe, the handcuffs that bind the rest of the world to U.S. policies and U.S. dollars are coming off.

"The Great Decoupling" is definitely under way.

That sounds a bit scary—and it is causing a great deal of consternation among those in the political realm and latter-day Luddites, who think the world should never change. But, for those in the know, the change represented by this decoupling is cause for great celebration. The history books show that changes such as this have ushered in every great "age"—from the Age of Exploration to the Information

Age and everything in between—and have clearly been the creative impetus behind mankind's greatest economic opportunities.

WHAT *DECOUPLING* REALLY MEANS

The term *decoupling,* while not new, is widely misunderstood—and, even more widely misapplied. Most people think of it solely in terms of financial markets. However, what it actually means is that global *economies* will disconnect, particularly as previously underdeveloped nations build up their own consumer bases. We're already seeing that these disruptions in the developed economies—the United States, Europe, and Japan—are having much less of an impact on growth in the developing economies.

For example, most major disturbances in the United States now cause only minor ripples in the Chinese economy, which has developed a strong consumer base of its own in recent decades. In fact, it's entirely conceivable that, in 50 years or so, China won't even need the United States or its products, instead relying solely on *regional influences* for its economic health—a trend that applies to other developing nations as well.

Since the mid-1980s, global-scale disturbances have become far less common as an influencing factor in the internal business cycles of the world's emerging countries. Recent data show that *regional* inputs are much more important—for two primary reasons:

1. The economies in emerging nations are being propelled more and more by their own growing customer base, as well as those in neighboring countries.
2. The current international slowdown, rather than being caused by systemic conditions worldwide, was largely driven by problems specific to the United States—particularly the housing bubble and issues related to currency valuation.

As a result, most of the stronger emerging countries will be in a position to almost completely decouple from the U.S. economy within the coming decade, based on:

- Continuing expansion of their own domestic consumer bases.
- Further development of their inter-regional trade connections.
- A lessening of global disturbances as the developed markets begin their own economic recoveries.

Only then will true decoupling be seen in the financial markets as well—at which point, we may well have to revise that famous old adage. You know, the one that says, "When the U.S. economy sneezes, the rest of the world catches cold."

In the future, it may be far more accurate to say, "When the U.S. economy sneezes, it should take two aspirin and call Beijing in the morning."

WHAT THIS MEANS FOR YOU

Obviously, though, we're not at that point yet—but we will be within our lifetimes, and probably most of the way there a mere 10 years from now. So what should you do to get ready? I provide some answers to that question in Part II, just to set the stage for the meatier, more specific advice coming in Part III.

How can I do that? Well, for one thing, I remind you that, as bad as events have seemed recently, it's really nothing new. As you'll learn in Chapter 5, America has experienced a whole host of economic calamities in the past, and it has recovered from *every one of them*. You'll also see that, though the dips are typically less severe than this one, downturns in the economy are actually normal—part of a natural cycle of business that has extended back for as long as there has been business.

Sadly, we'll also take a look at some things the United States, particularly our government and monetary leaders, *didn't learn* from past experience—things that undoubtedly contributed to both the severity and extended duration of the current crisis. Things that must be learned this time around if America is to maintain a continuing leadership role in the world's new economic order, which I cover in Chapter 6.

Finally, in Chapter 7, I look at the primary forces that should lead the global economy toward recovery, as well as the key areas of the globe I think you should watch to see the initial signs of this emerging rebound. Chief among those, of course, is the Red Dragon—China.

I firmly believe China is already well on the road to global economic (and perhaps even monetary) dominance, and I close out Part II by explaining why—dispelling some of the myths you've no doubt heard and detailing some of the powerful realities that make one thing perfectly clear:

If you hope to succeed as an investor in what I believe will be the next "Golden Age of Wealth Creation," you absolutely must make a well-thought-out China strategy an integral part of your overall financial plan. And that's what Part III will help you create.

CHAPTER 5

WAIT A MINUTE!

We've Seen This Before
(But We Still Haven't Learned)

This is like deja vu all over again.
—Yogi Berra

Investors, by their very nature, are an optimistic lot. If they weren't, why would they put up their hard-earned cash to buy stocks, bonds, gold, or whatever? Not because they think prices are going to go *down!* (Okay, we all know there are short sellers and put option buyers, but even they are optimistic—optimistic that the market they're playing will tank.)

Alas, optimism has a dangerous side effect—it causes an extreme loss of memory. Once prices start moving in their favor, optimistic investors think they're going to keep going in that direction forever—*even though they never have before.* That's why they're nearly always surprised when the markets turn, or the economy as a whole does a great big belly flop—which it most certainly has this time around.

In reality, though, they shouldn't be. Cycles are an essential part of economic life—and have been for as long as man has had anything resembling an economy. It's *normal*. Just as a long-distance runner must slow down every so often to catch his breath—and occasionally even stop for a short while—so must economies pause at fairly regular intervals. They need to rest a bit, digest recent overindulgences, refuel with innovative technologies and growing markets, and plot an appropriate new course before they can resume their jog to the future.

About the only thing that doesn't routinely cycle into a new phase is the loss of memory. Just as investors forgot that the rallies weren't going to go on forever, they also forget the subsequent slumps will eventually end as well. But they *always* do—and this one will, too.

A LEISURELY TRIP DOWN RECESSIONARY LANE

To help convince you of that, I want to take a quick look at some of America's past downturns, some of the things that caused them and the truly great opportunities they created for building new wealth. Obviously, any review of U.S. economic crises in terms of severity would rank the 1929 market crash and ensuing Great Depression and our current meltdown at the top (order yet to be determined). But, it probably makes most sense to review past problems chronologically.

As an indication of just how enduring America's sporadic financial crises have been, you have to go all the way back to 1819 to find the first one. That disruption, rather unimaginatively called the Panic of 1819, featured high inflation, foreclosures, widespread bank failures, a steep rise in unemployment and even a sharp drop in prices on America's first stock exchange, which had been founded in 1790—in Philadelphia.

The Panic was blamed on—and this will sound eerily familiar—heavy borrowing by the government to finance the War of 1812, followed by a tightening of credit by the Second Bank of the United States (basically their equivalent of the Fed—though Congress back then had the good sense to give it just a 20-year charter) in response

---

FISCAL FLASHPOINT

Note to Democrats: You can't blame Republican free-market policies for the Panic of 1819; the GOP wasn't even founded until February 28, 1854. The Panic also predated many other notable events. For example, it came 10 years before the birth of Levi Strauss, credited with manufacturing the first blue jeans—perhaps the most enduring symbol of the power of "Made in America" to consumers around the world. It also came 12 years before the first true validation of the U.S. banking system—on March 19, 1831, Edward Smith executed the country's first bank robbery, hitting the City Bank of New York for $245,000. (History doesn't record what weapon he used, but it definitely wasn't a "Saturday Night Special" since Samuel Colt didn't get a patent for the first revolver until 1836.) He was caught and sentenced to five years in Sing Sing—which *did* exist back then, proving that crime has been an equally enduring feature of American life. Finally, it predated by 16 years an event that was almost certainly predictive of today's activities by the Fed—on June 2, 1835, P. T. Barnum began his first circus tour of the United States.

---

to risky lending practices by wildcat banks in the West (which in those days meant Ohio, Kentucky, and Missouri, not California and Nevada).

But, setting a strong precedent for the future, the economy made a fairly quick recovery, fueled by continued westward expansion, the acquisition of new territories (Florida), increased literacy and education (the first women's college was founded in 1821), and rapid technological advances. The Erie Canal opened and the first steam locomotive went into operation in 1825, and massive fortunes were made by those who invested in the shipping and railroad companies that followed. International trade blossomed, even over land. Missouri trader William Becknell carried a wagon train of U.S. goods down the Santa Fe trail to Mexico in 1821 and made such a huge profit that he negotiated a trade agreement with the Mexican governor and repeated the trip yearly for more than a decade. Stock prices soared and trading mushroomed in both Philadelphia and New York.

While there were several minor ups and downs, the U.S. economy ran fairly smoothly over the next four decades as rapid growth—in both territory and population—and technological innovation helped create both business and personal fortunes. Then, all purely economic concerns got pushed aside for almost a decade as the Civil War interrupted. Although filled with inconsistencies and injustices, Reconstruction fired the economy back up—until the next major panic hit in 1873.

A HORSE IS A HORSE, OF COURSE, OF COURSE . . .

Ask an expert for the reasons underlying the current crises and you'll get a list almost as long as your arm. However, the economy was simpler in the 1870s and the 1873 Panic was essentially caused by one thing—horses.

At that time, despite steam engines and other "modern" technologies, the U.S. economy still depended heavily on horsepower. The real kind. Horses unloaded and carried cargo from ships, pulled carriages and city trolleys, worked farms and ranches, pulled fire wagons and ambulances, and transported troops and military equipment. American society—and the U.S. economy—couldn't function without them.

But, in late 1872, roughly 99 percent of the horses in the United States came down with equine influenza, which had crossed the border from Canada and spread to the West and Deep South in just a few months. Horses everywhere went down, coughing uncontrollably and too weak to work. The consequences were almost unimaginable by today's standards. Drays disappeared from city streets, and stores emptied of goods, halting commerce. Business and social travel ground to a halt. Frontier troops had to go into battle against the Indians on foot. A fire to rival the later Chicago conflagration raged through Boston for three days, destroying more than 700 buildings at a cost of $73.5 million and killing 20 people—because there were no horses to carry water to firefighters. Even the railroads stopped running because the coal they ran on was hauled to the tracks by horses.

In the end, more than 20,000 businesses folded, including a third of the nation's railroads; the stock market crashed as profit numbers plunged; and unemployment rose to 15 percent. By the following spring, most of the horses had recovered—but the economy suffered for more than five years.

Once again, however, it rebounded strongly—and even greater fortunes were created. Driving forces included new states and new people, transcontinental railroads, a second round of silver strikes in Nevada, gold strikes in Alaska, oil gushers in Texas, and human ingenuity in the form of the telephone, functional electric power systems, early automobiles, and the beginnings of the age of aviation—all of which created new companies, new stocks, and rising prices for all of them.

FISCAL FLASHPOINT

Another event with long-term economic impact came during this period. In May of 1886, workers across the United States started a general strike, seeking laws to mandate an eight-hour workday. The strike went bad three days after it began when a bomb went off during a rally in Chicago's Haymarket Square, sparking a riot that led to dozens of injuries and hundreds of arrests. Later that year, 25 unions joined together to form the American Federation of Labor (AFL) and, over the next 15 years, unions pushed through eight-hour days in industries ranging from textiles to mining. This led to increased job creation, as well as a strong push for more efficient manufacturing methods.

A PROVEN CASE OF GREEDY CAPITALISM

Many people have tried to blame our current troubles on greedy capitalists—specifically bankers and mortgage lenders—but, while they certainly contributed, it's unlikely they were the total cause. However, America's next major economic panic, in 1907, was definitely inspired by a greedy capitalist.

Augustus Heinze was a multimillionaire, having made a fortune mining copper in Montana. Believing he had sufficient control over the industry to corner the copper market, he enlisted the aid of several major banks and initiated a scheme to buy all the shares of United Copper. However, his dream exceeded his grasp, and the scheme fell apart, bringing down Heinze, United Copper, the banks—and thousands of stockholders.

The failure of the banks in Heinze's deal stoked concern about the soundness of all U.S. banks, and investors began pulling their money out, triggering the collapse of one of New York City's biggest trust companies. Panic resulted and the stock market crashed. Congress called for a bailout but, since there was no U.S. central bank at the time, they had no way of instituting one, no means of injecting money into the economy—and no extra cash to inject.

On the plus side, the financial system was saved when millionaire banker J. P. Morgan organized (with more than a little arm-twisting) a group of leading financiers, who stepped in and used their own resources to prop up the banks and rekindle upward fire in the stock market.

Morgan, who could be ruthless, has gone down in history as saying, "I owe the public nothing"—but it was his single-handed action that reversed the financial panic that began on October 23, 1907, with a run on the Knickerbocker Trust Company. Acting with all the force and effect of a central bank—conducting business largely from the antiquities-laden library of his Madison Avenue mansion—Morgan pulled together teams of analysts and money men to determine which financial institutions could be saved, and then channel funds to them. At one point, Morgan even resorted to locking leading New York trust company presidents in his library overnight in order to negotiate deals to support the financial institutions.

Morgan obtained pledges from the Bank of England, John D. Rockefeller, and other major financiers, and he personally interceded to prevent New York City from defaulting on its short-term bonds by arranging a $30 million bailout and drawing up a contract on the spot.

On October 24, Morgan saved the New York Stock Exchange—which faced being shuttered unless massive rescue funds could somehow be provided to 50 brokerage firms verging on collapse. To stem the panic, Morgan quickly assembled a group of bank presidents, got them to pledge a cool $25 million within minutes and, by 2:16 P.M., had a team assembled on the Exchange floor to announce that "call money" was now available with an interest rate of just 10 percent.

Morgan's emergency injection of liquidity into the banking system undoubtedly prevented an already bad situation from getting still worse. And, by taking command and rallying other bankers, Morgan succeeded in restoring confidence in the U.S. economy.

On the negative side—very, very negative in my opinion—the politicians were totally dismayed by their lack of control in the situation. In response, they created the Federal Reserve System in 1913—and the first income tax was instituted in the same year so the newly formed Fed would have some money to play with. Rue the day!

A CONSPIRACY OF COLLUSION: HOW THE FED WAS BORN

As the central banking system for the United States, the Federal Reserve is best known for its effect on interest rates. But, since the Fed isn't the most transparent of institutions, many people believe that unseen hands are actually controlling U.S. monetary policy. Coupled with suspicions aroused about just *who* has been benefiting from all the recent bailouts, many of the old suspicions surrounding the Fed's cloak-and-dagger birth are being conjured up anew.

It's true that bad times tend to bring out the conspiracy theorist in just about everyone looking for somebody (or something) to blame. And it's also true that Americans have always been suspicious of central banks, going back as far as colonial times. But the history of how the Fed came to be can easily be read as the tale of a financial cartel,

(continued)

conceived and dedicated to the proposition that all men are *not* created equal—especially fat-cat bankers and their wealthy friends.

Following the Panic of 1907, Congressional demands for banking and currency reform led to the establishment of the National Monetary Commission to recommend a new system of controls. The chief commissioner, Senate Republican leader and financial expert Nelson Aldrich, supported centralized banking—an idea that was met with fierce opposition by politicians wary of Aldrich's close ties to wealthy bankers. (His daughter was married to John D. Rockefeller's son.)

To sidestep the opposition, Aldrich loaded the assistant secretary of the Treasury and executives representing the banks of J.P. Morgan, Rockefeller, and Kuhn, Loeb & Co. into a sealed railway car, blinds drawn, on the night of November 22, 1910, and hustled them away from Wall Street for a trip to "Destination Unknown."

A writer named Bertie Charles Forbes (who subsequently founded *Forbes* magazine) later described the trip thusly: "Picture a party of the nation's greatest bankers stealing out of New York on a private railroad car under cover of darkness, stealthily hieing hundreds of miles south, embarking on a mysterious launch, sneaking onto an island deserted by all but a few servants, living there a full week under such rigid secrecy that the names of not one of them was mentioned lest the servants learn the identity and disclose to the world this strangest, most secret expedition in the history of American finance."

The destination turned out to be Jekyll Island, Georgia, where the financiers remained ensconced in seclusion for 10 days. They discussed "the matter of a uniform discount [interest] rate," agreed on a detailed currency system for the United States, and hammered out a plan for what they called the Federal Reserve System. The results of that meeting became reality three years later when, in December 1913, President Woodrow Wilson signed the Federal Reserve Act into law.

Frank A. Vanderlip of the Rockefellers' National City Bank of New York finally broke his silence about that meeting in his autobiography, *From Farmboy to Financier*: "I was as secretive, indeed, I was as furtive as any conspirator. Discovery, we knew, simply must not happen . . . If it were

(continued)

to be exposed that our particular group had got together and written a banking bill, that bill would have had no chance whatever of passage by Congress . . ."

Little surprise then that, even today, conspiracy theorists continue to view the Fed as a real threat to our Constitutional right to the pursuit of financial happiness—a collusive marriage between corrupt corporate forces and their flunky political friends that speaks volumes about the lengths to which the rich and powerful will go to bury the truth.

Note: If you'd like to find out more about the origins of the Fed, the shroud of secrecy has been shredded by several authors, most notably libertarian economist Murray Rothbard in his *The Case Against the Fed,* and G. Edward Griffin in *The Creature from Jekyll Island: A Second Look at the Federal Reserve.*

Despite those still-existing handicaps, the economy proved its resilience once more, riding wartime industrial production, a postwar explosion of enthusiasm and consumerism—built largely on the purchasing power of women celebrating suffrage at last—and more technological gains (including Ford's assembly lines and radio broadcasting) to the heights of the Roaring Twenties. Uncounted fortunes were made in countless enterprises. (Note: Reflecting how overall attitudes have changed in the past 90 years, in November 1920, the first vote in which women could participate, they helped elect Republican Warren G. Harding in a landslide over Democrat James M. Cox.)

CRASH!!! THE MARKET FALLS AND DEPRESSION FOLLOWS

Then, of course, we all know what happened. The stock market crashed in 1929 and the Great Depression followed. *Because* we all know what happened, I'm not going to devote more time to the causes of the Crash and the Depression, nor will I repeat information covered earlier regarding how World War II and the postwar boom completed America's next economic cycle.

FISCAL FLASHPOINT

There is one story regarding the Depression that I'd like to recount—
because it's both amusing and reflective of how politicians think.
Near the end of his term in 1932, President Herbert Hoover, under
whose watch the Crash occurred and the Depression started, invited
former President Calvin Coolidge to lunch at the White House. There are
no Nixon-like tapes to prove it, but the after-lunch conversation supposedly featured a lengthy round of complaints by Hoover regarding how
ungrateful the public was for not appreciating everything he'd done for
them.

   Finally, Coolidge had had enough, so he interrupted, saying,
"Mr. President, you cannot expect to see calves running in the field the
day after you put the bull in with the cows."

   To which Hoover reportedly replied, "No, but I would at least expect
to see a lot of happy cows."

Source: Smith, Richard Norton, and Timothy Walch. "The Ordeal of Herbert
Hoover, Part 2," *Prologue* magazine. Washington, DC: The National Archives,
Summer 2004.

What I will comment on is the fact that the Depression was responsible for the birth of the "bailout mentality" among federal politicians—
and, eventually, the "government-as-parent" school of thought that
makes so many people now believe it's their *right* to be bailed out.
Don't get me wrong. It's not that the people didn't *work* their way
out of the Great Depression, because they did—and folks of that era
deserve tremendous credit for it. However, they also had plenty of
government help in doing it.

   Hoover had indeed tried to help the country recover, asking
Congress in December 1930 to pass a $150 million public works proj-
ect to boost the economy and increase employment. Then, in early
1932, he pushed through creation of the Reconstruction Finance
Corporation to help restore confidence in the country's banks and
leading businesses. But, in spite of those efforts, unemployment

worsened, reaching 12 percent, and Hoover was soundly beaten in November 1932 by Franklin D. Roosevelt, who rallied the country against the Depression with his, "We have nothing to fear but fear itself," inaugural speech.

With a solid majority behind him, FDR called a special 100-day session of Congress and, over the next four months, a mountain of "New Deal" bills avalanched to approval, including the Federal Unemployment Relief Act, which created the Civilian Conservation Corps and put more than 2.5 million men back to work. It also laid the foundation for creation and funding in 1935 of the Works Progress Administration, which provided almost 8 million jobs from then until 1943. Other notable FDR initiatives during that period included:

- Establishment in 1934 of the Securities and Exchange Commission (SEC), which was authorized to oversee securities regulation, quell speculative activities, and restore confidence in the stock market.
- Passage of the Social Security Act in 1935.
- Enactment in June 1938 of the Fair Labor Standards Act, which set the first national minimum wage (25 cents an hour) and mandated time-and-a-half pay for overtime.

ALONG CAME THE 1970s

With only a couple of minor burps, the economy easily digested post-war prosperity and America moved relatively smoothly through the 1950s and 1960s. Then came the 1970s, when the growing costs of another foreign war combined with soaring energy costs to set the stage for another recession, triggered by uncertainty following President Nixon's forced resignation.

The recovery this time was slow and difficult, hampered by inconsistent interest-rate policies and monetary objectives, as well as four swings in political control over a 12-year period, which made Congress generally ineffective. But it did come, with a new boom getting under way shortly after Ronald Reagan's 1980 election.

From our perspective now, the most notable feature of this recession—and absolute proof of my contention that the government has learned *nothing* from past economic misadventures—was the first "official" federal bailout of a private corporation, actually labeled as such. On November 1, 1979, at the strong urging of President Jimmy Carter and Treasury Secretary G. William Miller, Congress approved the "_____ Loan Guarantee Act of 1979."

It provided a $1.5 billion bailout for, fill in the above blank . . . wait for it . . . that's right, Chrysler Corporation!

Looking at it now, about all I can say is, "Oh, yeah, *like that really worked!*"

What's more, I'm reasonably sure the bailouts approved in response to our current catastrophe will be equally effective—meaning they won't really work, either.

ANOTHER DECADE, ANOTHER CRASH

The next milestone was the 1987 stock market crash, in which the Dow Jones Industrials fell 508 points, or 22.6 percent, in one day (Black Monday) and a terrifying 770 points, or 30.7 percent, over a four-day period. The rest of the world followed, with some markets (Hong Kong) losing more than 45 percent.

This was the first computer-linked market collapse, with most experts blaming it on "program trading," in which technical indicators generated electronic sell orders, forcing a decline that resulted in margin calls (demands for more collateral), which forced more selling that turned the decline into a rout.

Although the Fed did pump $2.2 billion into the economy to improve liquidity and the stock exchanges made some changes (such as "circuit breakers" to curb program trading and the imposition of uniform margin requirements), there really wasn't time for government action to aid the market because the recovery was quick. The Dow finished 1987 with an overall gain, and had recovered its full October loss by mid-1989.

INTRODUCING THE "PLUNGE PROTECTION TEAM"

One other result of the 1987 stock market crash was the establishment of the President's Working Group on Financial Markets—or, as it
is sometimes referred to today, the "Plunge Protection Team." Created
by Executive Order No.12631, signed by President Reagan on March
18, 1988, the Working Group was set up to analyze situations and recommend legislative and private-sector solutions for "enhancing the
integrity, efficiency, orderliness, and competitiveness of [U.S.] financial
markets and maintaining investor confidence." The Secretary of the
Treasury (or a designee) serves as chairman of the Working Group, which
also includes the chairman of the Federal Reserve Board, the chairman
of the Securities and Exchange Commission, and the chairman of the
Commodity Futures Trading Commission.

While that's the official function and composition of the Working
Group, many financial professionals and analysts hold that the Plunge
Protection Team (PPT) is something entirely different. Rather than just
being a nickname for the Working Group, they contend the PPT is
actually an unacknowledged offshoot of the Working Group—a collection
of high-ranking government and private financial specialists secretly
working behind the scenes to:

- Prevent market crashes, particularly as a result of man-made or
  natural disasters.
- Stop major market declines before they turn into crashes.
- Maintain large market up-trends and prevent them from reversing.

Both the Treasury and the Fed have explicitly denied the existence
of this clandestine team, sticking to the nickname story. However,
the Working Group itself is mysterious enough. Often referred to as a
"shadow agency," the group's meetings are generally unannounced and
their recommendations disseminated only by authorized statements—one
of which was issued in October 2008. In it, the group indicated it was
"taking multiple steps in order to attempt to stabilize the financial

(continued)

system"—though the actual government purchase of shares in private companies to help support stock prices was denied.

Obviously, final results on the success of the Group's "multiple steps" aren't yet in—but I have my doubts . . .

Source: Fromson, Brett D., "Plunge Protection Team," WashingtonPost.com, 1997.

THE SECOND BIG BAILOUT BONANZA

The damage to the economy was a bit longer lasting as the loss of capital assets and a related lack of liquidity were among the reasons cited for the savings and loan crisis, in which more than 740 thrift institutions around the country failed. (The Tax Reform Act of 1986 was also a factor, as it did away with many real estate tax shelters, sharply reducing the value of properties developed for that purpose with the use of S&L financing.)

In the face of billions in losses and the near-cessation of home-mortgage lending, the government stepped in and, in August of 1989, the Savings & Loan Bailout Bill (formally titled the "Financial Institutions Reform, Recovery and Enforcement Act of 1989") was passed by Congress and signed by President George H.W. Bush. The bill changed the entire regulatory structure for U.S. savings institutions, authorized up to $400 billion over 30 years for government purchase of "toxic assets" (not a term used then), and created the Resolution Trust Corporation (RTC) to sell off those assets. The ultimate cost of the crisis was put at $161 billion, roughly $125 billion of which came directly from the federal government.

All of that worked so well that it took barely 15 years for the entire mortgage-lending world to wade into even hotter and far more costly water (must have been the bottled stuff). So, though we had most certainly been there before, we obviously hadn't learned our lessons.

BUT LOOK WHAT HAPPENED ANYWAY

Those last couple of segments were a bit discouraging, so let's take a quick U-turn to the brighter side. In spite of all the problems of the

1970s, 1980s, and early 1990s (there was another minor recession I skipped), stocks still produced tremendous amounts of new wealth for American investors. On Black Monday, 1987, the DJIA closed at 1738.34. Less than 12 years later, on March 29, 1999, it closed above 10,000 for the first time ever.

And, if you want longer-term proof that the U.S. economy and the U.S. markets have always come back—regardless of the severity of intervening downturns—just look at Figure 5.1. It shows the course of the Standard & Poor's 500 Index from 1871 until 2007, punctuated by the major crises we've talked about and other notable events. When it comes to demonstrating the resiliency of the U.S. stock market, this is really the *only* chart you need to see.

Now I know a number of sharp-penciled readers are going to make all sorts of noises about seeing an inflation-adjusted chart, but settle down a moment. The important thing to understand is that the markets have a decidedly upside bias. How you deal with inflation is

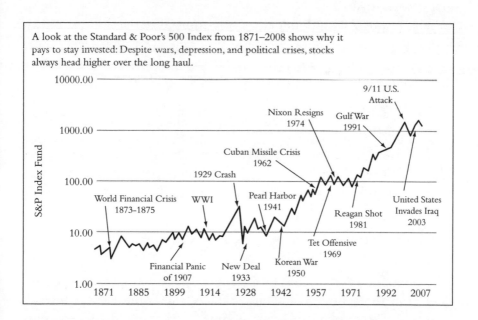

FIGURE 5.1 Staying the Course: The Only Stock Market Chart Investors Need to See

Source: Fitz-Gerald Research Publications, LLC; Robert Shiller, Yale University.

FISCAL FLASHPOINT

While panics and recessions have historically created some of the most profitable buying opportunities for stock investors, that doesn't mean I advocate holding your stocks *through* such periods. The reason? On average, had you held the portfolio you had at the start of each recession since 1950 and ridden it all the way to the bottom, it would have taken you nine years to get back to even—and even longer to get ahead—assuming you made the S&P 500's average annual return of 9.7 percent (since 1926). But, had you sold early in the recession, then bought back in one year after it started, your return over the next two years would have exceeded 25 percent. That's why, as you'll learn later, I recommend that you *always use stop losses* as a primary portfolio-management tool.

---

a tactical asset decision, not a means of disputing the markets in general. I cover that later.

The future will undoubtedly bring more wars, political scandals, financial panics, recessions, depressions, and even global economic crises—but, over the long run, stock prices will almost certainly continue to move higher, for two key reasons:

1. People are remarkably resilient—which means our financial markets will be, too.
2. As it has in the past, nearly every instance of financial turmoil that sends stocks lower will ultimately prove to be a remarkable new long-term buying opportunity.

A QUICK LOOK AT THE ECONOMIC CYCLE

As I mentioned at the start of this chapter, the other reason I'm confident both the economy and the markets will come back is that it's *normal*—at least as normal as anything in the world of economic theory can be. Since Day One, academics and economists have studied how economies work—not just in the United States, but everywhere in every time—and they've always found essentially the same pattern. It looks like a series of waves, repeatedly moving from trough to peak and back to trough. From depression to boom, back to depression, back to boom.

Of course, "modern" economic theory paints a more complex picture of the waves, just as "modern" economies are far more complex than the old agrarian ones. The National Bureau of Economic Research (NBER) is the arbiter of economic statistics in the United States, and it factors a wide array of features into its long-term wave models. These include such items as capital formation, household income, growth of GDP, unemployment rates, and the like. As a result, rather than being just a simple up-and-down pattern, NBER's picture of economic cycles looks like the one in Figure 5.2.

As you can see, this model—rather than talking in terms of booms and recessions—views the economy as shifting from periods of contraction to periods of expansion, based on improving sets of data being reported. NBER's basic contention is that economic cycles are *more* than just simple fluctuations in economic activity; that they're

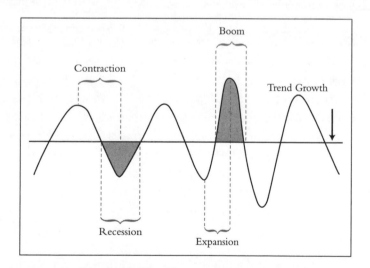

FIGURE 5.2 A Five-Phase View of the Economic Cycle
Source: The National Bureau of Economic Research.

indicators of actual changes in the nature of the economy that, when averaged out over longer periods, show developing and waning trends in economic growth. Makes sense to me . . . I think! (Be aware, as well, that the NBER's model is a bit skewed by its exclusion of stock markets . . . which could be why so few government officials actually understand them.)

Sarcasm aside, in a modern economy, expansions (or booms) typically feature above-trend growth in GDP, rising employment, higher disposable incomes, and increased consumer spending. Contractions (or recession/depressions) are marked by below-average GDP growth, rising unemployment, lower disposable incomes, and reduced consumer spending, usually due to inflationary pressure, especially in markets for basic commodities such as oil and food stocks.

FISCAL FLASHPOINT

A recession is generally defined as "two consecutive quarters of declining or below-average GDP growth." That's fairly clear, but with one problem for investors—by the time the definition is fulfilled and a new recession announced, its effects have already been priced into the markets. Indeed, in three of the past four recessions (1980–1981, 1991, and 2001), the S&P 500 had already reached its recessionary lows at the time the announcements were made (another reason to use stop losses rather than waiting for economic reports). Historically, recessions have had a time span of 18 to 24 months, but the average since 1900 has been just 14.4 months—though that average will no doubt rise as a result of the most recent contraction, which was already in its 17th month when I wrote this. (The NBER made the "official" recession call on December 1, 2008, based on third-quarter data, meaning the actual start was somewhere around March 2008—though my numbers indicate it was actually a few months before that.)

Many investors complain about our economies being locked into these cyclical patterns—especially as they approach a time (like retirement) when they will need their money. They ask, "Why can't the markets just keep going up?"

Of course, as nice as that may sound, it would actually be *a bad thing*—proof that growth is artificial, the markets are "fixed," and the economy is being controlled, rather than just guarded, by our governments. "Free-market" economies would no longer be—free, that is.

THE DANGERS OF UNLEARNED LESSONS

The possibility of such government control—or even increasingly tight guardianship, as we've seen lately—is why it's so dismaying to see that so few of the lessons of past recessions and market downturns have been learned.

In virtually every case we've examined, it has been individual initiative and hard work—or external events such as wars—that ultimately fired the economy and the country to new levels of prosperity. But people today don't want to hear this—not when their jobs, their retirement funds, their entire financial futures may be among the casualties of the economy and the markets following their natural cycles. They pound on government's door, pleading for it to do "something . . . anything." The cacophony is deafening, the noise driven by people's naive fear that the government—their ultimate "parent"—will desert them.

The politicians, by nature even more fearful they will lose their jobs come election time, hear this noise and try to hide the truth that they don't know what to do, either—that there is actually just as much panic in the halls of power. They just know they must do *something*—and, failing to take an honest look at history, more often than not do the wrong thing.

FISCAL FLASHPOINT

The world has gone through equally severe periods of economic disruption in the past, many based on the same mistakes made this time. But we still haven't learned the most important thing from our experience: *No nation in recorded history has ever hauled itself out of recession by doing what we are doing now for anything other than an extremely short period of time.*

This is why the government, led by legions of economists and advisers, has so ardently pushed the current bailouts—and will no doubt encourage even more in the months and years ahead.

Federal bureaucrats, the mainstream media, average citizens, and even some of my fellow Wall Street prognosticators express confidence that the government stimuli and a continuation of accommodative Fed policy will work—that it will eventually revive the economy.

My expectation is the reverse. I feel certain the next few years are going to be tougher than almost anybody can imagine—all because of the lessons *we haven't learned*. I simply cannot see how any rational person, armed with accurate data and a knowledge of history, can honestly believe the government intervention we've seen will be the long-term solution the markets need—especially when it is the government that actually caused most of this mess.

It never fails to amaze me how Congress can pass economic stimulus packages that really stimulate nothing but inflation—then hold hearings to investigate *why* oil prices are rising. It adds insult to injury when our government creates a problem, then compounds it by wasting still more taxpayer money trying to determine its cause. In the end, Americans will be on the hook for all of the added losses, either directly through higher taxes or indirectly through more inflation.

That's why it makes far more sense to rely on our own merits than on the federal "tooth fairy" when it comes to our financial futures. And, let's be clear. In spite of all I just said, I remain optimistic about our potential for future financial success. At least about the success of investors willing to think outside the box—and outside the United States.

The coming decade will witness a radical transformation in the world economic order—a transformation filled with tremendous opportunities all over the world. If you recognize this, follow along as the changes occur, maintain your perspective (and your courage), and invest accordingly, you will be able to rebuild your portfolio—not to mention capture some spectacular returns.

I have much more on exactly *how* to "invest accordingly" in Part III.

CHAPTER 6

AMERICA'S ECONOMY AND ITS PLACE IN THE NEW WORLD ORDER

The best way to destroy the capitalist system is to debauch the currency. By a continuing process of inflation, governments can confiscate, secretly and unobserved, an important part of the wealth of their citizens.

—John Maynard Keynes, economist

As you've already seen, when it comes to economic affairs, the world undergoes notable changes on a fairly regular basis. And, in the past, citizens of the United States—as well as those of our global trading partners—have generally trusted that this country's leaders would act on those changes with great confidence, integrity, and intelligence. Until now, we were seldom oversold.

This time, however, the changes we've seen have fostered an unprecedented level of financial anxiety—and the political and economic leaders of the United States (and most of our free-market allies) have responded by doing *exactly* the wrong things. Things that could ultimately spell the end of the American Dream as we know it, forcing the United States to relinquish its global role as the Land of Opportunity, full of the promise of prosperity for all.

Certainly, the triggering financial crises have been severe, but much of the present anxiety is due to the confusion engendered by the increasingly incomprehensible explanations offered by the most powerful figures in government, academia, and commerce. If you listened to any of the speeches of Fed Chairman Ben Bernanke over the past couple of years, you know what I mean. The large words resonate, but the high-falutin' concepts he was floating just never quite coalesced into any kind of meaningful plan.

This is evidenced by some of the counterintuitive policies the Fed has adopted. For example, over the past few decades, approximately 3 billion new people have entered the global economy—people with a similar frame of mind as the American pioneers of the nineteenth century. This has created incredible inflationary pressure, especially on commodities and raw materials.

Yet, instead of raising interest rates to combat this inflationary surge, the Fed has been obsessed with trying to stimulate the economy and solve our financial problems by maintaining artificially *low* rates. True, low interest rates are usually perceived as positive (except by those, like retirees, who rely on interest payments for their livelihoods)—but, in this case, they're merely serving as a smoke screen to cloud the true impact governmental actions are having on the economy.

Foremost among these adverse actions are the bailouts. Efforts to combat recession through stimulus measures mean more money chasing a given supply of goods. That may help the direct recipients of the bailout money—but, being the very definition of inflation, it simply pushes up prices for everyone else, while doing nothing to actually improve the underlying economics.

As I've said before, we should *never* have begun the bailouts. The concept of "too big to fail" is a total myth. History is littered with failed institutions of all kinds—from banks and brokerage companies to automakers and airlines. In the end, U.S. taxpayers will be on the hook for all of those bailout costs, either directly through higher taxes or indirectly through still more inflation. Add in interest, and the cost will be far more than the original crisis itself—even more than all of America's past financial disruptions combined. If you don't believe it, check out Figure 6.1.

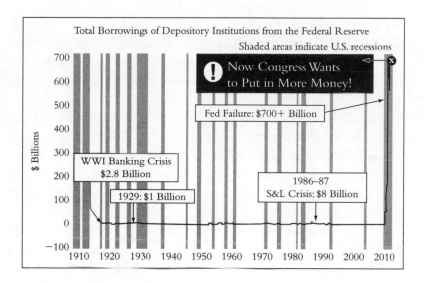

FIGURE 6.1 America Bails Out

Sources: Board of Governors of the Federal Reserve System; research.stlouisfed.org.

FISCAL FLASHPOINT

As evidence of the power of the U.S. economy to recover—even *without* bailouts—consider this: Despite the devastating losses in the Black Monday stock market crash of October 1987, economic reports issued by the Department of Labor for 1988 indicated an annual growth rate of 3.8 percent, the largest in four years, and an unemployment rate of just 5.3 percent, a 14-year low.

THE PENALTIES OF DOING "THE WRONG THING"

My view, of course, is that the government should have taken a "hands-off" approach. The politicians and the bureaucrats should have let the markets work out the problems the markets caused—let those who failed fail, and those who succeeded prosper from their success. Instead, the latter must now support the former—and the taxpayers must support them both.

It may well be that it's already too late for the government to change course. I suspect it is. But, if some attempt to change directions isn't made, America's problems could extend to the point that it will make Japan's infamous "Lost Decade" look like a "Lost Couple of Years."

Because I live in Japan for part of each year, I'm extremely aware of the impact of Japan's prolonged financial crisis—but, just in case you're not, I'll provide a brief review. My hope in doing so is that it will help you recognize some of the mistakes the United States is in danger of repeating, as well as how quickly things can go bad when you refuse to face facts.

In a fashion similar to what happened this time around, the Japanese crisis began with the collapse of price bubbles in both real estate and the stock market. On December 29, 1989, the Nikkei 225 Index topped out at 38,957.44. Within nine months, it crashed by half—and never recovered, ultimately bottoming out at just 7,830 in April 2003. At the end of the second quarter of 2009, the index still stood at a paltry 9,958.44—a staggering 74.5 percent drop from its peak 20 years before.

The destruction rippling across Japanese society ever since has been enormous: An estimated $20 trillion in stock-market and real estate wealth vaporized. Failed "zombie" banks, propped up by Japan's government to prevent collapse, stopped lending. Starved of loans, the Japanese economy tanked. In Tokyo's Ginza district, prime office space, once selling for $139,000 per square foot, now sells for less than one one-hundredth (1/100th) of its peak market value. Huge stimulus projects, designed to build infrastructure and jumpstart the economy, went bust. Japan's debt tripled, reaching a staggering 170 percent of GDP, and the country lost its coveted AAA bond rating (though, as you saw in our discussion of mortgage derivatives, those ratings don't seem to mean that much anymore).

Trust me, though, as terrifying as the damage to Japan sounds, the U.S. financial crisis will wind up being worse. America's economic trauma will take much longer than a "Lost Decade" to resolve itself—and cost much, much more.

But here's a small secret: Just as Japan didn't have to spend the better part of 15 years in the financial hoosegow, the United States doesn't have to endure a decade or more of wasted time, missed opportunities, and watching countries like China, South Korea, and India, among others, start to gain a real economic advantage on us. That may happen anyway—but the sooner we begin to do things right, the less inevitable it becomes. Granted, that's hard to do politically since populism is its own worst enemy right now, but it's not impossible.

Look at it this way. Back in the late 1980s and early 1990s, the United States survived a savings and loan collapse, about the same time Japan suffered the first hit in its banking and stock crisis. Today, the S&L crisis barely merits an isolated entry on America's collective web site, whereas Japan's Lost Decade is a part of global financial lore. The reason for this disparity is simple.

We attacked the S&L industry with tremendous energy, shuttered or sold off ailing thrifts, and decisively enacted new guidelines to avoid such problems as under-funded state insurance pools, inadequate capital requirements, and gaping regulatory loopholes. (We also did some ill-advised bailing out, but that's another story.)

Japan did nothing. For the first five years of its crisis, it refused to acknowledge the magnitude of its problems, partly because banks there are part of complex cross-linking societal arrangements known as *keiretsus,* and partly because taking action would have forced Japan to admit it had mishandled the sector. When the government finally realized the troubles had reached do-or-die proportions, the problem was so ingrained and the losses so large that it was too late for decisive action. Only time and long-term policy changes could provide the required fix.

Despite our experience in successfully resolving the S&L crisis and the lessons brought home with such force by Japan, we still didn't learn. When the current crisis exploded, the Fed chose to take the "prop-it-up" approach rather than act more decisively. After much hand-wringing and a whole lot of fire-and-brimstone, "It'll-never-happen-here" speeches, it did—happen here, that is.

Then, instead of allowing the free markets to fix the subprime mortgage crisis after it broke in late 2007, the Fed launched one of its most aggressive rate-cutting campaigns ever, slashing borrowing costs at a time when, in my opinion, it really should have been raising them.

The Fed then set a dangerous precedent by stepping into the Bear Stearns breakdown, brokering a combination bailout and buyout "shotgun marriage" with JPMorgan Chase & Co. With that as a precedent, the Fed had a virtual obligation to rescue Fannie Mae and Freddie Mac when their imminent collapse came around—a rescue that legendary investor Jim Rogers describes unabashedly as "an unmitigated disaster." Though the bailout brakes were finally applied with Lehman Brothers, the Fed remains in the precarious position of "presumed lender of last resort" should more failures occur—the Federal Housing Administration, or FHA, being a prime candidate.

You only have to consider one fact to figure out that Jim Rogers is almost certainly spot on in his description of the Fannie/Freddie fiasco: This bailout adds *$6 trillion* to the U.S. debt load—a liability that's equal to nearly half the output of the U.S. economy for an entire year.

A DIFFERENCE OF OPINION

In fairness, my *Money Morning* colleague and Contributing Editor R. Shah Gilani disagrees—to a point. He argues that the bailouts of Fannie and Freddie, while as undesirable as we say, were probably necessary to prevent a total collapse of the financial markets. That might make them the only valid exception to my firm "no-bailouts" stance—though I'm still not totally convinced.

BETRAYING THE SYSTEM THAT FEEDS US

By slashing rates, pumping up the money supply, and rescuing misman-aged enterprises, Fed Boss Ben "Helicopter" Bernanke has essentially thumbed his nose at the free-market system—as if to say the central bank can do it better. He's wrong. The financial markets are remark-ably resilient—and if financial ventures are so poorly run they're poised to fail, free-market doctrine says to let them do so. Sure, there will be pain—and a broad ripple effect—but, in the end, the marketplace will have flushed the poorly run venture away, freeing up capital that well-run, opportunistically rich companies can use to grow and create jobs.

But Bernanke and Co. can't stomach failure (though they'll ulti-mately have to deal with their own). They cling to a policy of artifi-cially low interest rates, which may be a balm for the short-term pain of this financial crisis, but over the longer term will continue to put an intense downward pressure on the U.S. dollar—pressure that will fuel further increases in food and energy prices and prolong the America's economic malaise for years to come.

FISCAL FLASHPOINT

Bailouts will never restore the United States to its former economic strength. For that, we must allow for capital formation and encour-age entrepreneurship, both of which have fueled every past recovery. Individuals all over the world are clever, resourceful people. What their gov-ernments need to do is simple: Lead—or get out of the way. But not hobble the initiative that has made this and other free-market countries great.

FISCAL FLASHPOINT

In a minor variation of a point I stressed in Chapter 5, let me reiterate: On anything other than a short-term basis, no nation in recorded history has *ever* bailed itself out by debasing its currency like the United States has been doing. *Ever!*

REALITY CHECK: WHAT YOU DON'T WANT TO HEAR—BUT WILL ANYWAY

We already know that the financial meltdown was an unmitigated disaster (stealing a phrase from Jim Rogers). But the eventual depth of the overall economic crisis remains to be seen.

I'm not part of the doom-and-gloom crowd—but then I'm not known for pulling punches, either. So, go get a stiff drink. This won't be a politically correct couple of paragraphs that's been sanitized for easy reading.

Historically, U.S. economic cycles have *always* been a case of "the deeper the gloom, the bigger the boom." As such, it's important to recognize that each of the troubling things we're dealing with today are, in fact, forming the basis for the opportunities I see coming up tomorrow.

My original guess, and one I haven't revised much yet, is that this U.S. economic collapse may become the toughest in recorded history—far more destructive in financial terms than the Crash of 1929 and the subsequent Great Depression.

To be clear, this doesn't mean we're all going to be in bread lines or marching across the country's logging roads as part of a New New Deal, but it does mean the rules of money have changed forever. There are a variety of reasons for this appraisal. For one, the U.S. population is much more urbanized today—and hence far less self-sufficient than it was 80 years ago. Millions of people survived the Depression by raising *all* of their food and making most of their family's clothing—both impossibilities today. People then were also much more self-reliant. Today, we have a subculture of people who are permanently dependent on the U.S. government for economic survival, as well as an institutionalized welfare system that didn't exist back then. FDR-era regulations—though strict—don't hold a candle to the skyrocketing levels of government control and (dare I say?) interference that we deal with today.

Taxes are also far higher now than back then. In 1929, the maximum tax rate was 23.1 percent—and that was only at the million-dollar income level (the equivalent of $12.77 million in 2009 dollars). In addition, few states levied an income tax, there was no Social Security tax, and the multitude of excise, sales, and other taxes we pay were unimagined in those days. This leaves fewer fiscal resources in the hands of citizens and more in the coffers of governments—governments that usually have that money spent before they even get it. And not spent all that well, I might add.

Despite gobbling up so many resources from its citizens, the government is at least doing everything it can to publicly dispel the notion that it doesn't care. Sadly, given Washington's definition of "caring," benign indifference would surely be preferable.

Take, for example, the three-headed, economy-crashing catalyst that pushed us into recession—otherwise known as Congress, the U.S. Treasury, and the Federal Housing Administration (FHA). The Housing and Economic Recovery Act of 2008—miraculously passed by both the House and Senate in just weeks, and signed by President George W. Bush at the urging of then-Treasury Secretary Henry Paulson—was the equivalent of lobbing a grenade into a gasoline warehouse.

The law allowed 400,000 homeowners in danger of foreclosure to refinance their mortgages into 30-year, fixed-rate loans, with the FHA guaranteeing $300 billion of those. The loans require down payments of only 3 percent (which can be borrowed as well), a move designed to encourage those who can to actually refinance rather than walk away from their properties. The whole deal sounds great—except for one thing. Many borrowers, who got into the homes on liar loans in the first place, still can't afford the new payments—and, with "no skin in the game," will eventually default, anyway. That will leave the FHA holding billions in subprime and junk mortgages, necessitating another federal bailout.

In effect, then, Congress, the Treasury, and the FHA have elected to take out a subprime mortgage on the economy's future—with already strapped taxpayers footing the bill. (Maybe they can sign up for one of those easy, pay-as-you-go loans from the fast-money shops at the mall—but I doubt it.)

The Final Bill Will Be Horrendous

And, speaking of that bill, most folks are still fixated on the $700 billion number cited for the October 3, 2008, bailout package. However, that's actually just a drop in the reality bucket. What started in March 2008 as a $39 billion set of loan guarantees in the Bear Stearns deal was already approaching an estimated eventual cost of $5.2 trillion in mid–2009, thanks to bailouts for banks, insurance companies, car companies, state and local governments, community housing agencies, you name it. Assuming the Census Bureau is correct in its tally of 105,480,100 U.S. households, that breaks down to a cost of $49,298 per household.

A SWELL IDEA—FELLED BY AN F IN ARITHMETIC

A couple of months after the initial news came out about all the big bailout bucks Washington was throwing around, a proposal started circulating on the Internet that quickly received wide and well-deserved support. (Actor Russell Crowe even pitched it to Jay Leno on *The Tonight Show*—and he's not even an American.)

Unlike anything the government might think up, the idea was quite simple: Rather than handing out billions of dollars to obviously *undeserving* banks, brokerage firms, and big corporations (which were just going to give the money to executives as bonuses anyway), why not *instead* give each and every *obviously deserving* American—all 300 million or so of us—$1 million apiece! Tax free! There would only be one small set of strings attached. The money would have to be used to:

- Buy a new home if you didn't already own one, which would rescue both the housing market and the construction industry.
- Pay off your mortgage and your credit card bills, which would return the banks to solvency and free up all sorts of credit for new purchases and business investment.
- Buy a new car (fuel-efficient, of course; maybe even a hybrid) and a whole houseful of new appliances, which would restore the automakers to their former glory and put all those jobless folks in the Rust Belt back to work in the manufacture of durable goods.

(continued)

- Take a trip (for which you'd need new clothes), buy lots of souvenirs, eat every meal at a restaurant and hit all the attractions—which would, of course, put still more of the unemployed to work and create a boom in the sagging retail, dining, and entertainment sectors, not to mention reviving the airlines and cruise companies.
- Invest the rest—assuming you didn't make like the government and spend it all.

What a super, super idea! Solve nearly all the country's economic problems, enrich every American's life and . . . well, you get the idea. Besides, it couldn't cost any more than the government was already planning to waste on stimulus packages. Or could it?

The one failing in *every* version of the proposal I saw—and there were plenty—is that no one bothered to do the ultimate piece of arithmetic (perhaps explaining why our kids are doing so poorly in math relative to those from Asia).

If you multiply $1,000,000 by 300,000,000 Americans, you *don't* get $300 billion as many said (and you *certainly don't* get $300 million, as Russell Crowe said on *Leno*). What you get is: $300,000,000,000,000!! (My apologies to those of you who may suffer from "zero-phobia.")

That's right—*three hundred TRILLION dollars*. And, as hard as it might be to believe, that actually makes the $5.2 trillion this mess has cost us so far seem like pocket change.

What's worse, that could be conservative—many analysts peg the eventual cost of all the stimulus and bailout packages at nearly $15 trillion. My own guess is that this is a $50 trillion problem before all is said and done. This is compared to the $14 trillion annual output of the *entire U.S. economy* (which, thanks to the recession, is most likely lower than that now). It also dwarfs the cost of all past U.S. financial crises, such as the World War I banking crisis ($2.8 billion), the 1929 market crash ($1 billion), or the 1986–1987 savings and loan (S&L) crisis ($8 billion).

THE FREE MARKET COULD HAVE DONE MUCH BETTER

Again, what the Fed is doing by bailing out private enterprises makes no economic sense and flies in the face of history. The past is littered with failed institutions—roughly 43,500 U.S. corporations declared bankruptcy in 2008 alone. That's not a surprise given the state of the economy, but consider that more than 32,000 companies failed in 1999, when the market was booming and the dot-com bubble was still inflating. And, historically, we're not talking about just mom-and-pop operations, either. Remember Packard and Studebaker, Pan Am, Bethlehem Steel, WorldCom, even Texaco, to name a few?

And banking certainly hasn't been exempt. In fact, there have been only two years since 1934 when no U.S. bank failed—2005 and 2006. Only three U.S. banks failed in 2007. But, apart from that three-year stretch from 2005 to 2007, you have to go back more than 75 years (to 1934) to find a time when so few U.S. banks failed, as illustrated in Figure 6.2. Even at the peak of the S&L crisis, when thrift institutions were failing at an average rate of two every business

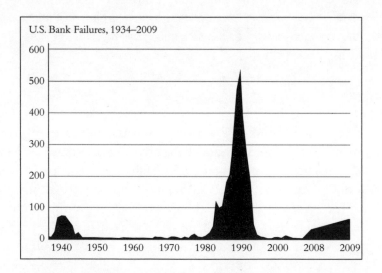

FIGURE 6.2 America's Past Is Littered with Failed Institutions—Especially Banks

Sources: FitzGerald Research Publications; Robert Shiller, Yale University.

day for two full years (more than 1,000 banks and S&Ls failed in 1988 and 1989) the economy survived. (Note: In the eight-plus months ending September 11, 2009, regulators had shuttered 91 banks.)

WHAT CAN WE EXPECT NEXT?

As I've already said, given the current course of action the government is taking, the length of this economic calamity could extend for longer than Japan's Lost Decade, with residual effects being felt 15 or even 20 years down the road. Many others agree, some having used sports analogies to express their opinions:

Buyout specialist Theodore "Ted" Forstmann, the chairman of IMG and one of the players in the "Barbarians at the Gate"/RJR-Nabisco saga, told *The Wall Street Journal* that, "It's hard for me to believe it gets fixed without [further] upheaval in the financial system. Things are going to fail. Enterprises are going to fail. The economy is going to slow . . . I think we are [only] in the second inning of this."

Noted *Contrarian Investing* columnist Bill Fleckenstein, writing for *MSN Money*, related the prediction of one of his industry sources, whom he simply refers to as "The Lord of the Dark Matter." He said the Lord admitted that, while he wasn't sure what inning the financial crisis was in, he was certain "it's going to be a double-header."

I couldn't agree more.

THANK YOU, MR. LETTERMAN

In an effort to inject a little humor into this dismal accounting of what's going on in the economic world, I decided to steal an idea from David Letterman. So, here are . . .

The Top 10 Ways You Can Tell the Economy Is in Real Trouble

10. CEOs are now playing miniature golf.
9. I got a "pre-declined" credit card offer in the mail.
8. I went to buy a toaster oven and they gave me a bank.

(continued)

7.   The Hot Wheels car company is now trading higher than GM in the stock market.

6.   Obama met with small businesses—GE, Pfizer, Chrysler, Citigroup, and GM—to discuss the bailout package.

5.   McDonald's is selling the Quarter-Ouncer.

4.   The most highly paid job in America is now jury duty.

3.   Chinese students laughed at Treasury Secretary "Turbo" Tim Geithner when he told them their money was safe in America.

2.   Former Countrywide CEO Angelo Mozillo is still making house payments.

And the best indicator of all:

1.   If the bank returns your check marked "Insufficient Funds," you have to call and ask if they mean you—or them.

WHAT'S THE SECOND HALF OF THE TWIN BILL?

Actually, we're already entering the second game of the double header. We survived the initial mortgage and housing meltdowns, and stocks have rebounded a bit. We're somehow working our way through a recession, with its accompanying spike in unemployment. But, a few positive signs notwithstanding, the economic crisis is still in full swing—and it's steadily eroding the standing of the United States in the "New World Order."

There'll be even more hell to pay when all the money the Treasury is printing for bailouts and stimuli finally undermines the value of the dollar. It may not happen today or next week or next year, but once the world starts doubting the stability of the U.S. dollar and the Fed's ability to support it, things can only get worse. Look at recent charts for the foreign-exchange (forex) markets and you can readily see how the dollar has been struggling against the strengthening euro and Chinese yuan (also called the renminbi, literally translated, the "people's currency").

That's because the world's central bankers have created trillions of dollars out of thin air. Short term, this was all about maintaining liquidity—but it is hyper-inflationary, and it will eventually affect the entire planet. So, longer term, it will become a case of "valuation preservation or die." When liquidity becomes less of an issue and people stop hoarding cash, history suggests they will spend that cash as fast as possible and begin hoarding hard assets instead. The dollar will crater—and growth currencies like the yuan will rise even faster.

How it all unfolds—or unravels—and the exact timing are anybody's guess. But, until the Fed stops printing money—or Congress starts hiding the paper and ink—the end result will be undeniable: A decimated dollar, more inflation (or even hyperinflation), and higher interest rates.

WEAK CURRENCY, STRONG ECONOMY—NO WAY

The U.S. government's bailout policy was ostensibly pushed through to bolster the sagging American economy—but, historically, that equation simply doesn't work. As already noted, printing money and pumping it into the system to artificially stimulate the economy is highly inflationary—and inflation is the *pocket proof* of a devalued dollar.

I'm not alone in that assessment, either. Steve Forbes made the same argument in a February 2008 article in *Forbes* magazine titled, "It's the Dollar, Stupid (And Taxes, Too)." He urged the Bush administration to abandon its Carter-like policies for weakening the dollar to boost the economy, concluding by admonishing: "No *strong* economy has a *weak* currency."

Bob McTeer, former president of the Federal Reserve Bank of Dallas and currently a fellow at the National Center for Policy Analysis, reiterated the point in a *Wall Street Journal* commentary criticizing the actions of both Fed Chairman Alan Greenspan and his successor, Ben Bernanke. However, he also warned that the reverse isn't necessarily

(continued)

true—in other words, strong currencies don't *always* guarantee strong economies.

Still, the concept is so ingrained that one of the fundamental rules of the foreign-exchange markets is that "strong economies have strong currencies." You'll find that axiom in the first few paragraphs of every single guide to forex trading out there. Case in point is the Online Trading Academy's web site for new forex traders, which says: "When we trade the forex markets, we are trading *economies.* Supply and demand for a currency depends on the current and perceived health of a country's economy."

The reasoning is simple. When an economy is performing well, it means that corporations are making profits, all but a small percentage of the workforce is employed, and, in most cases, interest rates are going up because there's a strong demand for funds for growth and expansion. All of that benefits the associated currency.

Which is why, with China's economy advancing, the yuan is steadily rising in value and, with the U.S. economy in the tank, the dollar is drowning—in spite of all the "stimulus."

As I predicted way back in the earliest issues of *Money Morning,* the dollar's eroding value has already transformed the United States into the "World's Biggest Garage Sale." And I'm not just talking "trophy" properties here—I'm talking critical U.S. infrastructure.

According to statistics compiled by the Council on Foreign Relations, a nonpartisan think tank based in New York City, foreign companies already own most of the ships, containers, handling equipment, and port facilities used in our domestic shipping industry. Approximately 80 percent of U.S. port terminals are leased and operated by foreign companies. Of the 517 domestic airports offering commercial passenger travel, 13 have management contracts with private companies that have significant foreign ownership or involvement.

Out of approximately 54,000 publicly owned water and wastewater systems, nearly 2,400 (5 percent) contract with private firms having foreign parent companies to provide operational and mainte-nance services. Most of the 15 percent of the U.S. population being served by 20,000 private, regulated water and wastewater utilities receive monthly bills from companies owned by domestic subsidiar-ies of foreign firms.

And, although the phenomenon of privatized highways is rela-tively new to the United States, the City of Chicago recently leased the 7.8 mile Chicago Skyway to the Australian-owned Macquarie Infrastructure Group and Spanish-owned Cintra Concesiones de Infraestructuras de Transporte, S.A., for 99 years at a cost of $1.8 bil-lion. The same firms were selected as the preferred bidders for the 75-year, $3.85 billion lease of the Indiana Toll Road.

Japan faced a similar ordeal, having to dump off virtually all the trophy properties it grabbed up during its artificially created salad days—properties like the Rockefeller Center in New York City. But, when you're the United States—and you constantly spend more than you make in the form of the twin deficits of budget and trade—you have to finance your shortfall somehow. And you do that by selling off your best—even your most critical—assets to your overseas credi-tors, just like we're doing now.

THE (CASH) COWS MAY COME HOME AGAIN

If there is a silver lining to the sale of important U.S. assets to foreign buyers, it's that they're probably not gone forever. If the United States gets its act together, the economy recovers, and the dollar regains its strength, most of these assets will come back to U.S. owners—just like Pebble Beach, Rockefeller Center, and other trophy properties, which were sold to the Japanese in the 1980s and later repurchased by U.S. interests when the economic tables turned. Thus, while such asset sales make for flashy headlines, there's probably no reason to worry too much about it.

THE FLIP SIDE OF THE DEVALUED DOLLAR

Of course, the other side of any devaluation in the dollar is the inflation it causes. Already, it's so rampant that the government now calls a jump of 2.3 percent in the Consumer Price Index (CPI) "acceptable." In my pocketbook, that's hardly acceptable! But, I suppose if I'm the Fed and I prefer to pay more attention to "core" CPI, which ignores food and energy prices, then the 3.8 percent annual rate of inflation in 2008 wouldn't ignite any deep concerns with me, either.

Then again, since I both eat and drive, as well as heat and cool my house, it does raise concerns—concerns I'm sure you share. To get the *real* inflation figures, based on unadulterated data, check out Shadowstats.com. They recently reported actual inflation rates are running closer to 9.0 percent—a lot more like the level of pain we're feeling in our wallets.

The weaker dollar also affects both employment and personal incomes. While companies may be showing higher gross revenues in dollars, the real value of those revenues is falling. Before long, that translates into downsizing and cuts in wages and hours for existing workers. As a reflection of how much of that has happened already, the Department of Labor reported that unemployment in July 2009 had climbed to a 26-year high of 9.5 percent (16.5 percent if you count laid-off workers who had stopped looking for work or taken part-time jobs), and personal-income growth had fallen 8.6 percent when discounted for inflation. The Fed spends a lot of time and PR ink trying to manipulate the public perception of the job it is doing—to gain and keep our confidence in its ability to stem inflation, keep the economy from dropping into a recession, and support the greenback, all by adjusting interest rates. But, as hindsight now clearly indicates, it has achieved none of those objectives.

What's worse, its own actions have trapped it, crippling its ability to battle these problems. It can't lower rates to stimulate growth because that would escalate the already dire inflation situation—and it can't raise rates to combat inflation because that could set off a repeat of the chain-reaction explosion that leveled our capital infrastructure from 2006 to 2008. A rate hike would trigger higher rates for adjustable-rate mortgages (and credit cards) . . . which could set off a new round of housing defaults . . . which could force more bank write-downs . . . which could . . . which could . . . which could.

In the face of that, the Fed's only real option is to leave interest rates close to where they are, hoping the current level of liquidity will be enough to rekindle demand and jump-start the economy. Fighting inflation and restoring the value of the dollar will just have to wait.

From an investment standpoint, this means that, more than ever, we're on our own—which is actually quite exciting. Yes, you read me right—*exciting!*

In fact, history strongly suggests that what's happening now could set up the greatest buying opportunity of our lifetime. Of course, you can't recognize that opportunity by following Wall Street's traditional buy-and-hold mantra, nor will a diversified portfolio let you achieve new wealth. To do that, you will need to look across the oceans, go long resources, and hedge against inflation—all strategies that are covered in specific detail in later chapters.

WHERE DOES AMERICA GO NOW?

Having taken one small step back from the edge of the economic precipice, the U.S. government must figure out how to effectively balance its new domestic role as guarantor, lender, and even investor of last resort. And, it must do so immediately—there will be no learning curve here. The government must also address just how difficult its massive intervention in America's private sector will make it for the United States to continue to intervene or exert its influence in the political and economic affairs of other nations.

At the same time, individuals must stop the guilt by association and the *argumentum ad absurdum* or *ad hominem* attacks. Everybody—from radicals to moderates to conservatives—ultimately wants a better world. So, this is the ideal time to engage our fellow man—literally and economically.

Many of the lesser-developed nations around the globe have so far been spared the worst of the world's economic crisis. Having resisted the seemingly lucrative (and lightly regulated) financial innovations that undermined the strength of the U.S. financial markets, their politicians and central bankers can now be grateful that their economies have not yet been pummeled like America's has been. As they advance their own economic agendas, the Chinas and Indias of the world will learn much from the painful experiences of the United States, Western Europe, and Japan—and this knowledge will help them become even stronger players in international finance.

Capital flows will also look far different as the New World Order continues to develop. No longer will money move primarily from developed to developing nations in payment for raw resources and cheap manufactured goods. While those flows will surely continue to grow, the emerging nations will also be exporting large quantities of capital, bringing in new goods and services to their growing consumer populations.

From the U.S. perspective, this flow of capital will be accelerated by the weak dollar. But rising domestic prices will not be just limited to imports. Prices for all goods still produced in the United States but capable of being exported will also increase. Strengthening foreign currencies will give overseas consumers an edge, enabling them to outbid U.S. citizens for their own production. Domestic producers, seeking to maximize profits, will sell more of their goods abroad—meaning that if U.S. residents want to continue past rates of consumption, they'll have to bid up to compete. Given lower employment and reduced incomes, this could further impede America's recovery.

Don't get me wrong, though. It will take time, but I firmly believe America *will* recover and still be a major force in the world economy. However, it may no longer be the *leading* force—and the dollar may not retain its position as reserve currency for the world—both based on factors I discuss in Chapter 7.

Global economic leadership has its privileges—and, as Washington is discovering, it also has its obligations. With our economic troubles at the center of the global financial vortex, the United States must think outside the box if it hopes to revitalize its financial system, control inflation, reduce reliance on foreign creditors, and regain the confidence of our economic partners.

With a more integrated global financial system, the playing field will look different and the rules of the game will change, creating new challenges for American investors. But, with a clear perspective on the world and a careful plan like the one you're about to learn, even greater success will be possible.

CHAPTER 7

CONSUMERISM ON THE MOVE

An Engine for Recovery

When you've got them by their wallets, their hearts and minds will follow.

—Fern Naito

Since the end of World War II, the theory has been that the heroic American consumer was carrying the rest of the world along in the bed of his half-ton pickup truck. However, the current global economic crisis has finally shattered that myth. Rather than being the source of global prosperity, the U.S. consumer—high on unrestrained credit and unrealistic home equities—was more accurately a leading force in its destruction. A liability by any other name.

Some are betting American consumers will soon show renewed signs of past resiliency, once again spending with unrestrained glee. But I take a different view. I believe those who make future stock and real estate investments based on faith in U.S. consumerism will quickly lose their naiveté—along with much of their money.

135

Don't get me wrong. I *do* believe strongly that consumerism will be a major factor, if not *the* major factor, in the world's economic recovery—it just won't be *American* consumerism.

Over the past decade, a number of so-called "emerging nations" have actually emerged, turning into major players on the global economic stage. Increasingly, they have become leading suppliers of both goods and services to the developed world—North America, Western Europe, and Japan—resulting in a massive transfer of capital into their coffers. Increasing prices for oil and other commodities have also contributed—so much so that, at the end of 2008, holdings of the world's emerging nations accounted for one of every 20 dollars in the global system, triple what they held in 2000.

Because of the success of the "emerging nations," some economic commentators have called for abandonment of the term—but others disagree. "People started using it more loosely, and . . . it lost a little bit of its original meaning," says Wharton School of Business Management Professor Gerald McDermott, "[but] I think it continues to convey a reality . . . about countries with great promise and great potential. They're growing, but they're still not there."

THE ECONOMIC WORM IS BEGINNING TO TURN

And, thanks to those growing capital holdings, the economic worm is beginning to turn. The emerging nations are developing their own consumer societies, fueled by the transformation of their populations from low-wage producers to middle-class customers. Those consumers are going to want the same trappings of success middle-class families everywhere want—from the newest electronic devices to the latest designer fashions—and many of those things will come from the United States and Europe.

These countries are also engaging in a rapid campaign of infrastructure improvements—roads, power systems, sanitation services, rail lines, airports, and the like. You name it, they are ready to build it. But they need help. Lacking the expertise, the technology, and the equipment for really big-ticket projects, the emerging countries will

> **FISCAL FLASHPOINT**
>
> The key to investment success in the years ahead will not be so much about investing in companies located *IN* the emerging-market countries, but rather about investing in companies that are growing *because* of emerging-market economies.

be buying those things from Europe and the United States, which is particularly well-positioned as an exporter right now because of weakness in the dollar.

WHO'S LEADING THE CHARGE TO RECOVERY?

So, who are the most influential new rising stars at the center of this historic transfer of wealth and economic power? China, of course, heads everyone's list, but the countries of Eastern Europe and the Middle East have also been raking in huge sums of private capital in recent years, capital they're now exporting again to buy Western goods and services—$450 billion worth each year, according to recent accountings.

My *Money Morning* comrade, Contributing Editor Martin Hutchinson, reports many analysts also pick South Korea and Taiwan to vigorously emerge from the ongoing global financial turmoil—with some justification. After all, China and the two smaller Asian "tigers" share several alluring characteristics:

- A highly competitive and innovative manufacturing industry.
- Excellent government and workforce discipline.
- Limited debt from fiscal and monetary stimulus (or, in China's case, a substantial *surplus*)—repayment of which would ultimately impede future growth.
- An export orientation positioned to benefit quickly as order is restored in the global trading economy.

Of course, the Asian leaders aren't alone. You'll find the same or similar characteristics among other nations in other regions of the world—characteristics that will help their economies bounce back from the recession with almost as much vigor. But, since China is the obvious first choice right now, let's begin by taking a closer look at the Red Dragon. Then, we'll come back and check out a few of the top prospects elsewhere.

CHINA—DANGEROUS MYTHS AND CRUCIAL REALITIES

It's often said that the Chinese symbol for "crisis" combines two pictograms—one representing danger and the other opportunity. While this translation isn't quite correct in the literal sense, the sentiment certainly is. The next chapter in China's economic saga will be filled with more opportunity—and potential crisis—than any decade in the last 100 years.

As should be evident by now, I'm a *strong* China booster. Much work remains to be done, but I firmly believe China will become the dominant force in global economics within the next generation. I also believe that, if you don't have a well-thought-out China strategy for your investment portfolio, you will wind up *falling far, far behind*.

Lately, of course, we've been hearing some really bad news about China—but much of that is based on a combination of sour grapes and misinterpretation. In truth, the country has 1.3 billion people, a progressively more stable and realistic government, a rapidly expanding middle class, an increasingly educated and technologically savvy populace, and virtually unlimited potential for growth.

As the new century turned, that potential transformed investors into drooling idiots, with many piling in at the very top of the most recent market cycle (January 2007)—and, predictably, paying a terrible price (see Figure 7.1). Those investors have gone through the classic emotional stages regarding investment in China: anxiety, denial, fear, desperation and, finally, panic. Now, having bailed out completely at the height of their panic, they've totally written China off.

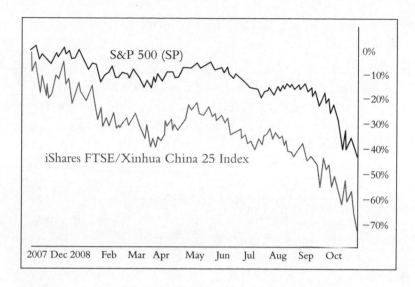

FIGURE 7.1 Many Early Chinese Market Investors Paid a Terrible Price
Source: YahooFinance.com.

But, if you examine the situation more closely, you begin to ask yourself if recent events in China are really all that bad. Relative to that question, here are two things you need to recognize:

1. What has been happening in China is actually part of the *normal* investing cycle.
2. To be successful in China, you must separate hype from reality.

Don't Believe the Hype

With respect to that latter point, five of the biggest myths you may have recently heard about China are discussed here, each followed by the reality as I see it.

Myth 1: China's Economy Is Failing

China's economy is *not* failing. It has slowed—but it is still growing. (By contrast, the U.S. economy has suffered its worst declines in a generation—and is still falling.) Here are some statistics to support my contention:

- China currently maintains the world's highest growth rate—even after taking steps to slow things down.
- China's GDP remains on track for unprecedented growth of 10 percent over the next 30 years. Add in 5 percent to account for the unofficial "cash" economy, and China's average growth rate is closer to 12 percent—at least 10 times the U.S. average for more than 30 years running.
- History suggests that China is just getting started. Right now, they're about where we were in 1900. Per-capita income now is roughly 10 times what it was in 1950. To put that into perspective, the growth of living standards only two decades after China launched market reforms is greater than the nation's cumulative progress over the last 2,000 years.
- The views of many investors are clouded by misconceptions about China—that it is a communist backwater, a primitive society with a lack of freedom and low income. But history shows otherwise. For 18 of the last 20 centuries, China has had the world's largest economy—and it will again.

Myth 2: Chinese Consumers Are Broke

Many think that Chinese consumers are tapped out—but it's not true. Consumer spending rose 21 percent in 2008 to $2.1 trillion—and growth of 15 to 19 percent was expected in 2009. China's National Bureau of Statistics reports the nation's middle class is now bigger than the entire U.S. population—and that's 330 million. The Chinese also save far more (35 percent) than Americans and have increasing disposable income, whereas disposable income is falling in the United States. Seventy percent of the U.S. economy is consumer powered, versus only 30 percent in China (imagine the potential as they come up to similar levels).

Myth 3: Communism Can't Work

But it is—thanks to regulatory controls designed to foster growth and build a consumer-driven economy. Chinese-style communism, as opposed to the much hated and rightfully feared Soviet variety, has

FISCAL FLASHPOINT

Meet the *Chuppies.* China's middle class—the equivalent of America's yuppies—is on a consumption binge. Chinese retail sales were up 21.8 percent in 2008 to US$1.59 trillion, or 10 trillion renminbi (RMB). Annual per-capita urban incomes grew 14.5 percent to 15,781 RMB; rural incomes rose 15 percent to 4,761 RMB. In 2009, the *RISE* in China's consumer spending was expected to outpace growth in the United States, the Eurozone, and Japan combined.

Source: National Bureau of Statistics—China.

actually proven to be a critical element in China's rapid modernization—and it will continue to be for years to come to the extent that central planning is both *needed* and *implemented.* There *will* come a day when the need for central planning vanishes, but don't expect it any time soon. Instead, take advantage of the stability it provides to the country at a time when Western nations are undeniably fractured.

The stability will be enhanced when Fifth-Generation Chinese leaders consolidate power in 2015. They are Western educated, with training in law, politics, and economics. They are starkly different from the Fourth Generation's social engineers, and thus much better equipped to deal with economic changes.

Myth 4: Falling Exports Will Kill China

False. Exports are down, but the impact will be far smaller than many think. In spite of the "Made in China" evidence you see on thousands of products sold here in the United States, only 6 percent of China's total workforce is involved in exports, accounting for between 8.5 and 9.0 percent of GDP. By contrast, roughly 43 to 45 percent of the Chinese GDP is generated by government spending on infrastructure and property improvement, and another 32 to 35 percent is driven by consumer purchasing.

Between 2000 and 2009, the annual rate of growth in China's exports fell by a massive 35 percentage points—yet China's overall

GDP growth slowed by less than one percentage point . . . little more than a rounding error. Sadly, most Western analysts continue to ignore these figures, still painting China as a country that will live and die by exports.

Myth 5: The Markets Stink

Yes they do—but probably not for long. Why? China sits on the world's largest pile of cash reserves—$2.3 trillion—which means that China can literally *spend* its way out of the current economic slump, whereas the West is functionally bankrupt. In contrast to the past, the Chinese will spend this money *despite* the subprime mess . . . or a weak U.S. dollar . . . or deficits.

Recognizing the truth about Myth 5 is the real key to investing in China without unacceptable losses. In contrast to Western markets, where investments follow profits, the situation in China is the reverse—in China, *profits follow investments.* (China is a consumption model; the United States is a production model.) We know from history that Chinese markets follow state investment cycles—which means we want to invest *when* and *where* Beijing is investing, taking our cues from the Chinese government's growth initiatives at any given moment.

FISCAL FLASHPOINT

Unlike the United States, where the markets are typically driven by corporate profits, the Chinese markets follow *state* investment initiatives. This means we don't just want to invest IN China—we want to invest *when* and *where* Beijing is investing. In other words, *because* of China; a point I made earlier.

Ninety-nine-point-nine percent of Westerners don't understand this, so they'll make the mistake of investing *IN* China when it's *because* of China that really matters. And, that means they will probably miss the greatest wealth-creation opportunity in the history of mankind (again).

A RED DRAGON ON THE ROAD TO DOMINANCE

The rise of China is a totally unprecedented phenomenon, raising questions about global economics and power relationships that the world has never before faced.

—Daniel Burstein and Arne de Keijzer, Big Dragon

What the truth underlying the myths just discussed means, translated into numbers, is that China is on track to create *700 percent growth* in per-capita income over the next two decades. This has never before been done in recorded history. Because of that surging economic power, there won't be an industry or business segment on the planet that China will not substantially influence—if not completely dominate—in 20 years.

That's why I continue to emphasize—over and over—one simple fact: *If you don't have a clear China strategy embedded in your investment plan, you are toast!*

Though far too many Western analysts ignore it, continuing to focus on China's export business as a sign of weakness, recent numbers give a clear picture of the building strength that will lift China out of the worldwide slump well ahead of other major players. While America and the rest of the developed world staggered through the first half of 2009, beset by ongoing waves of economic uncertainty, China powered ahead like a gigantic steamroller. For example, Chinese government reports released in July 2009 indicated:

- Domestic retail sales rose 14.8 percent year over year in April—then boosted that mark to 15.2 percent in May.
- Industrial output from China's factories rose 7.3 percent in April—then climbed by an even stronger 8.9 percent in May.
- China's gross domestic product expanded by 7.9 percent in the quarter ended June 30, 2009, up from an already strong 6.1 percent increase in the quarter ended March 31.
- Inflation, rampant in many other parts of the world, actually declined in China. The producer price index (PPI) fell 7.8 percent

in June 2009, on top of a 7.2 percent decline in May, while the consumer price index (CPI) fell 1.7 percent in June after a drop of 1.4 percent in May.
* Government and private investment in urban areas for assets like roads and new housing rose 40 percent in May versus spending in the same month of 2008.

Given this growth—and the prospects that it will not only continue, but increase at rates far greater than in other parts of the world—it only makes sense that we should channel our investment dollars into industries and companies that will service this growth. I have more specific discussions in Chapter 11 of some key sectors and companies poised to benefit, but for now just consider this one broad assessment:

Almost everything *China does* has some effect on the world economy—and that effect will do nothing but *grow* in the years ahead.

How can I say that with such certainty? Actually, it doesn't require a lot of deep analysis. A simple common-sense look at some obvious situations tells the tale. For example:

* *Low-Cost Labor:* China has the world's largest population and, though working conditions and pay scales are rapidly improving, that population still represents a major pool of lower-cost labor for the rest of the world. Thus, any time a Western company thinks of outsourcing any of its labor functions, China is among the first places it must look.
* *Strong Savings:* In spite of their low-cost status in the global labor market, China's consumers have been able to continue their buying throughout the worldwide recession because of both steadily rising incomes and the huge savings pool they have to draw on. On average, Chinese workers save more than 30 percent of their incomes, versus a savings rate of less than 7 percent in the United States (a rate that, according to the U.S. Bureau of Economic Analysis, actually stood below 1 percent for most of the past 20 years).

FISCAL FLASHPOINT

The companies that offer the greatest potential for growth in China will *not* be the ones in low-margin, labor-intensive industries focusing on export business. There is simply too much competition and that business model is too easy to copy. Companies that want to prosper in the new Chinese economy will have to have a visible advantage over the competition, be it superior management, a technological edge, or a strong brand name.

- *Lending Boom:* That huge domestic savings pool, coupled with the country's massive accounts surplus, means China has tremendous amounts of money to spend on major projects, and they're spending it. Or, more accurately, they're lending it to those prepared to spend it. In its midyear report, posted on its web site in early July 2009, the People's Bank of China said lending for June was 1.53 trillion yuan ($224 billion), double the lending for May. It also said total lending for the first half of 2009 had shot up to 7.4 trillion yuan ($1.083 trillion)—somewhat shocking given the Bank's original lending target for all of 2009 was just 5.0 trillion yuan.
- *Stimulus Superiority:* These large amounts of bank lending are providing a level of economic stimulus unseen in the Western world, where banks are still beset by huge losses on past lending and are thus reluctant to make all but the safest of new loans.
- *Luxury Demand:* Because much of China's "new capitalism" is centered in urban areas with youthful populations, there is a growing demand for high-end and outright luxury items. Sales of automobiles, for example, were expected to rise by more than 10 percent in 2009, versus an 8 percent decline in the rest of the world—in part because autos in China are more than just transportation. They're a symbol of wealth and success—a sexy status symbol. One's social position can be determined by the type of vehicle one owns and flaunts. That's why, despite high luxury taxes, China is currently the globe's hottest market for foreign

sports cars such as Aston Martin, Ferrari, and Lamborghini. (The Beijing Ferrari owners club is the world's second largest.) The same is true of top fashion brands (although counterfeiting of such products remains a large problem for legitimate manufacturers and importers). In short, China is no longer just a place to "import from"—it's now a major market for international companies to "export to."

- *Washers and Dryers, Too:* Don't forget the more mundane items, either. There are nearly 330 million middle-class Chinese consumers who simply want to buy washing machines, modern stoves, televisions, stereos, and other everyday items we take for granted. Their desires will dramatically rewrite the standards of consumerism.

- *Cell Dominance:* Consumer electronics are also in growing demand thanks to the shifting demographics. China recently became the No. 1 company in the world in cell phone ownership and usage, and it ranks second in the number of Internet users. The Internet offers a wide marketing doorway to China for companies in e-commerce. Despite government efforts to limit Internet "self-expression" through blogs and networking sites, when it comes to personal technology, the proverbial genie is out of the bottle.

- *Energy Expansion:* China's increasing wealth, urbanization, and demand for the trappings of modern society has exacerbated a growing energy shortage, but the government is using its financial resources to attack this problem. It has financed a number of joint-venture exploration and production projects, including a liquefied natural gas facility in New Guinea and refineries in Indonesia, and has sought major stakes in leading international oil companies, including a failed bid for Unocal in June 2005.

- *M&A Maneuvers:* China's mergers and acquisitions activity has not been limited to the energy sector. China's giant Lenovo Group bought IBM's personal computer business in late 2004, and its Haier Group Co. was barely outbid by Whirlpool in a 2005 attempt to acquire Maytag. To facilitate future M&A activities, China set up its own state foreign-exchange investment firm in 2007, and that new firm recently took a $3 billion position in Blackstone Group, a U.S. private equity firm.

- *Pollution Fight:* China is responding to international criticism with strong new regulations to combat both air and water pollution, and laws (in conjunction with the United States) to limit the "dumping" of pollutants such as old electronics equipment and chemicals used in the manufacture of such products as paper. This will require major spending initiatives on new and refitted power plants, water treatment facilities, and various other "clean" technologies.

Altogether, these activities and circumstances fully justify my earlier statement. It's simply *impossible* for so much to be going on in China without it affecting virtually *every* aspect of the global economy.

WILL CHINA'S YUAN BE THE NEXT WORLD CURRENCY?

One vitally important aspect of both doing business in China and investing in companies that do business there is the strength of the Chinese currency—the yuan (or renminbi).

Indeed, the true value of the yuan has been a hotly debated issue for years, with many analysts arguing the currency was severely undervalued versus the U.S. dollar following the abandonment of the Bretton Woods agreement. To counter that argument, China tied the value of the yuan to the dollar in 1994, fixing the exchange rate at 8.27 yuan per dollar. That valuation, supported by restrictions on the number of yuan Chinese businesses could exchange for foreign currencies, worked well until the turn of the century, when U.S. economists and government officials again complained the currency was undervalued. The United States threatened trade sanctions unless China converted the yuan to a floating exchange rate, which it did in July 2005. (Actually, rather than being completely free floating, China's government said the yuan's value would be "adjustable, based on market supply and demand with reference to exchange-rate movements of currencies in a basket," the basket to include the dollar, the euro, the Japanese yen, and the South Korean won.)

As a consequence, the yuan has steadily risen in value against the dollar, with the exchange rate moving to a ratio of 6.83 yuan to $1.00 in July of 2009, a reflection of both the economic downturn and the ill-advised U.S. stimulus and bailout packages—which, as I've already noted, are highly inflationary and debase the U.S. currency.

This has led to a new chorus of cries for a yuan revaluation—but there's a major debate over whether its value should be increased or decreased. U.S. officials, worried about China's continued accumulation of dollar reserves, contend the yuan is still undervalued in

---

FISCAL FLASHPOINT

The increasing strength of the yuan has been a major factor in China's ability to amass its current cache of foreign currency reserves. When Chinese companies receive foreign currencies in payment for their exports, the Bank of China uses yuan to buy that currency for the Chinese treasury—to the tune of $20 billion per month over the past few years. As a result, China's foreign currency reserves topped $2.3 trillion in early 2009, with an estimated half of that sum in U.S. dollars. As a percentage of GDP, China's reserves are the highest of any nation on Earth, nearly 33 percent at last count. By contrast, U.S. reserves (an estimated $71.515 billion) are just 0.5 percent of GDP. That means China can spend its way out of this mess, while our only hope is to *print* our way out.

FISCAL FLASHPOINT

China actually invented paper money, which was first used by tea merchants in the early seventh century and could be exchanged for actual goods or tax credits. The earliest date that state-issued paper money can be traced to is 1024 in Sichuan province. You can see many of these early notes first hand in the spectacular Shanghai Museum in the People's Plaza of Shanghai, at the intersection of Yan'an Dong and Henan Nan roads in central Shanghai.

Source: Silkroad Foundation, www.silk-road.com/artl/papermoney.shtml.

relation to the dollar, while other analysts argue the yuan is actually overvalued versus the dollar because of the dollar's own drop in value.

Where China Stands on the Issue

While the Chinese listen politely to U.S. complaints about the low value of the yuan—mostly because they don't want to risk an angry Congress imposing new trade sanctions—they are actually more concerned about the low value of the dollar. It's estimated that, in addition to its currency reserves, China is holding more than $700 billion worth of U.S. debt. And, with that kind of exposure, they obviously don't like it very much when the U.S. government continues to devalue their investment by printing more money and engaging in all kinds of bailout chicanery. For example, the dollar fell by more than 10.5 percent from March through May of 2009, meaning China suffered a corresponding drop in purchasing power over the same period.

Given that, it's easy to imagine why they're upset—but how far will they go in pressing the issue? Some U.S. observers—theorizing a Chinese conspiracy to undermine the United States—claim China is suddenly going to quit buying U.S. debt and unload what it already holds because the dollar is such a wreck.

I disagree—for one simple reason. While the dollar is indeed a wreck, there is no way China can unload its U.S. debt because there isn't another currency in the world with enough liquidity to absorb everything the Chinese would want to sell. Therefore, China will probably grit its teeth and think of new ways to beat Washington at its own game—like buying oil, gold, and other commodities that store value.

It's also highly unlikely China will rock the world currency boat right now because, over the long term, the Chinese want the yuan to become a dominant world currency. As such, they will avoid any rash actions, taking carefully measured steps to bolster its appearance of stability and acceptance around the globe.

Although many Westerners are struggling to come to terms with the notion of a dethroned dollar—which becomes more of a possibility every day, few can even imagine the idea of world markets

---

FISCAL FLASHPOINT

It's my firm belief that the Chinese yuan is at the heart of the world's financial future. It may well replace the U.S. dollar as the global reserve currency within our lifetimes.

---

being dominated by yuan-based currency settlements. To most, it seems about as likely as us putting another man on the moon.

But, it's already well on its way to becoming reality. At a time when the West is still busy handing out Band-Aids in an attempt to deal with the greatest financial crisis on record, China is quietly reinventing itself with a series of international swap agreements and trading relationships intended to boost the yuan's status as an internationally accepted currency. As reported by *The Wall Street Journal,* China signed currency-exchange agreements worth more than 650 billion yuan (US$95 billion) in the first four months of 2009 alone. Those pacts were with a host of nations more than glad to move away from the increasingly shaky U.S. dollar, including Argentina, Brazil, South Korea, Indonesia, Malaysia, Belarus, and Hong Kong.

INTRODUCING THE YUAN-CARRY TRADE

One of the steps China is taking to bolster worldwide acceptance of its currency is its effort to create a yuan-carry trade—much like the yen-carry trade. (It's not technically a carry trade, but it might as well be because the impact is going to be equally significant.) For those unfamiliar with a *carry trade,* it is a strategy in which an investor sells one currency with a relatively low interest rate, and then uses the money to buy a different currency yielding a higher interest rate. The goal is to capture the difference between the rates, and profits can often be substantial, depending on the amount of leverage the investor uses.

(continued)

Here's an example: Assume a trader borrows 1,000 yen from a Japanese bank, converts the funds into U.S. dollars, and then buys a bond for the equivalent amount. If the bond pays 5.5 percent and the Japanese interest rate is set at 0.5 percent, the trader stands to make a profit of 5.0 percent (5.5 – 0.5 = 5.0)—as long as the exchange rate between the currencies does not change. If the strategy is done using leverage, the gains can become very large. For example, if the trader in this example uses a leverage factor of 10 to 1, he can make a profit of up to 50 percent.

The big risk in a carry trade is the uncertainty of exchange rates. In this example, if the dollar fell in value relative to the yen, the trader could lose money. And, because it was done with heavy leverage, even a small adverse move in exchange rates could result in a large loss (unless hedged with another vehicle such as a futures or option contract).

China's Been Left with Little Choice— Strengthen the Yuan

While some may question China's motives, it's hard to question its rationale. By mid-2009, the United States had injected trillions of dollars into the ailing American economy—collectively worth more than 35 percent of the entire GDP. And more "stimulus" was in the offing—hardly a comforting prospect. So, China is being forced to take steps that ensure its own survival.

Unfortunately, the blockheads in Washington don't seem to understand this. They keep taking actions that only make matters worse when they could be actively working with China and the world community on developing exchange-rate equity. It's like Washington is in denial of the coming fact that the yuan will undoubtedly be elevated to global status, in line with the current major currency trading pairs for settlement purposes—and could even become the world's next reserve currency.

I've raised this issue frequently in recent years and, most of the time, received blank stares in response. People just aren't prepared to deal with the idea that the U.S. dollar could be finished and that

WHAT THE YUAN'S RISE COULD MEAN TO INVESTORS

A major factor in the current dollar-yuan valuation debate is that, because of China's huge reserve position, Washington has lost its ability to dictate future international monetary policy. This loss of U.S. monetary power is evident if you look back a bit. In 1990, the reserves in the U.S. banking system were roughly 2.5 times larger than the Chinese banking system's reserves. Now, the situation has reversed and compounded— China's central bank has *25 times* the reserves of the Federal Reserve.

What's worse, the top dogs in D.C. don't understand the implications of this—and, sadly, they're virtually the only ones in the world who don't. They think they can continue to use monetary policy as a weapon, when most of the rest of the world now thinks the U.S. dollar is a liability. However, China's massive reserves will no longer allow that. More and more, China is demonstrating the ability to blunt Washington's monetary moves—a pattern that will intensify as the Chinese sign currency swap agreements with more and more countries, enabling the Chinese to trade directly with those nations wanting to make payments in Chinese yuan, while receiving huge discounts in the process.

This is a major reason (among others) I believe the world's next reserve currency is likely to be the yuan. I've said this for years (and been roundly criticized for my remarks), but even I've been stunned by the ferocity of the recent Chinese drive to increase the acceptability of the yuan—which, as Washington rightly points out, still isn't freely tradable. Beijing knows the dollar is currently a liability and they've stepped up efforts to take advantage of that.

To that end, the Chinese recently put together a meeting in Moscow attended by Brazilian, Indian, and Russian representatives, among others. The express goal was to reach agreements that would supplant the dollar as the world's reserve currency (or at least knock it off its pedestal), replacing it with a yuan-led basket of currencies—or with the yuan alone.

An agreement wasn't reached, but more attempts will undoubtedly be made, which raises this question: What are the real risks if China succeeds?

There are a variety of implications, some admittedly apocalyptic, but most are just new wrinkles on already existing concerns, such as:

(continued)

- The dollar could go into freefall. If countries no longer have to hold dollars, they won't. Instead, they'll dump them as fast as they can—which will drive the dollar even lower and further damage our economy.
- Inflation will strike the United States with a vengeance as anything bought, sold, or priced in dollars instantly rises in price to offset this decline.
- With the dollar as the world's *de facto* currency, U.S. companies bear very little exchange-rate risk when it comes time to repatriate assets or make currency-related adjustments. That would change overnight, and prices throughout the value chains would rise sharply to compensate.
- The cost of money itself would rise. If the dollar falls, not only will there be massive selling pressure against it, but the cost of borrowing it will rise dramatically as lenders raise rates to offset the increased risk of dollar-based transactions.
- Finally, if there is *another* reserve currency, other countries will no longer have to buy U.S. debt—and you can guess where that will lead us . . .

My best guess is we won't see any one of these things in isolation, but rather a blend of each. To the extent that China continues to absorb our inflationary influences, buy our debt in measured doses, and maintain its reserves, we'll probably have a slow-paced decline in the dollar—but not the catastrophic fall many in the doom-gloom-and-boom crowd are predicting. At the same time, I also see the IMF changing course over the next few years to reflect increasing Chinese influence and monetary power.

On the individual level, this clearly provides a new set of influences most investors have yet to grasp. Many will perceive the changes as threatening, but I think there are real opportunities at hand. Some are obvious, like investments in currencies and commodities that are of interest to the Chinese. Others, like direct investment in the Chinese yuan, require a leap of faith.

Either way, there will be an upside for individual investors—even if it's not a popular one.

another currency could replace it after more than 100 years of global dominance. But they better get used to the idea—in a hurry.

China, of course, is acutely aware that not having international currency convertibility hampers its development and its relative ability to flex its capital-market muscles, especially in transactions involving dollar-yuan exchange rates. This is inconsequential to most Americans, but it's a very real problem for Chinese businessmen like Chen Xianbin, chairman of the Guangxi Sanhuan Enterprise Group. He told *China Daily* that, in the past three years alone, he estimates he has lost more than $150 million on international trade because of exchange-rate shifts between the yuan and the dollar. So he's keen to see yuan-based foreign trade that will reduce exchange-rate risk or eliminate it entirely.

Given that internal pressure and a lack of recognition of the problems among Western leaders, China has been left with little choice but to elevate its own currency—and it will continue to do so whether the United States helps in that process or not. That's evident in statements issued by Chinese President Hu Jintao and others. The words may not be precise, but when you've been in Asia as long as I have, you learn very quickly to listen not to the literal translations, but to the metaphors behind them. Do that and you'll quickly recognize that President Hu Jintao is telling us what he's going to do, point blank—which is strengthen the yuan.

To that end, I believe the yuan is still the best currency investment on the planet—even if it's going to have some bumps along the way.

FISCAL FLASHPOINT

Opportunity is not totally about GDP growth and production. One of the most important elements in defining the investment potential of an emerging-market country is the strength of its economic and political institutions in maintaining the rule of law, establishing even-handed regulatory controls, and endorsing the enforcement of contracts. And, believe it or not, the roster of nations with those characteristics includes China. It may be primitive by Western standards, but it is developing rapidly.

History shows that strong economies tend to have strong currencies—and the actions China has taken recently only reinforce that.

And by the way, when I said the possibility of the yuan becoming the world's dominant currency seemed as likely as us putting another man on the moon, I forgot to mention . . . China's planning to put a man on the moon by 2020 or sooner.

Don't Even Think of Dismissing China

So, in conclusion, if you're tempted to dismiss China within the context of your overall investment strategy, take a cue from Al Pacino in *Donnie Brasco* and "fuggeddaboutit!" I can't think of a worse mistake you could make at this point in our history—especially with a global economic recovery finally starting to build.

Obviously, there will be challenges—but, as I've said often in our *Money Map Report* and *Money Morning* newsletters, the benefits of growth far outweigh "Band-Aid capitalism" when it comes to cornering the best global economic trends. And it will be just such growth-driven trends that lead you to the recovery and expansion of your personal wealth in the years ahead.

THE RISING TIDE IN EASTERN EUROPE

Now let's take a quick look at some other areas of the world where you should find opportunities as the global economic recovery progresses and more and more nations transform from *developing* to *developed* status.

While Germany can hardly be classified as *emerging,* it will probably lead the rest of Europe—including the still-developing Eastern European economies—back out of the depths of recession. The German manufacturing industry is the envy of the world and, because of that production power, the German balance of payments surplus soared to $205.8 billion in the 12 months through April 2009. While most of the rest of Europe was running trade deficits, the World Economic Forum (WEF) estimated Germany's surplus would be 4.4 percent of gross domestic product for all of 2009. Unlike the United States and Britain, the German government resisted the urge to splurge on huge stimulus packages. Consequently, it was expected to run a budget deficit of only 3.9 percent of GDP in 2009 (though the Bundesbank predicted the ailing world economy could cause it to rise to 5.9 percent in 2010). That ratio is far smaller than in other G-20 economies and should be fairly easy to finance, freeing up more capital for investment by German business. Chancellor Angela Merkel also indicated quite strongly to the highly conservative European Central Bank (ECB)—whose primary purpose is to support the euro currency system—that it had better *stay* conservative to keep the lid on inflation.

Of course, there is a flip side to Germany's more conservative fiscal stance. Because it didn't provide substantial stimulus, it has suffered a deeper recession than many other countries, as evidenced by a 6.9 percent drop in first-quarter 2009 GDP from the year's prior quarter. By comparison, year-over-year GDP output declined only 2.5 percent in the United States.

However, preliminary figures showed German manufacturing orders stabilized in the second quarter of 2009, and most analysts predicted Germany would likely experience a return to growth in the second half of 2009. The Center for European Economic Research (ZEW) indicator of German economic sentiment for June 2009 came in at 44.8—up more than 13 points from April to a three-year high.

Because of Germany's cautious fiscal and monetary policies, its continuing economic rebound is likely to be healthy, without resurgent inflation or bond market turmoil. The World Economic Forum (WEF) ranked Germany among the top 10 countries (out of 134 global economies) for competitiveness in 2009—and ranks it first in the world for the quality of its infrastructure, particularly transportation and communications.

A good starting place when looking for European recovery plays.

Eastern Europe's Boom Has Gone Quiet

In the years following the breakup of the Soviet Union, Eastern Europe rode a rising tide as newly independent nations restructured government and economic systems and their citizens went on a buying spree for all sorts of goods they'd been denied under the repressive communist regimes. Industry blossomed as well, with many of the countries making strong advances in the world's commercial hierarchy.

Now, however, the global crisis has caused Eastern Europe's rising tide to ebb somewhat. Midyear numbers indicated GDP growth for all of the Eastern European countries would likely be negative for 2009. Even those least affected by the crisis—Poland, the Czech Republic, Slovakia, and Slovenia—were expected to show a GDP decline of between 2 and 5 percent. Bulgaria, Romania, and Ukraine were likely to post double-digit declines in GDP. As a group, the drop in manufacturing output was expected to be at least as severe as that seen by Asian nations during that region's economic upset of 1997–1998. Additionally, the European Union's "Economic Sentiment Indicator"—a monthly measure of how well each member nation is handling the economic crisis in its respective industry, service, construction, and retail sectors—projects Hungary as the worst performer.

If you're looking for an outside appraisal, Fitch Ratings forecast that Emerging Europe as a group would suffer a 3.1 percent contraction in GDP growth in 2009, but would post a modest 1.4 percent recovery in 2010. That's encouraging, but it pales when compared to the 6.8 percent average growth from 2002 to 2007, and even the 4.0 percent growth in 2008. Fitch warns, however, that you need to look beyond the averages because there is a huge divergence in prospects— for 2009, Azerbaijan was expected to grow by 2.5 percent, while Latvia was projected to experience a 12.0 percent *contraction*.

Of the 21 countries it includes in its Eastern European analysis, Fitch predicted 2009 GDP would contract in 19 of them, be flat in one (Poland), and grow only in Azerbaijan. The two largest economies—Russia and Turkey—were expected to contract by 3.0 percent. In spite of the initiatives for trade and arms control floated by President Obama in July 2009, the investment message on Russia is clear: "If you want long-term profit plays, don't spend a lot of time looking here." However, if you're nimble and focus on the areas I discuss in Chapter 11, it's still possible you could make at least a small fortune fairly quickly.

Obviously, Russia isn't a great global growth market like China, India, or Brazil—and without major policy changes, it never will be. But, if you've got the moxie, it can be a wild and profitable ride.

A Hidden Gem from the Former U.S.S.R.

Of the non-gainers in 2009, there is one "comer" flying under the radar that you might want to keep a close eye on: The former Soviet state of Estonia. Ever since the European Union expansion in 2004, the competitiveness of this new Eastern European member has strengthened. GDP per capita increased an average of 5.0 percent each year, with the pace of GDP growth steadily doubling. That makes Estonia's well-functioning markets the most competitive of the emerging Europeans by a significant margin.

Estonia's GDP growth slowed in 2008, up only 1 percent at $23.2 billion, and analysts were predicting a slight contraction in 2009 because of unemployment and budget deficits of 2.5 percent of GDP. However, accumulated reserves should offset that, and the Nordic banks that dominate the Estonian banking sector (Swedbank, SEB, and Norder) should be able to withstand the slowdown and continue funding expansion. The Central Bank forecast recovery in 2010, when Estonia was expected to adopt the euro.

Estonia's economic emergence has centered on its remarkable ability to adapt new technologies to enhance productivity. For example, take Teeme Ära 2008, founded by Estonian millionaires Ahti Heinla (the chief architect of the Skype Voice-over-Internet Protocol) and Rainer Nõlvak (founder of Microlink and Delfi). Their newest venture essentially scrubs the country clean, using software based on Google Earth to map illegal dumping sites, and then calling on 40,000 of Estonia's 1.3 million citizens to clean it up. Projected increase in waste recycling? Eighty percent. Cost of doing business? Next to nothing. Value to the environment? Priceless!

Because of innovations such as that, the World Economic Forum (WEF) ranks Estonia Number 17 globally for a government that "manages public finances adeptly and has been successful in its efforts to make [Estonia's economy] one of the most aggressive." The WEF also ranks Estonia Number 32 in the world for competitiveness—making it another good place to look if you want a true emerging-market player from Eastern Europe in your portfolio.

THE INFLUENCE OF MIDDLE EAST CASH BARONS

Another region that will help fuel the global recovery is the Middle East and Persian Gulf, simply because they have so much petroleum-based income to work with. Admittedly, petrodollars aren't as important now as they were a few years ago, but when looking for overseas investment opportunities, you can't afford to ignore the countries that have them.

The power of this oil money becomes clearly evident when you look at the tactics of some of the foreign government-controlled sovereign wealth funds, which are investing billions in America's blue chip companies. The funds are making their moves with an almost surgical shrewdness. They're grabbing up manufacturing firms that own key technologies, taking stakes in financial firms that control key market segments and buying into such strategically positioned ventures as stock exchanges (presumably willing to send good money after bad so they can better learn the art of financial dealmaking, which America once dominated because we were so good at it).

In mid-2009, William Patalon III, another *Money Morning* contributor, reported in his column that Dubai had spent $800 million for a 90 percent stake in New York's vaunted Chrysler Building—the first in what figures to be a long line of trophy purchases by foreign buyers. Trust me when I say you'll be able to watch many more such deals as the sovereign-wealth heavyweights from emerging Asia, Eastern Europe, the Middle East, or cash-laden China—with its $2.3 trillion in foreign reserves—begin to snap up high-profile U.S. properties.

They're Shopping in Europe, Too

Plummeting real estate prices, low interest rates, and a weak currency—not to mention West End theater—have made London a prime target for Middle Eastern real estate investors as well. In March 2009, Landmark Property, a Dubai-based firm, opened an office in London's swanky Mayfair Hotel to take advantage of deals it claimed were 25 percent more affordable through exchange rates alone. Several sovereign wealth funds have also hired specialist property managers to cater to their appetites for tasty Euro-real estate.

One interesting side note: In showing such a keen interest in acquiring British distressed assets, the sovereign funds from Dubai and other oil-based economies have also inadvertently sparked a major program of green construction and rehabilitation across the United Kingdom's commercial property sector. Since environmental performance is now such an intrinsic part of the value of a building, demand for greener buildings is being driven by the influential role now played by these funds—and British commercial property managers are under growing pressure to deliver energy-efficiency improvements.

In France, sovereign wealth funds from the United Arab Emirates and Saudi Arabia have attempted to build minority stakes of up to 5 percent in Areva, the state-owned nuclear power company. Areva, the world's largest producer of nuclear reactors, needs new capital to maintain its leadership position—and France, which owns 90 percent of Areva, wants to establish some influence in the Middle East. As such, investment from the Middle Eastern funds could prove beneficial for all parties.

Elsewhere around the Middle East, the economic competitiveness of most Gulf countries shows a robust upward trend. Chief among them is Qatar, which has been buoyed by the country's well-assessed institutions, the functioning of its financial markets, and enhanced innovative capacity. One threat that could add risk to Qatar's future is rising inflation, which reached almost 14 percent over the past two years. The World Economic Forum ranks Qatar twenty-sixth in the world for 2008–2009 competitiveness.

The United Arab Emirates also caught the WEF's eye, moving up six positions in the 2008–2009 rankings to thirty-first place. Overall, the country improved in all categories tracked, with a more stable macroeconomic environment and a higher-quality educational system

EMERGING ECONOMIES ARE GROWING MORE BOLD

In the past, the Western world pretty much took what it wanted from the lesser-developed countries—and those countries let them get away with it. No more.

According to Wharton School of Business Management Professor Witold Henisz, today's emerging countries—particularly those rich in natural resources—have begun to revise their approach to the global economy. They are still willing to integrate with the international markets and allow foreigners in to help build their economic infrastructure—but, emboldened by success in today's booming commodity markets, they are demanding a greater share of the benefits.

Unlike in earlier colonial periods, these countries aren't claiming they're being exploited. Henisz says their new approach is more sophisticated. "They are saying, 'We're still going to work with you, but we will do it on *our* terms.'"

In other words, they're trying to be more like the United States and play by the same rules we do.

(though the percentage of young Emiratis going on to higher education remains low by global standards). The country's institutional environment is positive, characterized by a low regulatory burden (fifth), high public trust in politicians (eighth), and reliable police services. In addition, the use of advanced technologies is becoming more widespread, with the UAE rapidly catching up with the rest of the world in IT and communications systems.

Turning Apparent Liabilities Into Assets

Middle East economies also stand poised to capitalize on the region's two biggest resources: its unprecedented geologic gift in the form of oil (the price of which I believe could easily top $200 a barrel in the not too distant future), and a demographic gift in the form of a huge youth population. Though high oil prices and large numbers of unemployed youth are frequently viewed as contributing to economic volatility and social instability, in the Mideast these characteristics could actually be twin dividends leading to greater global prosperity and security.

Among all the world's regions, the Middle East contains the highest proportion of youth, who make up almost a third of its total population. With two working-age people (ages 15 to 64) for every one nonworking-age person (under 15 or 65 and over), the region has a historic opportunity to increase per-capita incomes, bolster savings, and improve social welfare. In addition, unlike the mostly hard-line older generations, a majority of the region's young people want to see their countries offer individual economic opportunity and achieve global integration.

BEWARE OF *DE-MERGING* COUNTRIES

Not all emerging nations go on to achieve developed status. Sometimes they backslide—particularly in the more unstable regions of the world. Africa, for example, is peppered with nations that initially did well in post-colonial days, but then got into trouble under extended self-rule.

The Mideast also has a notable example in Lebanon. In the 1960s, it was one of the premier destinations on the Mediterranean, luring countless international tourists and enjoying strong trade relations and high per-capita incomes. Then it descended into civil war, becoming a bombed-out hulk of its former self, and most likely unable to ever recover its former place in the economic world.

Argentina is another mystery. In the early twentieth century, it was one of the richest countries in the world. It went through a period of decline in the decades under Peronist rule, but again became a star with a strong 1990s campaign toward privatization, a well-educated public, and a wealth of natural resources. However, it stumbled into a major financial crisis in 2001 and has yet to recover its economic footing.

That's why looking for a stable government and economic infrastructure with a firm rule of law is so vital when ferreting out emerging-market opportunities.

SPENDING WILL SAVE US ALL

In summary, then, the engine that will drive the global economic recovery is spending. No, not the kind of mindless "stimulus" spending the U.S. government is so recklessly engaging in—and not just consumer spending, either.

No doubt, the growing consumerism movement that will accelerate as more and more emerging economies actually emerge is critical to the recovery. But so is the reasoned, growth-directed spending the governments of those nations will engage in. Money allocated to infrastructure improvements, better utilization of energy and other resources, and such societal concerns as education, health care, and clean air and water will compound exponentially in terms of both economic growth and investment opportunity. If you look at who is doing the spending—and on what—and then follow that money, your investments will likely grow even faster than the developing economies underlying them.

I provide specifics in the remainder of this book on just how to identify those money flows, the new rules that will drive them, the countries and industries where you're most likely to find them, and a host of strategies you can use to best take advantage of them.

So, emulate the countries I've been talking about and "emerge" from Part II into the "developing" realm of increased wealth-building opportunities to be found in Part III. It's easy—just turn the page.

PART THREE

DR. FITZ-GERALD'S AMAZING HOME REMEDY FOR HANGOVER RELIEF

A wise man will make more opportunities than he finds.

—Sir Francis Bacon

In the first two Parts of this book, I've tried to provide some factual history and analytical insight into how we got into the mess we're currently experiencing, many of the things we're still doing wrong, and some of the factors that should eventually lead us out of our troubles and into an era of renewed prosperity. That's all well and good—but, from a practical standpoint, it's of very little personal benefit going forward.

That's why, in this final section, I try to focus on more specifics—actions you can begin taking almost immediately to recover from the fiscal hangover we're now experiencing, prepare for the world's new economic realities, and ultimately achieve the three goals this book

165

was designed to help you meet. With this information at hand, you should be able to:

- Soothe the aches, pains, and mental anguish you developed from having watched much of the value of your past investments go spiraling down the drain.
- Regain confidence in your ability to make future investments that will reclaim your former wealth and provide you with life-long financial security.
- Sleep well at night because of renewed faith in both the quality and the safety of your investment strategies.

If you've been among the hardest hit by our economic reversals, you may have trouble believing me when I say you *can* recover your past losses and achieve even greater prosperity in the years ahead. However, let me assure you that it's true—and I think I have the track record to prove it. While I heartily wish I had been dead wrong, I was *dead on* in calling the crisis we're now living through. Beginning in the late 1990s, I started warning private clients, public audiences, and newsletter readers alike that—despite the soaring economy, a recovery in housing prices, the dot-com boom, and a prolonged bull market in stocks—we were on the verge of one of the worst financial meltdowns the world would ever see.

To most who heard me or read my missives, that message appeared outrageous—or downright impossible—and I was laughed out of more than a few boardrooms and conferences. Sadly, those people aren't laughing now. However, the few who *did* listen—who heeded my warnings and took the appropriate actions to protect their assets and plan for the worst—are almost certainly smiling today. They're already ahead of the game—and they stand to gain even more ground as we move into the coming global recovery.

However, their success doesn't mean that you have to be left behind. While there's little doubt in my mind that the next few years are going to be tougher than even the pessimists among us can imagine, we are also going to be presented with *tremendous opportunities*— opportunities that are already appearing on the horizon as I write. If you maintain a clear perspective, screw up your courage, and prepare to capture them, *you will be able to restore your portfolio, recover your sanity, capture some spectacular returns, and rebuild your financial dreams.*

It will be a vastly different financial world that emerges from this crisis—but, as has been the case in the wake of economic crises throughout history, this new world will offer *the greatest chance for wealth creation we will see in our lifetimes.* What you learn in the remainder of this book will allow you to take full advantage of it.

CHAPTER 8

THE WORLD'S CHANGING INVESTMENT LANDSCAPE

Toto, I have a feeling we're not in Kansas anymore.

—Dorothy Gale in *The Wizard of Oz*

Your first step in preparing for a return to personal prosperity and future investment success is to recognize that the financial world awaiting us on the other side of this crisis will be far different from the one we've known in the past. As the old car commercial proclaimed, "This isn't your father's Oldsmobile." The investment landscape will have an entirely new appearance, with new markets to explore, new power players to compete with, and new risks to guard against.

It will be a far cry from the financial scenery we saw for most of the nineteenth and twentieth centuries, during which the business, banking, and investment activities of the world took place in the United States and the money centers of Europe (with Japan joining the ranks in the mid–1960s). As late as the 1980s, most of the developed world still wore financial blinders. When Americans wanted to purchase a bond, they'd limit their search to the offerings of the major East Coast or San Francisco investment bankers. When they wanted a stock, they'd call up their local brokerage office and place an order for an NYSE or American Stock Exchange issue—or, if they were more aggressive, something traded on NASDAQ or over the counter. The truly adventurous might look overseas for a little added diversification, selecting something listed on the London Stock Exchange or putting a bit of cash in an international mutual fund.

Average investors were discouraged from trying anything beyond those choices—and the big-money pros weren't much more "a-broad minded." After all, most securities exchanges away from the United States, Europe, and Japan were badly organized, with limited access, weak regulation, and poor liquidity, and the companies whose stocks and debt they traded lacked quality management and verifiable fundamentals, plus they did business in weak or developing economies with limited growth potential, often unstable governments, and suspect currencies.

Why even bother was the general attitude. Why chase too little reward with too much risk?

Today, the situation is reversed. The United States and most of the rest of the world's developed nations are in financial disarray, beset by oppressive government and personal debt, dwindling business revenues and profits, mushrooming unemployment, declining currency values, and concurrent inflation, particularly in prices for oil, commodities, and other raw materials. What's worse, the leaders of these nations are taking exactly *the wrong steps* to deal with the crisis—steps that will prolong our period of pain for much longer than any of the pundits predict.

By contrast, many of the world's so-called emerging nations are enjoying growing—or at least comparatively stable—economies, driven by an expanding middle class, increasing domestic consumer demand, and steadily rising expenditures for infrastructure improvement. Because of revenues for past and ongoing exports of both finished goods and raw materials, many also have low debt—or, in the case of China and a few others, actual surpluses—and strengthening currencies. They are also building more efficient markets and better business environments, thanks to shifts from repressive past regimes to more modern democracies and other moderate government forms that have fewer arbitrary rules and better legal and regulatory systems.

What this means is simple: If, as an investor, you want to profit from the coming global recovery, you should look toward the *developing nations* and the *emerging markets*, not at the traditional financial venues of New York, London, Western Europe, and Tokyo.

FISCAL FLASHPOINT

On June 3, 2009, the Center for Economics and Business Research (CEBR) reported that the United States, Canada, and Europe were expected to account for *only 49.4 percent* of global economic output in 2009. In the same report, the CEBR predicted Western economies will decline to just *45 percent* of global economic output by 2012—much earlier than previous estimates, which forecast that the West wouldn't decline to below 50 percent until 2015.

This time around, it will be Wall Street that offers too little reward with too much risk, too little promise with too much uncertainty. More dependable, more rapid, and more dynamic returns will be found elsewhere—in the more lush, faster growing, and still developing areas of the global financial landscape.

FISCAL FLASHPOINT

As evidence of the increasing role of emerging nations in the global economy, consider this: When the World Trade Organization (WTO) was formed in early 1995, replacing the General Agreement on Tariffs and Trade (GATT) as the arbiter of international commerce, it counted 76 countries as members. By July 2008, the roster of member nations had more than doubled to 153.

THE NEW LANDSCAPE IS BARREN AT HOME

Though we've seen a few bright spots recently, the outlook for the Western world is still grim—as bad as it has been since the Great Depression—and the problems aren't going away any time soon. Despite the bailouts and stimulus packages, America still faces four critical risks:

1. An economic relapse that could throw us into an even deeper and longer recession.
2. A further surge in inflation as a result of ill-conceived and executed monetary policies.
3. A resulting devaluation of the dollar to levels even worse than seen in 2008 and early 2009.
4. A continuing credit crisis that would stifle each new push toward growth and recovery.

The chances of these risks being acknowledged and addressed by most individual investors are *near zero*. Hobbled by fear, yet still hopeful of an eventual recovery, they'll sit on the sidelines, playing it safe, until it's too late, at which time they'll move back into the same old stocks, bonds, and real estate investments they made before. While this approach is fatally flawed, it does compound the opportunities for those few investors *who recognize the truth*.

A big part of that truth is that the U.S. stock market won't rescue us from this mess or restore our lost wealth—at least not in the near term. Most investors think the markets in the United States topped out in late 2007 and, after trending lower (with the exception of a few bounces) ever since, should be ready for a new surge higher. That may be true in absolute terms—but, when you take inflation into account, the U.S. stock market is actually still mired in a secular bear market that's been going on for almost a decade.

Including the one that ran from 1906 to 1921, the United States experienced three similar secular bear markets over the past 100 years, and each eventually turned into a major bull market, with the United States leading the world to new levels of prosperity and creating more

---

FISCAL FLASHPOINT

Because of the prolonged secular bear market in U.S. stocks, some advisers—proud to claim the title of *contrarian*—have been saying now is the time to plunge headlong into U.S. stocks. While I'm not opposed to selectively buying good companies with strong fundamentals that have been unfairly beaten down, I'm not that big a fan of contrarianism as an overriding investment philosophy. In my experience, contrarians are great stock pickers at market tops and market bottoms—but the rest of the time, *they're just wrong.*

---

wealth than ever before. I firmly believe this will eventually happen again—but with one major variation.

This time, *it won't be the United States* that leads the recovery. This time, it will be the developing nations—with China at the front of the team—that pull the world's economy and its investment markets out of the mire. Emily Brandon, writing in a recent issue of *U.S. News & World Report*, summarizes why:

> No question about it. Ten years ago, we had the Asia financial crisis. Today we have the American financial crisis. Then, those countries had to be bailed out. Today, emerging markets sit on 75 percent of the world's foreign-exchange reserves. [Then,] they were dependent on the West for money, for management, for everything. Today, we would not be able to function without oil from the Middle East. Our interest rates would be higher without the Chinese to buy our Treasury bills.

Brandon went on to confirm my theme in much of this book— that the world really *has* changed and is tipping in favor of emerging markets. What we're seeing, she said, is a large group of what used to be very poor countries becoming middle class. America over-consumes, and it under-invests. They under-consume and over-invest. They help the United States make up the difference between what Americans save, which is not enough, and what Americans invest, which is also not enough. The emerging countries help us maintain our standard of living.

So, while it's tempting for U.S. investors to stay home, betting on a repeat of past U.S. market recoveries that will assuredly come, you will be leaving a tremendous amount of money on the table if you do because *the developing world will recover much, much faster.* In fact, many of the world's secondary markets are already far outperforming U.S. stocks—and did so even before the 2007–2008 collapse.

Figure 8.1 shows how the S&P 500 performed over the five years leading up to the U.S. market reversal as compared to the Top 10 performers among MSCI's single-country, regional, and international index funds. Depending on the time period, the S&P lagged top-ranked Brazil by 62.7 to 78.6 percent.

Similarly, Figure 8.2 shows how the S&P 500's five-year performance compared to MSCI's Top 10 one year *after* the U.S. market peak. Even though the U.S. market did better than most foreign venues during the first 10 months of 2008, it still lagged Number 1 Brazil by an even more dramatic 85.2 percent over the full five-year period.

Name	YTD	12 MO	3 YR	5 YR
MSCI Brazil USD	−8.53	59.27	51.43	56.32
MSCI Indonesia USD	−1.97	55.23	38.73	51.27
MSCI EM Latin America USD	−6.41	35.40	41.45	45.45
BSE SENSEX LCL India	−13.10	25.25	39.11	40.27
MSCI Argentina USD	−7.79	−11.43	32.31	39.48
MSCI Turkey USD	−23.58	21.06	17.97	38.65
MSCI World/Metals & Mining USD	−4.91	31.72	34.12	36.21
MSCI Mexico USD	−1.31	5.23	29.56	34.04
MSCI EM GR USD	−12.45	23.66	29.59	33.97
MSCI Chile USD	−1.98	13.72	23.13	32.36
S&P 500 TR	−6.00	−2.31	7.28	12.04

FIGURE 8.1 Average Annual Returns (in US$) for Top Foreign Markets to February 15, 2008
Source: Index Universe.

Name	YTD	12 MO	3 YR	5 YR
MSCI Brazil USD	−31.24	−22.69	19.33	34.92
MSCI Indonesia USD	−35.63	−24.39	22.68	24.95
MSCI EM Latin America USD	−27.58	−23.03	15.03	28.78
BSE SENSEX LCL India	−36.61	−25.62	14.20	23.63
MSCI Argentina USD	−19.77	−28.69	2.87	26.15
MSCI Turkey USD	−41.43	−38.04	1.81	21.71
MSCI World/Metals & Mining USD	−36.79	−40.13	8.82	18.72
MSCI Mexico USD	−19.79	−22.39	10.31	22.99
MSCI EM GR USD	−35.37	−33.01	8.69	19.05
MSCI Chile USD	−14.90	−16.64	6.74	17.17
S&P 500 TR	−19.29	−21.98	0.22	5.17

FIGURE 8.2   Average Annual Returns (in US$) for Top Foreign Markets to October 16, 2008
Source: Index Universe.

The World's Wealth Is Shifting

The superior performance of foreign stock markets in recent years has been one factor in a steadily growing transfer of wealth and power from industrialized to developing regions of the world. This shift on the national level was illustrated by the foreign reserve figures I cited in earlier chapters, but it's also evident in the individual ranks—not just on Main Street and High Street, but also among the world's wealthiest folks. According to the Merrill Lynch/Capgemini World Wealth Report, released in July 2009:

- Globally, the number of high-net-worth individuals—those with at least $1 million in investible assets—declined by nearly 15 percent in 2008. And, the ultra-high-net-worth individuals— those with at least $30 million in assets—did even worse, with their ranks plummeting by almost 25 percent.
- In the United States, the high-net-worth population declined by 18.5 percent.

- Despite the declines, the United States, Japan, and Germany remained the three countries with the largest number of high-net-worth individuals. However, China vaulted to number four—foreshadowing a continuing shift in wealth that, according to the study's authors, will see *the Asia-Pacific region surpass North America in the number of wealthy individuals by 2013.*

FISCAL FLASHPOINT

Much of this new individual wealth will be created by the Chinese stock markets. While they will undoubtedly experience some ups and downs in the future—as all markets do—the Chinese markets are growing so rapidly and have become so large that no serious investor can possibly justify ignoring them.

That last statistic is incredibly important because it verifies the strategy *you must take* in the years ahead if you want to keep up. If the number of wealthy individuals in the West is declining, while the number of wealthy individuals in China is soaring, you should obviously be investing *not in America,* but in *the same things* and *the same places* the wealthiest Asians are focusing on. (In case you're wondering what they're investing in and the themes they're following, stay tuned. I cover that a little further on.) Then, with the profits you make from those investments in hand, you can reinvest your increased wealth in America once fundamental economic reform takes place here.

If that doesn't make sense in the abstract, think of it this way. Today, people hang on every word Warren Buffett says, but tomorrow's investment icons may have Chinese names—names most Westerners haven't heard of, like Zhang Jindong, Yang Huiyan, and Zhang Xin, all of whom are under age 50 and, according to *Forbes,* already billionaires (Huiyan is only 27 and worth $2.3 billion).

Be aware as well that this advice is not limited just to more aggressive investors—those out for fast gains from increasing share prices. Even if you're conservative, more interested in a steady flow of income

New Zealand	NZSE50	8.7%	
Brazil	Bovespa	4.9%	
United Kingdom	FTSE 100	3.7%	
Australia	ASX Comp	3.6%	
Hong Kong	Hang Seng	3.1%	
Netherlands	AEX	3.0%	U.S. Market Lags Badly
South Africa	JSE	2.6%	
France	CAC 40	2.4%	
Canada	TSX Comp	2.2%	
Germany	DAX	2.0%	
United States	**S&P 500**	**1.8%**	

FIGURE 8.3 Dividend Yields in Foreign Markets Versus the United States
Source: Bloomberg LP.

from stable, dividend-paying stocks than in quick capital gains, you can safely look at the overseas markets—and you definitely should. (In fact, as you'll learn shortly, the foundation of my recommended portfolio—fully 40 percent of it—should be devoted to just such dividend-rich stocks.) A quick glance at Figure 8.3 should clearly illustrate why, since it shows that, as was the case with average returns, dividend yields are also much higher in foreign and developing markets than they are in the United States—which, once again, doesn't even make the Top 10.

A NEW DEFINITION FOR ASSET ALLOCATION

Given these market statistics—as well as the trends in the overall world economy—one thing becomes patently obvious:

The traditional asset-allocation models we were taught to follow to produce maximum rewards with minimum risks no longer apply.

It's no longer enough to keep some of your assets in stocks, some in bonds, and some in cash, with a few gold coins in the safety deposit box. Your stocks and bonds need to be split not just across various industries, but across various borders and interest-rate environments as well. Your cash needs to be not just in U.S. dollars, but also in stronger foreign currencies. And you need to recognize that gold isn't the only—nor perhaps even the best—hedge against inflation.

Virtually every investor in the United States today is dramatically underweighted when it comes to international holdings. Some recent surveys indicate average U.S. investors have just 10 to 15 percent of assets in international holdings; other studies suggest it's a mere 6 percent. Whichever is correct, they're severely underexposed. My view, given all we've discussed, is that 40 to 60 percent may be more appropriate. Here's why:

In 1985, the United States accounted for 34.2 percent of the global economy; in 2030, that will fall to just 17.1 percent. The U.S. share of world market capitalization is declining even faster. In 2004, U.S. stocks accounted for 44 percent of the value of global equities. By the end of 2008, this had fallen to just 28 percent, as illustrated in Figure 8.4.

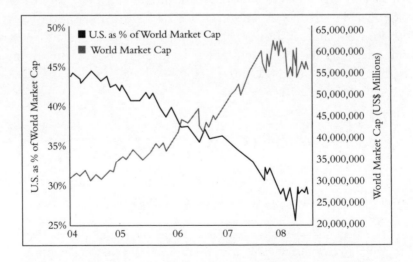

FIGURE 8.4 United States Market Capitalization as a Percentage of World Totals—2004 to 2008

Source: SP/Citigroup/Bespoke Investment Group.

The value of international diversification is evident not just in stock portfolios but in corporate performance as well. It's been acknowledged for several decades now that companies with an international business base produced higher returns on investment than strictly domestic firms during up markets—but that's now been proven the case in down markets as well.

According to the Bespoke Investment Group, a leading market research firm, U.S. companies with the highest international revenues outperformed companies with no international revenue by 7.37 percent (−11.88 percent return versus −19.25 percent) during the collapse of 2008. That kind of edge in incremental return adds up to a tremendous increase in wealth over time—allowing you to double your money in less than 10 years, *even if that's all you make*. Put it on top of an average S&P 500 return of 9.7 percent (since 1926) and you could double your money in just over four years.

FISCAL FLASHPOINT

The return differential cited in the main text—and the time to double your money because of it—are the stuff headlines are made of. Be aware, however, that the *true value* of international diversification—of "going global"—is not so much about the returns we reap today as it is about *the risks it will help us avoid tomorrow.*

With all of these statistics to support it, there should be little doubt that *every* American investor needs a global strategy if they hope to navigate their way across the world's changing financial landscape.

And, if that's not 100 percent true right now, it will be shortly. Why? Because, despite the current economic hard times, my research suggests that worldwide investments will *double* to more than $300 trillion within the next 5 to 10 years, with 60 percent of that coming from new global markets—twice the amount that will come from mature markets like the United States and Japan. That means, if you *don't* invest overseas, you risk forgoing large returns and leaving a potentially huge amount of money on the table—money that could spell the difference between a *golden retirement* and working under the *Golden Arches* in your latter years.

Perhaps even more compelling is the prediction by Antoine W. van Agtmael that, within the next 10 years, there will be *1 billion more consumers* in emerging-market nations than there are today—and, in 25 years, the output of the economies of the emerging nations will surpass the *combined* economies of today's developed countries.

WHO *IS* THAT GUY?

Just in case you're wondering who Antoine W. van Agtmael is and why he's qualified to make a prediction like the one just referred to in the main text, he was the guy who coined the phrase *emerging markets* at an investor conference in Thailand in 1981. He was, at the time, deputy director of the Capital Markets Department of the World Bank's International Finance Corp. (IFC). Today, he is the CEO and chief investment officer of Emerging Markets Management in Arlington, Virginia, which oversees $20 billion in institutional investments—in emerging markets, of course.

FISCAL FLASHPOINT

Relative to international diversification, there's one additional point I want to make—just to make sure there's no confusion. Do *not* abandon the American markets altogether. You still need U.S. equities in your portfolio because the U.S. economy *will* eventually recover. We are a nation filled with resilient, clever people and, although the chips are down, I wouldn't bet against America. In fact, when the history books are written, I guarantee the long-term analysis of the current economic situation will show that our present troubles are not so much about the United States getting poorer; it's just that so many of the world's other nations are getting richer.

SOME OTHER CHANGES TO WATCH FOR

When we emerge from the current crisis and move out into the world's new financial landscape, you'll most likely notice a number of other changes in a variety of different places.

One of the most significant will be a major reversal of the flow of goods from Asia—especially China—to America. For decades, the Asian economies have subsidized American consumption with their own lower standards of living—and some of them are now feeling the pain generated by the drop in U.S. spending because of the recession. However, they will recover quickly as they reallocate production resources and begin satisfying the consumption appetites of their own middle class.

Indeed, entire nations like Japan—which harbored dreams of economic domination only a few years ago—are now inextricably bound to China's future. The connection, as one of my friends put it, is like a complicated spider web with thousands of strands stretching out in all directions. The same is true of Indonesia, Taiwan, and even South Korea, which finds itself drawn into the economic web that is modern China.

With respect to China in particular, the change in the commercial relationship will be almost as bad as an unfair California divorce. The Chinese will win over the court, getting to keep *100 percent* of their property and *all* their factories, use all of the products they produce *themselves*, import what they *don't* make from America, and enjoy a dramatically improved lifestyle. America, like a former derivative trader's ex-wife, will have to scale back her lifestyle and reduce domestic demand to bring it in line with production. She'll also have to make hefty support payments in the form of *higher prices for the products she herself produces* if they're also in demand overseas.

Soon, instead of seeing "Made in China" on every other box on Wal-Mart shelves in Buffalo, "Made in USA" will adorn many product packages at the Silk Market in Beijing—and not just for the luxury items you see there now.

Even more startling to Americans, it won't just be the *new* stuff we produce that will go up in price. The cost of many *used* consumer goods we previously imported will also rise. For example, U.S. residents have a lot of cars, while the Chinese have relatively few. As the dollar plunges and the yuan soars, demand for cars will rise in China as it falls in the United States. With U.S. residents struggling to make ends meet, they will find a vibrant market in China for the cars they can no longer afford to drive.

Consumer goods will flow abroad, while a flood of dollars washes back up on our shores—in the best of cases. In the worst cases, merchandise will still head back overseas, but *without* a return of cash, as foreign suppliers begin repossessing the goods that they sold to America on credit.

COMMODITY PRICES WILL REMAIN AN ISSUE

Another post-crisis probability will be permanently higher prices and levels of demand for many commodities, particularly those that will fuel the burgeoning growth of consumerism around the globe. Many people may doubt this prediction, citing recent price declines for oil, metals, and many agricultural commodities (including such basics as beef and milk), as well as an apparent drop in commodity consumption caused by the worldwide recession.

The mistake most of those doubters make is that they focus on the demand side of the commodity equation rather than looking at supply considerations, which can both damage the economy and fuel inflation.

It's true that, in the midst of the recent financial meltdown, we witnessed the worst broad decline in commodity prices in history, but it wasn't a reduction in consumer spending that stalled demand and depressed prices. Actually, *total spending was up* because more and more people, hit by rising costs for housing, mortgages and other credit, were living paycheck to paycheck, trying to squeeze every last dollar out of their take-home pay just to keep their noses above water.

The difference was, while people had once spent on luxuries, they were now being forced to devote everything to necessities. That's why, for example, Wal-Mart's sales have remained strong throughout the entire financial crisis while high-end retailers are struggling—or failing altogether.

What few armchair analysts took into account then—and still don't recognize—was the long supply chain between the manufacture and the end demand for many products. At various points in the supply chain, there are sizable stockpiles of product. Under normal economic circumstances, these stockpiles serve as a buffer against supply disruptions and help to smooth out price fluctuations. Given that, when a commodity is in adequate (or even abundant) supply, the price may actually appear to be flat.

However, stockpiling supply requires operational capital. Money tied up in inventories is often just credit extended by banks—usually in the form of commercial paper—rather than actual cash in the corporate till. That's fine as long as the credit market is healthy and well-funded—but, in a credit crisis like we've been in, the supply chain gets cut. Borrowing money for stockpiling or ongoing business operations gets too expensive—or outright impossible—even for good producers. Without necessary operating funds, inventories must be sold and spending for raw materials and new equipment must be cut. And, when suppliers cut production spending, the destruction of the supply chain is triggered.

Inventory liquidations and the lack of purchasing of new production materials give the illusion of a supply surplus, which further depresses commodity prices and may prompt even more sell-offs. What's actually happening though is that supply is being *suffocated*—the supply chains are being squeezed *completely dry*. Everyone (with the possible exception of folks in the "oil bidnus") cheers the cheaper prices. But, as anyone who loves those "Going Out of Business!" sales knows, the best prices always come right before they lock the doors for good. After that, you can't find good prices anywhere in the neighborhood—which is what happens with commodities. With the supply chain stockpiles gone, there's no more buffer against supply disruptions—and no more supply. Prices skyrocket, and consumer shock follows—even when demand remains stable.

Add in the spike in demand we're certain to see as a result of the increased consumerism in developing nations, and higher commodity prices will unquestionably be a prominent feature of the world's new financial landscape for years to come. (Hence, my earlier prediction that we could see $200-a-barrel oil before all is said and done.)

THE CREDIT MARKETS WILL REMAIN TIGHT

Contributing to the ongoing pattern of higher commodity prices will be a continuation of the tight market for credit, which will make it ever more difficult for manufacturers to rebuild their inventories and refinance necessary supply chain stockpiles. You might think that, with all the bank bailouts and government programs to help mortgage borrowers and cut credit-card fees and interest rates, credit would be a lot easier to get these days—but it's not.

As noted earlier, the TED spread—the difference between the London Interbank Offered Rate (LIBOR), at which banks lend each other money, and the rate on three-month U.S. Treasury bills— reached previously unthinkable levels. What that meant is that, despite all the government support, *banks were still scared to lend money*—even to other banks, which should have been among the most reliable of borrowers around.

The TED spread as of publication time had fallen to a more normal 29 (anything under 50 is considered favorable), yet credit remains elusive. That's because the government failed to anticipate the other behavior that goes hand in hand with fear—hoarding. Right now, businesses throughout the world are hoarding cash because they don't know what's next. That includes banks, which are not anxious to be burned again.

Meanwhile, spreads between LIBOR and many other types of loans—including such items as Overnight Indexed Swaps (OIS), which provide guarantees for ultra-short bank-to-bank loans—are slowly returning to normal, but remain significantly out of whack compared to their historical norms. While there are a variety of ways to interpret this, it basically means that *banks still don't trust each other.* The net result is that there's less money available for interbank lending— and less money means higher interest rates ahead.

Then there are the LIBOR rates themselves, which are calculated for several currencies over periods ranging from overnight to one year. While well below the highs they hit in January of 2008, they are also still very high by historical standards. This affects the interest rates and prices for all financial contracts, which Bloomberg reported were valued at $393 trillion at the beginning of 2008 (roughly $60,000 for every person in the world)—and those prices help set the global rates for *all types* of consumer credit, from home loans to credit cards.

Comparing these rates might seem like an esoteric exercise to the man on the street, but the effect does filter down to virtually every level of business and commerce. As an example of just how large an impact high rates can have, consider that the Federal Reserve's January 2009 survey of senior bank loan officers found that 60 percent of domestic U.S. banks were reporting reduced loan demand—up fourfold from October 2008, when only 15 percent reported lower demand. Obviously, both individuals and businesses have quit asking banks for money—either because they know they won't get it or because they couldn't afford the interest payments if they did.

Similarly, credit-card issuers are reporting a marked reduction in card usage in the wake of new fees and higher rates that went into effect in the first three quarters of 2009, something that hardly bodes well for the economy in general and the retail sector in particular—not to mention the fortunes of the credit-card companies involved.

Between the inability of businesses to get financing for their own operations and the inability of their customers to get credit to make purchases, it's not hard to see why business conditions—in spite of some improvement—are still generally rotten. Almost every U.S. company, from the biggest to the smallest, has been affected in one way or another by this crisis. Profits have suffered, stock dividends have been cut, and employment has hit 30-year highs, with the term of jobless-ness for many stretching to Depression-era lengths. Personal debt defaults are still on the rise and consumer confidence, while off the bottom, remains in the cellar.

Given that sustained economic recoveries require consumers who actually *have money,* who have jobs, and who feel confident, it's easy to see why I continue to survey the foreign landscape for the best recovery opportunities—saving up profits earned there for reinvestment in the United States when the right time finally comes.

THERE ARE SOME POSITIVE SIGNS

When might that "right time" actually be? For now, the signals are far too mixed to make a firm prediction—but there have at least been a few positive signs mixed in with the bad news. Corporate earnings for the second quarter of 2009 showed a hefty rebound for some companies, especially in the financial sector (the result of those higher interest rates, bank fees, and more creative accounting, no doubt). This helped fuel a strong summer bounce in stocks, which had been looking for an excuse to rally after having given up nearly 50 percent of their value (and as much as 80 percent in some NASDAQ sectors) after hitting new highs in November 2007.

It was too early to tell whether that rally would be sustained, but it may have loosened up the purse strings of some investors—who, according to the Federal Reserve and studies by Money.net Inc., were reportedly sitting on the sidelines with as much as $9.5 trillion in cash, just aching for a reason to get back into the U.S. stock market. Private equity firms alone were said to be holding as much as $1.3 trillion. Personally, I'm not sure that much money is actually out there given the estimated $30 trillion to $50 trillion that was wiped out in the prior decline—but I won't argue my case at this point.

What I will do is note that, regardless of whether you choose to jump back into the U.S. market, follow my advice to go global, or do a little of both; the world's changing investment landscape has resulted in a wide array of new money rules that you'll need to follow if you hope to achieve the objectives I'm setting out for you in this book.

Those new rules are spelled out in detail in the next chapter, along with some tips on how best to follow them, so turn the page and keep reading.

CHAPTER 9

THE NEW MONEY RULES, AND WHY YOU MUST FOLLOW THEM

I always say that it's about breaking the rules. But the secret of breaking rules in a way that works is understanding what the rules are in the first place.

—Rick Wakeman, rock musician

In the previous chapter, I talked about the world's changing financial landscape and many of the features you will likely see as we continue to move out of the current crisis and into the new economic climate that lies beyond. In this chapter, I want to go over some of the new rules that will govern the world of money as a result of our recent catastrophes, and also provide a bit of direction regarding which ones you can profitably break—and which you absolutely *must* follow if you hope to succeed as an investor in the wake of this crisis.

Some cynics would argue that, in spite of the bubbles, bailouts, and overall brouhaha, nothing has really changed—that once the recovery progresses a bit more, it will once again be business as usual. I beg to differ. The world's moneymen—both in government and in business, both here and abroad—are changing the financial rules in ways the majority of investors have not yet even begun to understand. What's worse, the motives behind many of those changes are far from clear—and may not even be consistent. Some actions are allegedly aimed at stabilizing various markets, others at protecting consumers and investors—and some, it will turn out, are motivated by simple greed.

But, while the motivations may not yet be clear, the results are already being seen—results that may well change the nature of investing forever. Here are just a few examples:

- Market swings of 300 points used to be called *wild*. Now, daily rides of 500 to 600 points on the Dow barely make *The Wall Street Journal*'s front page.
- You'd expect gold—the only real "safe haven"—to be shooting through the roof, given recent events. But gold, against all expectations, has actually been flat to lower through much of the crisis.
- The U.S. government hands out several trillion in freshly printed dollars, devaluing the entire stock of American debt—yet the dollar, against all odds, actually *goes up* in the foreign-exchange markets.
- Banks take billions in government loans to free up credit—but, instead of lending the money, they use it to *buy* other banks. Are the inmates in charge of the prison?

Why are these things happening?

A big part of the reason is that government and financial officials don't really have a clue about what's actually going on. They don't understand *why* world markets and global economies are spinning out of control—nor do they know *what to do about it*. They are still operating on the same assumption that has applied since World War II and the era of Bretton Woods—that Keynesian economics works.

But that's no longer the case (if it ever really was). Everything these so-called experts have predicted was going to happen *hasn't happened*. And what *has* happened can't be explained by their tried-and-true theories. Central bankers around the world have thrown pasta at the wall, but nothing stuck. Thus, the old "rules of money" simply don't work anymore—and probably never will again.

THE *EFFICIENT-MARKETS HYPOTHESIS* IS A FALLACY

One of those old rules is the notion of an *efficient market*—which is one of the single biggest fallacies ever foisted on the investing public. Academics love this idea, which is why the "efficient-markets hypothesis," or EMH, is taught at all the leading business schools. The broadest version of this theory holds that securities prices already reflect *all known information,* thus making it impossible to outperform the markets over time—except by luck.

The reality, however, is that the markets are anything *but* efficient. In fact, not only are the markets highly *inefficient,* but—as many investors have learned the hard way—they are frequently completely irrational as well.

As rational market observers, what we need to ask ourselves is this: If the markets truly are this efficient, why do all the research? Why would we have an entire industry of analysts who are collectively paid billions of dollars a year to ferret out information that the efficient-markets hypothesis says is already reflected in current market prices? In fact, why would we even have the concept of *insider trading* to worry about, or be so concerned by AIG-type bonuses or government bailouts, both of which would be irrelevant if all of the data were truly "known?"

The inconvenient truth is that the markets are wildly *inefficient,* and can be for much longer periods of time than people realize—or that "experts" would admit. Moreover, as my own research shows, the markets are neither one-dimensional nor three-dimensional, nor are they characterized by *log-normal distributions.* Rather, they are *fractal*

THE BIRTH AND GROWTH OF THE EMH

First published in 1965 in *The Financial Analysts Journal,* the efficient-markets hypothesis was the result of a quixotic doctoral thesis penned by Eugene Fama. He theorized that the markets are characterized by multiple participants acting in a rational manner in an effort to profit. Fama believed—as the majority of EMH proponents do—that in an efficient market, competition among the participants leads to a situation in which the actual prices of individual securities—stocks, bonds, exchange-traded funds, and the like—already reflect the combined total of all known information. Given that, stock prices reflect reasonable intrinsic values *at all times.* One version of the efficient-markets hypothesis, the so-called "strong" version, actually holds that securities prices reflect *all* information—even information known only to company insiders and to no one else out in the marketplace.

The belief in market efficiency—as much as any other factor—is one of the single biggest justifications for all sorts of things that we take for granted today, including mark-to-market accounting systems, the concept of total returns, and even various stock-rating systems. Market efficiency even provides the underpinning for the so-called "prudent man" rules that are so critical to ERISA (Employee Retirement Income Securities Act of 1974) funds and the entire money-management industry, not to mention many of the Financial Accounting Standards Board (FASB) regulations.

creatures that can shift from trending to nontrending in an instant. They are also increasingly characterized by something called *fat tails.* When you hear that last term—which you will with increasing frequency in the years ahead—it will usually be associated with *huge market moves* that had previously been unthinkable, or regarded as *totally impossible.* (Nassim Nicholas Taleb, incidentally, does a great job of describing them as *Black Swans* in his book by the same name.)

FISCAL FLASHPOINT

Governments, from the federal level all the way down to municipalities, are in love with acronyms—those handy identifying nicknames formed from the first letters of the words in the formal name of an agency or program. Everybody recognizes FBI, CIA, DOE, DOT, and the like—and most of these are readily accepted and used with little verbal abuse. However, there are some exceptions—and ERISA, mentioned in the previous box, is one of them. At the time it was passed, the Act—formally titled the "Employee Retirement Income Securities Act"—was highly unpopular with businesses because of the costs and the extensive recordkeeping the measure required. Thus, it took only a few days for some creative Human Resources type to come up with an alternate definition for ERISA—and it will no doubt be forever casually referred to as "Every Ridiculous Idea Since Adam."

In an effort to devise a defense against improbable market events—and also profit from them—I've spent well more than a decade investigating pricing behavior and the impact of fractals in determining the direction and magnitude of market moves. It was this research that led me to believe, despite our current economic travails, that we are now on the verge of the greatest profit opportunity of our lifetimes. To help in determining who will win and who will lose as a result of the new money rules, I also devised a new analytical service I call "The Geiger Index."

I won't attempt to describe how it works here because, as I said, 10 years of work went into its creation and explaining it in detail would fill another book all its own. What I will do is note that, at the time of this writing, the Index had been correct—identifying profitable trades—on 16 of the 16 recommendations made. Perhaps even more important, the Index gave me an "early-warning signal" of the impending 2008 market collapse—well before the trouble was visible to even the smartest traders. That allowed me to advise my subscribers to get out of their positions—at the optimum prices—*long before the panic set in.*

WHAT ARE FRACTALS?

Fractals are mathematical expressions of the kinds of shapes we see in nature, although they are typically invisible to the naked eye—and to traditional statistical analysis. They tend to look random, but their hidden order makes them predictable when analyzed correctly. Even more interesting, they *adapt* on the basis of feedback from their environment, just as markets do. Natural shapes like the snowflake, lightning, blood vessels, and the pattern of peaks in mountain ranges are examples of fractals.

The term *fractal* was coined by mathematician Benoît Mandelbrot in 1975, but fractals were actually discovered in the twelfth century by Leonardo Pisano (known today as Fibonacci).

Obviously, I don't expect perfection to continue long term, but I do expect to maintain a level of accuracy in the 90 to 95 percent range. So, if you're interested in learning more about this proprietary advisory service, check out the information under The Geiger Index heading at www.moneymorning.com/money-morning-premium-content.

THERE'S A NEW DEFINITION OF *NORMAL*

For most people, the next few paragraphs will be a discussion best accompanied by a stiff drink, so you can skip them if you like. The important thing to understand—and to come to terms with in today's markets—is that the "impossible" happens a lot more than its name implies.

In years past, people became entirely too comfortable with the notion of *normal* markets. That's one reason so many investors are hurting so badly now. They came into 1999—and then into 2007—with portfolios that were too heavily weighted in stocks and other

---

FISCAL FLASHPOINT

Contrary to what most people think, the risks you take as an investor don't really matter that much. Instead, it's the risks you *AVOID* that rack up the big returns. Building long-term wealth under the new money rules will *NOT* depend on making huge profits, but on avoiding big losses in our more volatile markets. Effort spent making up what you had, but then lost, is effort wasted—sort of like stopping to tread water in the middle of a 100-meter freestyle race.

Hardly anyone recognizes the fact, but it is *much harder* to make up losses than it is to make gains in the first place. This is like going to the gym to work off a few pounds after eating too much. I'd rather go to the gym so I can eat what I want. To make a 25 percent gain in a year, you only need a 25 percent return—but, to recover a 25 percent *loss* in a year, you need a *33 percent return* over 12 months (and that doesn't even count the 6 or 7 percent cost of money). Take a 50 percent loss and you have to have a *100 percent return* (plus money cost) to make it up. Losing 70 percent requires a *233 percent gain* over a year—*just to get even!* So, avoid the losses and the gains will come—along with steady growth in your personal prosperity.

---

holdings that relied on *normal* market behavior and historical precedent. Those investors sealed their own fates by believing that the fancy diversification graphs they got from Wall Street investment houses and the Armani Army would protect them.

Instead, they discovered that diversification doesn't work when everything goes down together.

Research—mine and that of others who are a lot smarter than I am—suggests that conventional diversification theory based on lognormal market distribution actually *camouflages risk* rather than reducing it. That's why companies such as AIG, Lehman Brothers, and others got into so much trouble. By placing their trust in errant financial models, the analysts who were supposed to be protecting the hen house let in the foxes without even realizing what they had done.

The experts' mathematical models were supposed to account for normal conditions. Nobody asked what would happen when the improbable "black swan" showed up. (And, even if they did ask, they sure as heck didn't pay attention to the answers, because it might have ruined their plans for gazillion-dollar bonuses.) I can't tell you how often recently I've heard insiders protest—loudly and at length—that "the markets aren't supposed to do that."

This is really neither here nor there, though. For everyday investors, the critical thing to understand is that the markets *are* demonstrating behavior that's supposed to be *impossible*—and they're doing it on a much more regular basis than people realize.

Take, for example, a November 2008 study from Cook Pine Capital, LLC. Like my own research, the Cook Pine study showed that, in the last 82 years of Standard & Poor's 500 Index data, moves of so-called "three sigma" (or three-standard) deviations happened *more than 100 times.* Conventional log-normal modeling of the type AIG and others used heading into this crisis suggested that such events should have occurred *only 27 times.* Oops!!

And that's not even as bad as it gets. The Cook Pine study also demonstrated that the likelihood of a four-standard-deviation move on any given day is 1 in 100. Yet we've seen *43 of them* since 1927. Even five-standard-deviation moves, which are theoretically impossible from a statistical standpoint, have happened *40 times in the last 81 years,* including eight times in the six months following September 2008 alone. This is precisely why I frequently point out to investors that, while using conventional diversification is better than nothing, it's often akin to rearranging the deck chairs on the RMS *Titanic*—you're much better off just getting off the boat altogether.

As I've been saying, the rules of money have changed and these kinds of data suggest that it's not *how you diversify* your assets that's important, but *how you concentrate* your wealth that matters, particularly when it comes to avoiding the improbable—*and even profiting from it.*

> **FISCAL FLASHPOINT**
>
> Diversification, as it has traditionally been practiced, is nothing more than spreading your pennies around. What really matters in today's market environment is how you *concentrate* your money—focusing either on the areas that will carry the least risk when everything declines, or offer the greatest appreciation when everything rises (or *nothing else* rises).

THE NEW RULES DEMAND NEW TOOLS

One of the simplest ways to protect yourself against "impossible" market actions is through the use of noncorrelated investments—those that zig when everything else zags.

In the old days, that meant having exotic futures accounts or taking positions opposite to the markets by using margin accounts to sell individual stocks short, one stock at a time. But, unless you had a fair chunk of change to implement these strategies, chances were you couldn't effectively mitigate the risk of the unknown. (Of course, traditional Wall Street brokerage firms dismissed futures for a long time, so that didn't help. But that's a story for another day.)

Today, there's an entirely new class of "inverse" investments available to individual investors. They're structured like standard mutual funds and, unlike managed-futures accounts, there are no account minimums and no active management fees. They're found among the broad group of so-called exchange-traded funds, or ETFs, which can be purchased and sold just like stocks and are generally available through online discount brokers.

These inverse funds have been around for a number of years now, and I am amazed that more investors don't use them. Actually, *I'm absolutely astounded.* As their name implies, inverse funds go up in value when the markets go down. There are plenty of choices to consider, with funds linked to everything from the S&P 500 to specific sectors. There are even double and triple inverse funds, which use swaps, futures, and options in a fashion that allows them to move two or three times as much as the investment vehicles to which they are linked.

Of course, if the markets go up, the reverse is true, and these things can lose money in a real hurry, so one can't just pile in indiscriminately.

My research—and that from futures and options pros like the CME Group, Inc. (CME), and Chicago Board Options Exchange (CBOE)—suggests that an allocation equal to 1 to 5 percent of your overall assets is about right when it comes to using noncorrelated assets to enhance overall returns and lower portfolio risk.

FISCAL FLASHPOINT

While an allocation of 1 to 5 percent in noncorrelated assets is sufficient for most individuals, more aggressive investors may want to up the ante. Studies have shown that those who take on as much as 20 percent in noncorrelated assets can dramatically lower their drawdown in a bad market—from 7.5 percent for a diversified portfolio to 41 percent for a stocks-only portfolio—while increasing their overall returns by 7.4 to 8.9 percent, depending on the portfolio mix.

These are important lessons to take away from these troubled times. If you embrace such a strategy, chances are that you'll not only be smiling on days when stocks are down, but you'll actually come to *enjoy* the unpredictable markets we're now experiencing.

Of course, if you hope to be truly successful, the new money rules require more than just allocating a small portion of your portfolio to noncorrelated investments.

Some Broad Observations for Future Reference

For starters, you need to realize that there are a couple of factors in play now that weren't around a couple of decades ago. One is the technology of trading—and financial operations in general—which has increased both the pace and the scope of every little market action. The other is the willingness of government to step into the fray and try to fix things (or, in my opinion, further screw things up).

For reference in future crises, you should consider the following points made evident by this one:

- *Faster pace.* Technology and globalization have increased the frequency and spread of financial crises—but not necessarily the severity.
- *Quick intervention.* Early intervention by central banks is more effective in limiting the spread of economic disruptions than later moves are in correcting them.
- *Understanding required.* Even if early intervention is taken, it won't work if the people instituting the policies (read that as Greenspan and Bernanke) don't understand their implications. By keeping interest rates artificially low leading up to and in the early stages of this crisis, borrowers were rewarded and savers were punished; speculators got rich, while prudent investors were left wanting.
- *Lending secret.* The business of banking is widely misunderstood. It's not really about lending money at all; it's about getting paid back. As Mark Twain originally said—and Will Rogers echoed—"I'm more concerned about the return *of* my money than the return *on* my money."
- *Early uncertainty.* Nearly all financial upsets look the same at the beginning. It's therefore difficult to tell in the early stages whether a stock market crisis will have broader economic consequences.
- *Innovation wins.* Bureaucracy is much slower than capitalism— meaning regulators have little or no chance of keeping up with the pace of financial innovations (such as credit-default swaps) that might trigger a crisis. Or a recovery, for that matter.
- *Regulation coming.* In spite of this, the severity of the recent meltdown will result in much more regulation of the financial markets than in the past. Exactly what and how stringent that regulation will be after it works its way through Congress and the agencies

that must implement it remains to be seen—but, if history is any indicator, the markets will find a way to subvert it.

- *Act, don't react.* Merely reacting to emergencies is no way to live life—nor is it any way to invest. With careful planning and a strategy for loss avoidance, the fact that Wall Street experiences a crisis should not automatically create one for you, too.

New Money Rules Apply at Home, Too

You also need to realize that the new money rules aren't just restricted to national monetary policies, global economics, and the world's stock markets. They apply right there at home, at the kitchen table, where folks are paying their monthly bills and balancing their budgets. Here are some areas in which the rules for people on Main Street will be different, too:

- *Spending*—In the old days, people thought it was okay to spend up to *half their income* on discretionary items like cars, boats, clothing, eating out, and other things they wanted, but didn't necessarily need. Savings, once the backbone of this country, dropped so low they actually went *negative* for a while. Now that the national debt level has skyrocketed, along with personal debt, discretionary spending should be limited to *no more than 20 percent*—if for no other reason than to leave a reserve for the higher taxes that undoubtedly lie ahead.
- *Home mortgages*—Despite the fact that interest-rate hikes are baked into the cake longer term and the embers of inflation are glowing red hot, it's not inconceivable that Team Fed could lower rates further in the near future in a quest to keep the embryonic recovery going. Should that happen, all sorts of related interest rates would drop, too—including for mortgages. If the new rate is more than 1 percent below your current fixed mortgage rate, consider refinancing—but only if you plan to stay in your home at least as long as it takes the savings to pay for the closing costs and fees. The days of rapidly rising housing prices are over, so you can't depend on that to cover your expenses. If you have an adjustable-rate mortgage, consider converting to a

30-year fixed mortgage. That way you will avoid the threat to your lifestyle that could come later as rates start rising and your monthly payments go up by 30 to 50 percent—or more.

- *Retirement savings*—In the old days, people could count on a lifetime of employment, a silver pocket watch, and some nice bennies. Now, they're more apt to get a pink slip and Social Security. Save at least 20 percent of your income to offset the risks of shoddy pension plans, underfunded liabilities, and shorter retirement-plan payouts. Take full advantage of any employee matching programs and maximize any retirement savings vehicles available to you.

- *Investing for retirement*—It used to be that you could subtract your age from 100 and come up with a reasonable guess as to the percentage of stocks you should hold throughout your life. But that day is long gone. Because of rising life spans and increasing costs for medicine and terminal care, there's a real possibility many people will outlive their money. And that means you need to hold more stocks or income positions to make up the difference. Consider subtracting your age from 110—or even 125 if you're younger than 50 or have a high tolerance for risk. And by all means, stick to a protective master plan like the proprietary 50-40-10 Pyramid I detail in Chapter 12. Not only will it shield you if the markets come unglued, but it will accelerate your comeback as the recovery picks up steam, putting you far ahead of the game. Be sure, however, not to confuse speculating with investing. Many folks did over the past 20 years, and that's why they're hurting now.

- *401(k)s and company stock*—One of the reasons spectacular blow-outs like WorldCom, Enron, and, more recently, Lehman were so painful is that employees concentrated too much of their retirement holdings in their own company's stock—and paid a terrible price, losing both their jobs and their savings. Put no more than 5 percent of your holdings in company stock and factor your monthly salary into your diversification plan.

- *Emergency reserves*—It used to be you needed a reserve fund equal to six months of everyday expenses. Now, with the average job search taking a lot longer than it used to, your rainy-day fund should cover 12 months' worth of expenses. Make whatever short-term sacrifices needed to get there quickly. Then, as I said earlier, you won't be stuck in a situation in which all you can do is *react* to emergencies.

VIEW IT ALL AS A NEW OPPORTUNITY

So, if you want to be positioned so you won't be forced to react to emergencies, what should you do?

As I've noted numerous times already, this isn't the first financial crisis America and the world have experienced (nor, by any stretch of the imagination, will it be the last)—and, each time, the markets have emerged stronger, creating more new wealth than ever before. Similarly, this isn't the first time the rules of money have been rewritten—and, without fail, results of the past revisions have always been positive. If you don't believe it, just check out the summary presented in Figure 9.1.

As the figure should make clear, spectacular investment opportunities have followed each past rewriting of the world's money rules— and that will again be the case. Just check out the timeline of our current situation:

2003—Credit feeding frenzy.
2006–2007—Collapse of the housing and mortgage bubbles.
2007–2008—Global financial meltdown.
2009 and beyond—New money deployment featuring:
  • Intense social and institutional creativity. When the rules of money change, society itself changes, and people's attitudes toward money are altered.
  • Recapitalization of the world financial system.
  • A worldwide economic expansion with "unsaturated markets" like China, India, Indonesia, Eastern Europe, and the Middle East leading the way in a new era of golden growth that's unprecedented in its scope and tenacity.

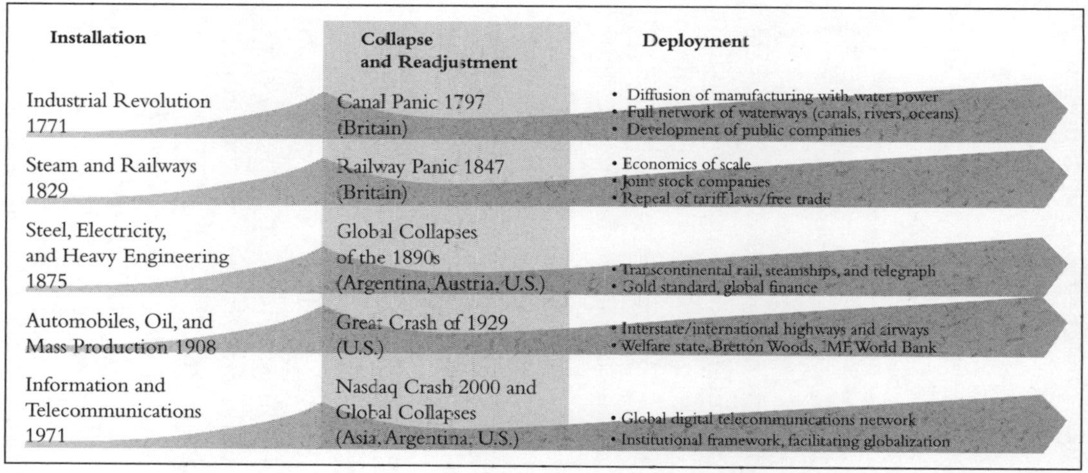

Installation	Collapse and Readjustment	Deployment
Industrial Revolution 1771	Canal Panic 1797 (Britain)	• Diffusion of manufacturing with water power • Full network of waterways (canals, rivers, oceans) • Development of public companies
Steam and Railways 1829	Railway Panic 1847 (Britain)	• Economics of scale • Joint stock companies • Repeal of tariff laws/free trade
Steel, Electricity, and Heavy Engineering 1875	Global Collapses of the 1890s (Argentina, Austria, U.S.)	• Transcontinental rail, steamships, and telegraph • Gold standard, global finance
Automobiles, Oil, and Mass Production 1908	Great Crash of 1929 (U.S.)	• Interstate/international highways and airways • Welfare state, Bretton Woods, IMF, World Bank
Information and Telecommunications 1971	Nasdaq Crash 2000 and Global Collapses (Asia, Argentina, U.S.)	• Global digital telecommunications network • Institutional framework, facilitating globalization

FIGURE 9.1 New Money Rules of the Past—and the Positive Results They Produced

Source: Based on "Technological and Financial Capital: The Dynamics of Bubbles and Golden Ages," Carlota Perez; IBM 2004 Annual Reports.

- More and more domestic U.S. companies determining that, as is the case with individual investors, it's time to "go global or go home." To that end, many U.S. executives are already intensely studying foreign markets and positioning their companies for future global growth.

In addition to that redeployment of money, actions, and attitudes in response to the new rules of money now coming into play, history also suggests we could see:

- *An end to the "Gordon Gekko philosophy" of investing, in which "greed is good"* (the premise of the film *Wall Street,* in case you're not a movie buff). Greed and avarice will be replaced by greater personal responsibility, a more dominant focus on risk management, and more individual savings. (Evidence of the latter had already begun to show up in mid-2009, with the U.S. savings rate climbing to near 7 percent—up from under 1 percent in 2006.)
- *The transition of financial regulation from reactionary to more preventative.* We could see a complete re-regulation of entire classes of securities and the actual outlawing of dangerous instruments (like credit default swaps) that produce no economic value at all. The SEC's decision in July 2009 to permanently ban "naked short sales" in the stock market is one of the early examples of proactive regulation growing out of the past crisis. Though Rule 204 could well be overturned in the future, it illustrates the type of regulation I'm talking about.
- *The stock market again becoming a place in which people invest to get ahead, rather than just "placing bets" hoping to catch a "lucky" move in stock prices.* As this happens, it could begin a recovery in which we will see gains of 10 percent a year or more again—*eventually.* (Sadly, many American investors will still be too disgusted by the losses they sustained in 2008 and early 2009, so they will miss it all.)

RECOGNIZING THE TURNING POINT

As America continues to struggle with its economic problems, we will see more and more evidence that decoupling is becoming a reality. This is good because it will give us an opportunity to once again begin investing in the U.S. stock market on its own merits. Although there are some exceptions among individual stocks, that time isn't here yet—*but it's coming.*

In looking for broad market turning points, I generally rely on four primary indicators that have proven themselves reliable in measuring the conditions most needed for a bull market. These indicators are:

1. *Sentiment.* Historically, the best buying opportunities occur when the Consumer Confidence Index is at its lowest point (below 60)—and right now it's still very near the record lows set at the start of 2009 (see Figure 9.2). Furthermore, history has shown that, with respect to confidence, the more gloom, the stronger the potential market boom. While we may not have

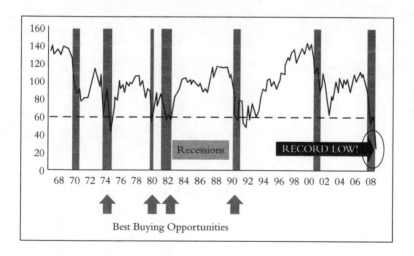

FIGURE 9.2 Best Buying Opportunities of the Past Based on Consumer Confidence
Sources: Fitz-Gerald Research Publications, LLC; Conference Board.

seen the absolute bottom, it's getting closer all the time—and, given the sense of doom that accompanied this crisis, odds are that history will look back at what's happening now as one of the great bottom buying opportunities of our lifetimes.

2. *Value.* Two good measures of market value are the ratio of bond yield to stock yield, and the ratio of the S&P Industrials price to book value. Legendary market rallies have all started when the key stock ratios, including the market's overall price-to-earnings (PE) ratio, were undervalued. Again, valuations may not be at their lowest, but they're becoming more realistic by historical standards and they're definitely near the "sweet spot"—the point at which past strong rallies have begun. The following puts that in perspective:

If you invest when the market PE is:	You can expect a return from stocks of:	Over 40 years you will compound your money:
40 (March 2000)	2.5%	2.7 times
21–26 (2003-2007)	2.7%	2.9 times
14 (Normal)	7.1%	16.9 times
7–10	14.3%	294 times

3. *Credit.* As noted in earlier chapters, a key credit measure is the LIBOR rate, and a key indicator is the relationship (or spreads) between the one-month LIBOR, three-month LIBOR, three-month U.S. Treasury bills, the U.S. Prime Rate, and the Federal Funds Target Rate (FFTR). When LIBOR ratios are rising, it means banks are having trouble; when it's falling, they are getting more confident and willing to lend. Watch for a narrowing in the TED spread as an indicator that the credit markets are becoming more accommodating, which could free up money for new investment and growth, which would be bullish for the stock market.

4. *The Coppock Guide*—This little-known momentum indicator is one of my favorite long-term technical tools, largely because it has such a powerful track record. Of the 17 rallies it has signaled since first being published in *Barron's* in 1962,

only one has failed to occur. That happened in November 2001, when the Coppock misread a bear-market bounce and gave a signal—18 months ahead of the actual turning point.

The underpinnings of the Coppock Guide are somewhat strange, it having been inspired by a clergyman's observation that deaths usually require a period of mourning by survivors that lasts 11 to 14 months. On hearing this, an economist named E. S. C. Coppock equated a bear market to a period of bereavement and designed the indicator (originally called the *Trendex Model*) as a means of measuring long-term movements in the S&P 500 Index (it's now used for a variety of other indexes, as well).

Without getting into too much technical detail, the guide is the sum of the 14-month and 11-month rates of change in the underlying index, smoothed by a 10-period weighted moving average. When the line created by this combination begins to curve *upward* from a level *below zero,* it is considered a buy signal. (Note: The Coppock is *exclusively* for bullish market turns; it does not identify market tops.) Figure 9.3 shows how the Coppock has tracked the movements in the S&P 500—or vice versa—over the past 10 years.

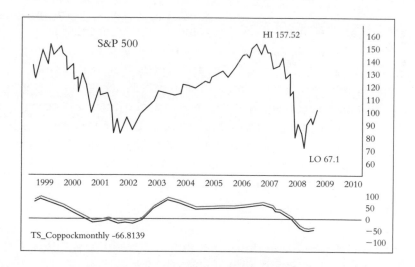

FIGURE 9.3 The Coppock Indicator Versus the S&P 500 Index over the Past 10 Years

Sources: Fitz-Gerald Research Publications, LLC; TD Ameritrade.

GETTING SAFELY BACK IN THE MARKET

The four indicators discussed in the preceding section should tell you when to start moving back into the U.S. market, as verified by upward moves in other key world markets. Remember, even though the entire world is still reeling from this catastrophe to some extent, the global markets will be critical to America's recovery.

In the meantime, if you want to get a head start, you can follow the smart money and begin taking positions in companies, based both here and abroad, that are globally diversified. But be selective—and maintain a defensive posture. Concentrate on companies that have real cash flows and strong earnings, not just a fancy business concept. Add to your layer of armor by limiting yourself to companies that have a minimum amount of debt, that are paying dividends of 2.5 percent or more, and that are positioned to profit from unstoppable global trends.

FISCAL FLASHPOINT

The combination of real earnings and a healthy dividend is vitally important in avoiding excessive stock market losses. Companies that reinvest earnings as a way of financing growth and ultimately enhancing share values are inherently more speculative than companies that pay out a significant portion of their earnings in dividends. Think of it this way: Dividends are not only a contract with shareholders, they're also a reality check for management, which has committed to a course of action for which top operating executives are accountable. It's an extreme example, but I don't believe the Enron debacle, for instance, would have happened had the company had a dividend that, in effect, forced them to prove their earnings were real by actually putting up the cash.

As an added safety valve in these uncertain times, try to pick out companies that are long resources and are hedged against or will benefit from inflation. The reason is, if the markets fall further from here, history shows these types of companies will *fall less.* Moreover, when a recovery really does take hold, their stocks tend to rise faster and higher than other choices—plus, many of them kick out substantial cash dividends. (Though it's hard to be precise with respect to prices and other details because of the time lag in getting a book to print, I offer some specific suggestions on stocks that meet these criteria in Chapter 11.) Generally speaking, stocks that qualify under this condition will be in one of three sectors:

1. *Petroleum, oil refining, or oil delivery systems* such as tanker or pipeline companies.
2. *Precious metals,* mainly gold—or, once the recovery begins speeding up, industrial metals that will be needed in growth and infrastructure projects.
3. Essential *agricultural products* that are needed to feed and clothe the world's growing population and provide raw materials for the products needed to satisfy the burgeoning consumer demands of the emerging nations.

Be aware, though, that the underlying market forces related to both resources and the course of inflation can be confusing. That's particularly been the case with commodities over the past couple of years, as the prices for many of them have behaved contrary to what would be expected. But don't be fooled. The plunge in commodity prices we saw in late 2008 and 2009 does *not* represent a fundamental change in the supply-and-demand relationship. Fundamentals *do not change* that abruptly in such a short period. Overall, the trend is still up.

The real reason for the decline was the global credit crunch, which squeezed out inventories in the supply chains, causing a momentary and false supply surge, which depressed prices. Such price-depressing effects are only temporary and will be corrected to the bullish side—most likely in violent fashion—once the false surge of supply is exhausted and the effect of inventory liquidation becomes evident.

As you saw in Chapter 8, stockpiling materials and rebuilding inventories requires money and credit—credit provided by banks in the form of commercial paper. This process works great when the credit markets are healthy and adequately funded, but not at all when they're locked up, as they have been. When lending resumes, business spending will again go up—and commodity prices will climb right along in tandem.

FISCAL FLASHPOINT

Investing directly in commodities with physical assets like gold—or indirectly, with funds, options, or futures contracts—can be as valuable for you in modest proportions as it is for the companies whose stocks you buy. Not only do commodities tend to lead the rebound when the economy reaches a bottom, but they tend to hold up better if the bottom is yet to come. To clarify, we've seen countless stocks—including some stalwarts like General Motors—go all the way to zero. To my knowledge, no commodity ever has.

With respect to inflation, the monetary policies I explained and complained about earlier are the driving force—and will be for some time to come. In an effort to stimulate the economy and rescue outfits deemed too big to fail, the world's central bankers have created trillions of dollars out of thin air—which can only be hyper-inflationary.

Right now, the focus is on preserving liquidity—which means *hoarding cash,* even if the new money being printed diminishes the value. A little bit further down the road, it will be about *preserving value*—which means hoarding physical assets. As liquidity becomes less of an issue, history suggests Americans will spend their cash as fast as possible. That will further devalue the dollar, which will crater relative to the globe's growth currencies, chief among them at this point the Chinese yuan.

BEGINNING YOUR WORK UNDER
THE NEW MONEY RULES

In summary, then, you can see that big changes in the world's economic equilibrium are under way, with new rules of money being written each step along the way—rules that require a change in conventional thinking and the implementation of new investment strategies.

I've given you my expectations for what many of these new rules will be, as well as some general ideas for what you can do while you're waiting for official copies of the new rule book to be handed out. (Wouldn't it be nice if that were *actually* the case—and everyone agreed to abide by it?) However, since I'm a bit anal retentive, *general* is never quite good enough. I believe every investor should have a disciplined and well-thought-out plan—which, at this point, should include the four elements on the following checklist:

1. *Make a wish list of the stocks you'd like to own,* based on your own research and beginning with the types of recommendations featured in Chapter 11. As specified earlier, these should be companies with strong cash positions, low or no debt, experienced management, attractive valuations, a good dividend, and a global reach. (If you're technically oriented, their charts probably won't be overly compelling, but that's to be expected when bottom fishing for candidates to lead the way in a market recovery.)
2. *Scale in.* Don't bet the farm on an all-or-nothing assumption that we've seen *THE* bottom for this market cycle. For some strange reason, most investors are programmed to jump in with both feet when it's really time to put *only a toe* in the water. Stocks had a nice midsummer bounce in 2009, moving back above 9500 on the Dow—but a thousand-point reversal could just as easily come before another similar advance if the economic numbers turn sour.
3. *Make the markets prove it.* Even if you're not a technician by nature, check out the charts of anything you're considering

using Yahoofinance.com or any of the half a dozen other free charting services on the Internet. Pick out the major resistance points for both the S&P and the stocks you'd like to buy. Wait for a move through those marks—preferably two or three closes at higher levels to demonstrate strength—before jumping in.

4. *Be clear in your motivation.* If you're still smarting from your earlier losses, don't confuse the desire to make up the ground you gave up with an actual long-term investing perspective. Before you jump the gun and plunge in, make sure you're actually going after your A-list companies, not just trying to recoup losses with stocks or strategies that require you to take on more risk than you'd otherwise be comfortable with.

What else you can do:

- Take advantage of new tools like the earlier-mentioned inverse ETFs. They can stabilize your income and your upside.
- Learn how to use options. They don't have to be high risk when used correctly—and they can let you harvest consistent gains when absolutely nothing else is working.
- Trust your own instincts and turn the sound off on the mainstream media. You'll find it will be a lot like watching *Animal Planet*—in other words, both will show strange creatures doing lots of wild and amusing things, but none of them will be saying *a single thing you can understand!*
- Relax—and breathe. No one knows exactly how long this economic vortex will last, but two things are dead certain: We've been here before—and, regardless of how bad things get, this too shall pass.

Oh, yes, there's one other thing you absolutely *must* do under the new rules of money—which is:

Go global—or go home!

And that's what I discuss in Chapter 10.

CHAPTER 10

———

GO GLOBAL OR
GO HOME

Where to Make Your Future Fortune

If you could kick the person in the pants responsible for most
of your trouble, you wouldn't sit for a month.

—President Theodore Roosevelt

The U.S. financial crisis revealed—in a terribly cruel way—just how much greed and avarice ruled the dark heart of Wall Street. It also demonstrated how foolish many investors on Main Street were.

One reason the financial crisis hurt so much is that a lot of investors took on entirely too much risk, not only in their portfolios, but in their personal lives, too. Whether this was done intentionally or unwittingly depends on your perspective. But the fact is that they did. And so did the rest of the world—which means that, when we ultimately emerge from this mess, chances are things will truly be different this time around. (As you saw in Chapter 9, many of those differences—in the form of new rules of money—are already becoming apparent.)

Recent studies show that a major reason risk levels for U.S. investors were so high was that they were dramatically *overweighted* in U.S. stocks, bonds, and money market funds, with most practicing little or no international diversification.

The market itself took care of the first part of that problem, reducing the weighting by wiping out a massive chunk of equity in domestic stocks and pushing many U.S. corporate bonds into default. Even the once rock solid money market funds were forced to break the buck at one point, dropping the fixed share value below $1.00. The fright factor also helped adjust the balance, as many investors were scared out of the market completely, moving their assets into cash (which is a pretty frightening option in its own right, given the government's inflationary actions and the dollar's perilous valuation position relative to the world's growth currencies).

Sadly, what hardly any investors have so far done in the wake of the meltdown is address the second part of the problem—the issue of global diversification. An analysis by Standard & Poor's in the first quarter of 2009 found that U.S. investors were still grossly *underweighted* when it came to foreign holdings—only 6.9 percent of assets, on average. My own research concludes the impact of this will be severe. Not only is the excess domestic focus far from safe in regard to risk exposure but, more importantly, it will likely cost U.S. investors *as much as 50 percent in potential returns* over the coming decade.

At the risk of sounding like a broken record, I'll repeat an admonition issued numerous times already: You *must* begin investing on a *global* scale, *with a special focus on China.*

Fail to do so and I can almost guarantee that you will be left *far, far behind.* It really *is* as simple as that.

If my telling you that isn't sufficient, take it from *Money Morning* Executive Editor William Patalon III, who's been handing out the same advice almost as long as I have. Indeed, he recently wrote: "International investments are no longer just a nice bit of diversification, or a way to 'spice up' your portfolio. They're a *necessity.* You go global—*or you get left behind.*"

Don't get me wrong. If you choose to ignore us and stay home or go with what you know, you may still do *okay*. After all, there will eventually be a U.S. economic recovery and a market rebound. But know this: You will have to watch others outperforming you by 50 percent, 75 percent, even 100 percent, or more—for years to come. And, you'll have to deal with the ever-present knowledge that *you could have been one of them!*

If you can live with that, okay—but most of the investors I know won't be able to.

FISCAL FLASHPOINT

A lot of traditional investors are reluctant to look at China because of the Communist government—but, as explained earlier, the Chinese version of Communism is far more moderate and business-driven than the ultra-repressive form practiced by the former Soviet Union. What's actually of more interest these days is the talk of socialist markets. Many believe the United States is slipping into that category—and with good reason. With the governments of the United States, Britain, and most other developed nations pushing bailouts for banks and other private companies—in essence, playing "risk-taker of last resort"—one could make the argument with a straight face that *the free markets are no longer free.* Even if that's becoming the case, Socialism in and of itself is not a big problem. What is—and the reason it exists—is that Socialism mirrors the underlying desires of society. It lives on because it embodies the deep-seated need for common good and individual survival—needs more and more governments these days seem ready to cater to.

THE U.S. MARKET IS STILL IN TROUBLE

Be aware as well that a full recovery by the U.S. market could still be a long, long way down the road. Although we saw a healthy rebound in stock prices in midsummer 2009, the overall outlook for the U.S.

market remains fairly grim, with many companies experiencing broadly lower revenues, uncertain earnings, and a questionable customer base thanks to still-rising unemployment figures and excessive personal debt left over from a credit spree that, in reality, extends all the way back to the mid-1990s.

Because of that, many individual stocks have further to fall or will continue to languish. A look at past hard times shows that, if the companies survive, most of these stocks *will* eventually recover—and, of course, there are also many good stocks already on the rebound. Still, present conditions in the U.S. market make picking U.S.-only winners an arduous task—and picking sure winners a virtual impossibility.

FISCAL FLASHPOINT

A major reason I say the U.S. markets are still in trouble is that the sentinels of the U.S. financial system haven't changed. I have a hard time believing that the same career government officials, market regulators, and credit-ratings agencies that were asleep at the switch when the financial crisis began have miraculously figured out how to fix those same problems—especially when many of those folks haven't got a clue about how the financial markets actually work, and most have never worked in them.

By contrast, it's much easier to make confident selections when you look abroad. The secret is buying a combination of clear value and high dividends in developed foreign economies that are enjoying strong growth. My personal choices—and the majority of my most successful recommendations—have involved real companies with real products, growing sales, and high current incomes. These companies have targeted resource-rich and developed, growing economies—and most of them have primary or supporting roles in the production process. All, of course, met my other fundamental investment criteria as well.

While it is also possible to find companies with similar characteristics in the United States, the opportunities are, in general, far greater overseas. Companies there can typically be purchased at lower multiples, and they pay higher dividends than their domestic counterparts. And, logically, it simply makes more sense to invest in foreign countries where wealth is growing than in the United States, Japan, or Western Europe, where the economies are contracting. (Note: It *is* still okay to buy U.S. companies, so long as they have a major portion of their sales coming from overseas markets.)

FISCAL FLASHPOINT

Whether you're buying stocks at home or abroad, always make sure you stick to real companies with real businesses and real products—not just nebulous concepts and pie-in-the-sky business plans. If you don't fully understand a company and what it does, why own its shares? "Keep it simple, stupid," really *is* an effective concept.

Current patterns of global money flow clearly reflect those conditions. Money is flowing out of the United States, Japan, and other developed nations and into China, Indonesia, India, and the like. And we want to *follow that money*—investing where the money flow is going—because more money means higher personal incomes, increasing GDP, and greater overall economic growth.

It's true that the decline in the dollar's value may cause short-term disruptions in the economies of Asia—but, largely unburdened with debt and with trade accounts firmly in surplus, those economies are still in much stronger shape fundamentally than we are. And, they will become stronger still as they continue to develop into their own best consumers, fueling future growth internally rather than through exports. And future growth will translate to better markets—and higher stock prices.

By contrast, countries that have amassed huge levels of debt in trying to borrow their way out of the recession will face a much harder time sustaining a recovery because there will be less credit available to fuel business growth. Figure 10.1 shows the countries—from the

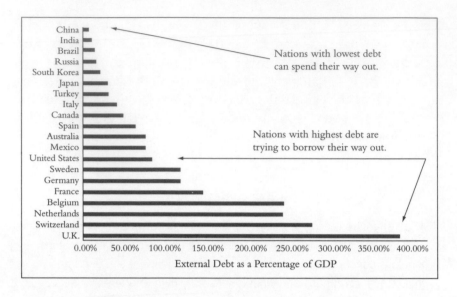

FIGURE 10.1 The Burden of Debt Affects Strategies for Economic Recovery

Sources: Fitz-Gerald Research Publications, LLC; Central Intelligence Agency; IMF.

United States through most of Western Europe—that face the largest debt burden, relative to their economic output.

That's why I firmly believe that, while still maintaining a diligent safety-first attitude, you should have at least 40 to 60 percent of your assets allocated to international investments or those that stand to benefit strongly from global growth areas like China. (In other words: focus 40 to 60 percent of assets on foreign markets.) Barring some unforeseen shift in current world economic trends, this strategy should be the major factor in creating your future fortune.

That view is shared by other notable experts as well. Wharton School of Business Professor Jeremy Siegel, who first gained national attention back in the mid-1990s for his book, *Stocks for the Long Run: The Definitive Guide to Financial Market Strategies and Long-Term Investment Strategies* (whew!), recently debunked the long-held conventional wisdom that international investments should comprise just 5, 10, or, at most, 15 percent of one's total portfolio value. U.S.

financial advisers had long preached that any more than that was foolhardy and way too risky.

Now, Siegel contends the truly foolish behavior would be to limit international exposure to *that small a percentage* of our assets. Like me, he says the biggest risk U.S. investors now face is *not* the possibility of losses when some foreign market plunges, it's the danger we'll get left behind financially because most of the world's growth in the decades ahead will be generated *outside U.S. borders*—by such countries as China, Japan, Taiwan, South Korea, India, Brazil, and soon even smaller players like Indonesia and Vietnam.

Given that, Siegel now believes U.S. investors should devote at least 40 percent of their total holdings to international investments.

His position—and mine—is further bolstered by the numbers. According to a report by the McKinsey Global Institute, global growth remains a huge investment opportunity—even allowing for the major losses in the recent meltdown. McKinsey calculated that the global value of all financial assets—stocks, bonds, certificates of deposit, and other securities—would still grow from $118 trillion in 2005 to $200 trillion by the end of 2010. That's an increase of 69 percent, the bulk of it owing to growth outside the United States and Western Europe. Going even further out, I believe we could see as much as $300 trillion by 2020—or sooner.

A different report from the World Bank, based on research from various analysts, had even worse long-term news for U.S.-only investors. In 2007, Asia and the United States each accounted for about 28 percent of the worldwide economy. By 2030, the U.S. economy will have more than recovered its recent losses, but its worldwide share will still have fallen to 24 percent. By contrast, Asia's share of the global market—with China leading the way—will have almost *doubled* over the same period, *rising to 55 percent!*

Think of it this way: In economic terms, the Asia of tomorrow will be *twice as powerful* as the United States is today—and almost 60 percent more powerful than it will be in 20 years.

Can you afford to miss out on that kind of growth and the profits it will bring? I think not.

FOUR TIPS FOR GETTING BACK IN THE MARKET

If you pulled in your horns during (or after) the collapse and got out of the market entirely, it's time to start thinking about re-entering because the changing times are creating new opportunities. However, to seize them, you probably need to adopt a different investment perspective. Here are four guidelines that should help you do better—and feel more comfortable—this time around:

1. *Not every stock is alike.* Above all else, what you don't want to do right now is pay cold hard cash for stocks that are clearly still trash. As I've said before, the best choices are companies with real products, real earnings, and solid sales growth, particularly those with exposure to China. Not only have such companies proven more stable during the entire financial crisis, but they're likely to continue to lead the broader markets higher.

2. *Clarify your objectives.* There is plenty of money to be made right now, but you have to know *what you're after* and *why*. Do you want to earn a specific level of income, or would you like to capture a specific dollar amount every month in appreciation? (Strategies for doing both are featured in Chapter12.) What is your target return this year, and how will you know if you've achieved it? Don't invest a dime until you can answer these questions and know exactly what role you want your investments to play in your financial future. My 50-40-10 Pyramid portfolio structure (also detailed in Chapter 12) is a good place to start for finding the answers.

3. *Focus on meeting them.* Once you've determined your objectives, identify what you need to do to meet them, and which areas of your portfolio you need to flesh out. Write this down on a note pad or in a journal (I use sticky pads on my computer monitor). Doing so will help you think more clearly, invest more efficiently, and produce consistently higher gains with fewer losses. An example might be, "I will invest only in dividend aristocrats offering a yield

(continued)

of 4% or more annually that have increased their dividends every
year for the last 10 years." And, yes, before you ask, there *are*
plenty of them out there.

4. *Guard your gains*. When the markets start to run, it's easy to forget
that stocks are most vulnerable during the early stages of a rally—
especially when things are still uncertain, as they are now. Make
sure you have trailing stops in place for every new purchase (more
on this later), and stick to them. That way, if future rallies fail, you
can easily head for the high ground while others have their dinner
dropped in their laps.

WHAT THE FUTURE WORLD MAY LOOK LIKE

In fairness, I should note that there's no lack of uncertainty about
the future path the world may take, though the risks to you as an
investor are more systemic than they are related specifically to a strategy of going global. In other words, if world turmoil increases from
this point rather than abating, the impact on investments will be negative whether they're here or abroad (though the strength of overseas
economic growth could ease that impact).

I'm a bit too focused on finance to make predictions about the future
of the world as a whole, but I am smart enough to find information
from those who do—and one such source is the National Intelligence
Center (NIC). The NIC is a think tank within the U.S. government,
reporting to the Director of National Intelligence. It provides the
President and senior U.S. officials with analyses of foreign-policy
issues, based on coordinated reviews of information from throughout
the intelligence community.

In a report presented in March 2009 for President Obama, the NIC
laid out three possible scenarios about the course the world might
take between now and 2025. While they're careful to note that these
are *not* predictions, just plausible alternative views about how the future
may develop, they do provide some interesting food for thought—
starting with the introductory summary, which reads:

Since 2002, *despite high oil and commodity prices,* the world has experienced *schizophrenic growth.* This growth has even surprised the most bullish economists and questions have arisen about its sustainability.

This economic growth was mainly driven by *a two-speed world economy* in which populous emerging markets, such as *China and India, were growing at more than 10 percent* and 8 percent, respectively. As a result, *an economic shift in gravity away from OECD [developed] countries to Asia is already on its way.* This . . . growth has resulted in an *unprecedented demand for ultimately depletable natural resources.* With population levels rising from the current 6.6 billion people to an estimated 8.0 billion people by 2025, it is evident that *change is inevitable* and that many stress points are likely to emerge in the future global environment.

The emphasis is mine, just so I can say, if that analysis doesn't verify nearly everything I've said so far in this book, then *I don't know what possibly will.* And, numerous elements detailed in the summaries of the three scenarios, which follow, also reinforce many of my key points.

Borrowed Time?

The first scenario is labeled "Borrowed Time," and it describes a world "following a path that, without major changes, leads to an unsustainable future. Ignoring, or giving insufficient credence to, the long-term consequences of their policy decisions, leaders leave an 'imperfect' or 'flawed' legacy for future generations. The result is a world ill-equipped to deal with complex global dilemmas." The timeline outlined for this scenario is as follows:

Mid-2009–2012: While the economic pace slows in developed countries, emerging economies continue to grow. Governments focus almost exclusively on problems with a clear historical precedent and are essentially incapable of finding creative solutions to newer problems (for example, climate change, global terrorism). Short-term, stop-gap solutions to problems requiring a long-term commitment are ineffective. Lack of global leadership only worsens conditions.

2013–2021: Lack of harmony in regulatory frameworks, in combination with a global leadership vacuum, results in difficulties in the West's adjustment to new geopolitical realities. The rules of the game are shifting and cracks appear in the system. OPEC falters, and a backlash results in immigration clampdowns.

2022–2025: Future generations are now set to inherit the many problems that have been allowed to fester. Economic swings, rising protectionism, and clear winners and losers in terms of growth characterize this world.

A World Beset by Woes?

That's sort of a good-news, bad-news compilation of possible events, but it's not nearly as scary as the second NIC scenario, which is called "Fragmented World." It features countries "struggling to manage problems against a backdrop of constrained growth combined with a lack of multinational solidarity. Neither individual nations nor the international system can keep up as the problems leave solutions behind." The timeline envisioned for this scenario is:

Mid-2009–2012: Traditional international institutions are weakened by the diffusion of state power and new entities challenging the status quo. The global economy slumps and nations are unable to manage security and environmental challenges.

2013–2021: The dream of the BRICs (Brazil, Russia, India, China, and other emerging nations) fades somewhat and global insecurity increases in the face of ethnic conflicts, natural-resource shortages, and a renewed Middle East arms race. Technology diffusion dries up. International cooperation is absent.

2022–2025: Poor economic performance, failed leadership, increased tensions and an absence of multilateral cooperation define this world. An overwhelmed international system is collapsing under its own weight.

Constant Renewal

Obviously, they forgot to consult the optimists on that one—but, thankfully, the final scenario, dubbed "Constant Renewal," paints a more promising possible picture. It features a world in which "nations realize that the international community must work collaboratively on a sustained basis to affect real change at the global level. Leaders system-atically adjust policies and frameworks as needed in support of shared global priorities. While the transition is not without difficulties, the world moves in the right direction." The timeline unfolds as follows:

> Mid-2009–2012: Political, economic, financial, and environ-mental shocks force changes in the mindsets of key players and pressure from civil society spurs change. Leaders and nations recommit to the international system.
> 2013–2025: A world in which societies reconnect with one another on local and global levels to tackle international prob-lems. Although problems persist, global communities come together (albeit with some hiccups) and the world sets itself on a path toward economic growth and shared responsibilities.

I'm not sure which, if any, of those scenarios will emerge as clos-est to the truth. While my experience suggests that Door Number 3—Constant Renewal—will be the course taken from here, I am quite certain that elements of each will shape the ultimate world reality.

What's important from our perspective is that each features con-tinued growth and economic development of nations beyond the bor-ders of the United States, Japan, and Western Europe—development your investments must profit from if you hope to take full advantage of the coming wealth-creation opportunities.

ASSESSING RISKS—KEY AREAS OF GLOBAL UNCERTAINTY

As with all investment strategies—global, domestic, or combination—uncertainties add to the level of risk, and the NIC report also evaluates the various areas of critical uncertainty we'll face in the generation ahead. They're broken down into five broad categories, with some specific concerns listed in each, as follows:

1. *Social Risks:* Intolerance and ethnic or religious tensions; health concerns and major pandemics; regional population distribution.
2. *Technological Risks:* Energy utilization and transitions to alternative energy; progress in genetics and life sciences.
3. *Economic Risks:* A two-speed global economy; China's decoupling from the U.S. economy; growth in energy demand; investment for energy infrastructure; the global flow of foreign direct investments (FDI); international trade; shifting prosperity levels; Russia's economic fundamentals; U.S. economic fundamentals.
4. *Environmental Risks:* Climate change and global warming; security of the food supply system; water scarcity and security.
5. *Political Risks:* The United States' global image; China's regional and world leadership position; global governance; market openness; terrorism; security of the energy supply; chemical and biological weapon proliferation; nuclear proliferation; religious fundamentalism; political corruption; U.S. moral leadership in the world.

Obviously, each of those areas carries with it an obvious degree of uncertainty, and adverse events in any of them could affect your investments. But, once again, the impact would almost certainly be universal—hitting both domestic and foreign markets—and your presence in overseas investments could actually shelter you against the worst of trouble.

BACK TO THE *REAL* SITUATION IN ASIA

As I said a few pages ago, the NIC report provides considerable food for thought for people who enjoy pondering tomorrow's what-ifs and maybes. If that's you, you can read the entire 64-page document by going to the NIC's web site at www.dni.gov/nic/NIC_home.html and clicking on the tab labeled "2025 Project." If nothing else, you'll be able to tell folks you know everything President Obama knows about the future of the world.

Personally, I prefer to deal with issues a little more selectively and concentrate on areas about which I have first-hand knowledge of what's going on. That's why I want to talk a bit more about China before we move on.

As somebody who's been stomping around in Asia for more than 20 years now, and who has spent much of my career deeply involved in analyzing the economics of the area, I wish I could be less blunt about the *absolute necessity* of investing there. But I can't! I've seen this economic transition coming for years now and have been practically screaming from the mountain tops telling people to get ready for it. To be fair, though, I didn't expect it to occur so dramatically, nor quite so soon. I thought it might be another 20 years before we would see China's full consumer emergence.

But like everything in that part of the world, this process, too, is accelerating.

What's more, as I just theorized about foreign investments buffering you against trouble, the growth in China is being driven specifically by the developed world's financial crisis. China, as hard as this is to imagine, is making hay while the sun *doesn't shine* on the rest of the globe. In accordance with the Confucian thought that governs much of their culture—and has for thousands of years—Chinese officials, business leaders, and consumers view the Western financial crisis as *a void that needs to be filled*. They're not out to conquer the world—but they are out to be a major partner in the world's economy.

What 99 percent of Westerners don't understand is that Beijing—and, by extension, many of China's leading companies—view the financial crisis as one big opportunity. *And we should, too!* They know that Western companies have been significantly weakened by the turmoil, and they are doing everything they can to expand while the competition is unable to. That's why you've recently been seeing, hearing, and reading news about everything from corporate acquisitions and resource purchases to new business in Taiwan and even the 2009 establishment of more than $200 billion in yuan swap agreements around the world.

The Chinese are developing not just a new nation, but an entirely new paradigm that incorporates elements of Western capitalism, even as it maintains strong ties to the country's 5,000-year history. Ideology remains a consistent and pervasive force there, with continued economic development and Chinese national growth a higher priority than the concept of personal freedoms—even among many individual Chinese citizens.

FISCAL FLASHPOINT

Relative to the country's 5,000-year history, tradition, and heritage, the current political and government structure—the People's Republic of China (or PRC)—isn't even out of diapers yet. In fact, it just celebrated its sixtieth birthday on October 1, 2009.

The Growth Just Can't Be Denied

It seems my message is getting out—the one about it being a situation of "get on board or get left behind."

Bloomberg announced last summer that, for the first time since it began compiling the data, Chinese share values topped $3 trillion on July 2, 2009. That was a 66 percent increase from the end of 2008, and marked the first time ever that Chinese market valuation surpassed that level.

At the same time, the MSCI Emerging Markets Index rose 35.0 percent versus a measly 2.9 percent increase in the MSCI World Index of developed economies. That's *a 1,106.89 percent performance differential* between emerging markets and their supposedly developed cousins.

When I said investors who elect not to participate better get comfortable being left behind, this is precisely the kind of information I was talking about. And, if it makes you uncomfortable reading it, good—because that means I've at least got you thinking.

Clearly the implication is that you can potentially make more money in emerging markets, especially China, than you can anywhere else on the planet in the years ahead. Obviously, it won't be a straight shot—but, longer term, the trend is *very clearly up.*

According to the Washington-based IMF, which noted in its April 2009 World Economic Outlook Report, the world's developed economies were expected to drop by −3.8 percent in 2009. At the same time, developing economies were expected to rise by 1.6 percent in 2009, and by 4.0 percent—or maybe even more—in 2010. This included all the usual suspects—China, Brazil, India, and Russia—plus a whole host of others not normally on the radar, including some in Africa and the Middle East.

FISCAL FLASHPOINT

While I strongly recommend exploring the entire world with your investments, don't make the mistake of enrolling in the Christopher Columbus School of Investing. You know, that's the one where you have no idea where you're going, don't know when you've arrived, and have no clue where you are after you get there.

But back to China. From 2003 to the end of 2008, its economy more than doubled to $3.8 trillion according to the IMF. At the same time, Bloomberg reported its market capitalization jumped more than fivefold. Indeed, China recently ousted Germany from its ranking as the world's third-largest economy—and it's fast closing in on Number 2 Japan and the Number 1 United States. My guess is we'll live to see China surpass both—and a lot sooner than most people think.

DOWN TO THE SPECIFICS—AT LAST

I talk more about China in the next chapter—as well as several other countries that I feel currently offer the best opportunities for going global. I also provide more specific guidance on which market sectors and individual industries you should explore—and even cite a number of companies that I feel have both excellent near-term promise and long-term staying power. Consider all of them the starting points in your bid to reallocate your assets toward capturing global growth and creating future wealth.

In the meantime—before you turn the page, that is—if you're really interested in the stability of the inevitable rise that is China and the emerging markets it will help propel to new highs, consider making the same sorts of investments China itself is now making: investments in resources, infrastructure, and metals.

Look to strapped companies like Canadian mining's Teck Resources, which recently sold 17 percent of itself for $1.5 billion to China Investment Corp. so it could reduce debt. Or head south to Brazil, where Chinese companies like Wuhan Iron & Steel Group are on the prowl for iron ore mining operations like MMX Mineracao e Metalicos SA, a potential $400 million acquisition being negotiated as I wrote this. In general, try to identify situations in which it would be helpful for resource-rich, but financially troubled companies to ink a deal with a patient, long-term partner.

Better yet, simply buy the best of the Chinese companies themselves—companies like those recommended on a more timely basis by me and my fellow analysts and commentators through our online advisory services, *Money Morning,* the *New China Trader,* and *Money Map Report.* Many of those Chinese companies are still going for bargain-basement prices despite sporting high double-digit growth rates—which is always an appealing combination. Plus, more of them than you'd think are traded right on the New York Stock Exchange.

CHAPTER 11

BRASS TACKS

Key Countries, Sectors, Industries, and Companies

A man's accomplishments in life are the cumulative effect of his attention to detail.

—John Foster Dulles

As an author and financial adviser, it's easy for me to make broad statements like "Go global or go home," which is essentially the message of this entire book. However, for you as an individual investor, actually acting on that theme is quite a bit more difficult. After all, though it's shrinking all the time, the globe we're living on is still fairly good sized, and I'm pretty sure you don't have enough cash to make at least one investment in every little out-of-the-way place on its surface.

So, in this chapter, I am a little more specific, talking briefly about the prime countries in which I think you should focus your search for value and future growth, as well as the market sectors and industries

229

that are likely to lead the way in those countries—and in the world as a whole. I even list some of the specific companies that I think are well-positioned for both short-term profits and long-term staying power.

FISCAL FLASHPOINT

Obviously, this book has a shelf life and circumstances can change at any time—but, in general, the companies I list later in this chapter are a great place to start. Some are already superstars and household names. Others are just coming onto the scene. All are meant as examples rather than specific recommendations. On that note, while I generally can't stand shameless self-promotion, if you'd like specific recommendations, you may want to sign up for my newsletter, *The Money Map Report,* by visiting www.keithfitz-gerald.com/fiscalhangover. It's $99.95 a year, and there's a special offer just because you're reading this book.

Finally, because finding global opportunities is sometimes easier for Americans than actually buying them, I talk about the various ways you can make foreign investments from within the United States.

SHOP IN THESE COUNTRIES FIRST

If you look closely enough, you can probably find quality investment opportunities of one form or another in a majority of the world's nations—but why work harder than you have to? There are more than enough worthwhile companies to choose from in the most advanced of the emerging-market countries, companies that will give you ample global diversification while also offering relative safety and, in many cases, a solid income through dividend payouts. And, there are plenty of candidates for filling that 10 percent of your holdings you'll want to devote to what I call *rocket riders*—investments with so much spectacular upside potential they can magnify the returns of your entire portfolio.

Obviously, You Should Start with China

I've made it no secret throughout this book that I believe China will be the superstar of any global investment initiative—simply because I believe it will be the superstar of the global economy in the decades to come. Most of the statistics relating to the emergence of China's own consumer base, the forward-thinking business attitude of its "neo-communist" government, that government's commitment to rapid infrastructure improvement, its vast stockpile of foreign currency reserves, and its spectacular overall growth have been detailed earlier in the book, so I won't repeat them here.

What I will do is point out that China is on track to create 700 percent growth in per-capita income over the next 20 years. This has never before been done in recorded history—by any nation, anywhere—and it supports my contention that, any time you have new money to put into the international portion of your portfolio, you should begin your quest with China-linked investments. By that, I mean you should focus on either growth companies actually based *IN* China or outside companies directly benefiting from *what China is doing* or how much *Beijing is spending*. I call these *because-of-China* choices. (I provide some more China statistics to support this when I discuss key sectors and industries on which to focus.) History has repeatedly demonstrated that the greatest opportunity arises in tandem with the greatest growth—and, as Figure 11.1 clearly shows, China eclipses the world in that category. Don't forget either that China's dominant position in these rankings comes in spite of recent government efforts to actually *slow* growth to prevent the economy from overheating.

Figure 11.1 also serves as loud testimony in support of my case for going global—and doing so among the developing nations, with a particular focus on Asia. If you choose to stay home instead, restricting yourself to the paltry growth rates—or even economic contractions—demonstrated by the United States, Japan, and the Western European nations, it's virtually preordained that you will fall behind more astute investors in the race for future wealth.

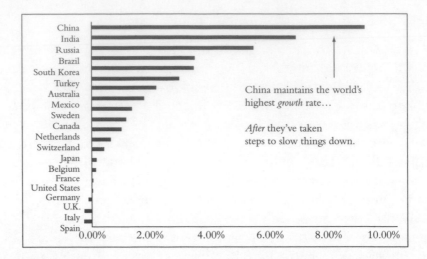

FIGURE 11.1   China's 2008 Growth Dwarfs the World's Other Leading Nations
Sources: China National Bureau of Statistics; International Monetary Fund.

FISCAL FLASHPOINT

If you do feel compelled to invest in Europe or among the developed nations, refer to the discussion of what's going on in Germany, featured in Chapter 7. The same applies to economic conditions and potential investment opportunities in the Middle East.

Next Stop, South Korea

Although there's some debate about whether South Korea should still be classified as an "emerging nation," it is demonstrating the growth of one. It also has many of the same social and economic characteristics that are driving other Asian dynamos, while more closely following the business and market models of the Western countries.

Because of its close business ties with the West, South Korea was plunged into recession in 2008 along with much of the rest of the world, with GDP falling to just $2.22 trillion, though it still posted a real growth rate of 3.8 percent (down from 4.9 percent in 2007),

THE DEVELOPING NATIONS NAME GAME

As I mentioned earlier, there's a trend among academics and analysts toward ending use of the term *emerging nations*. Goldman Sachs contributed to this when, in 2001, it began calling Brazil, Russia, India, and China the *BRIC* countries. (At the same time, it forecast they would make up more than 10 percent of global GDP by 2010. By 2007, they already accounted for 15 percent.) Goldman introduced another classification in 2005, dubbing a set of populous nations with the potential to have a BRIC-like impact on the global economy as the "Next Eleven" (N-11). The N-11 countries are Bangladesh, Egypt, Indonesia, Iran, South Korea, Mexico, Nigeria, Pakistan, Philippines, Turkey, and Vietnam.

However, with respect to South Korea, that designation is already getting some argument. Wharton School of Business Management Professor Mauro Guillen says, with per-capita income approaching $22,000 (well above most countries in Latin America and southern Asia) and an economy that has transformed from heavy industrial to one based on knowledge and technology, "It's about time we start thinking of South Korea as a fully developed economy."

thanks to continued government spending. According to Bank of Korea statistics, GDP growth resumed in the first two quarters of 2009, although the country remained officially in recession.

Still, that's a good sign South Korea is well on the way to resuming the strong growth it has maintained since the 1960s, when it was on the same economic level as poorer countries in Africa and Asia. By 2004, South Korea's GDP reached the trillion-dollar mark for the first time, and it now has roughly the same per-capita GDP as Greece or Spain. The growth was generated by strong government support of business through initiatives such as directed credit allocations, import restrictions, sponsorship of specific industries (such as auto production), and a strong labor education and training effort. The government also promoted the import of raw materials and technology at the expense of consumer goods, and encouraged savings and investment over consumption.

Today, South Korea's labor force of roughly 24 million is split among services (57 percent), industry (40 percent), and agriculture (3 percent). Leading industries are electronics, telecommunications, auto production, chemicals, shipbuilding, and steel. It had $371.5 billion in exports in 2007, dominated by products from those same industries. Imports totaled $356.8 billion, led by machinery, transport equipment, and electronics. Top trade partners are China, the United States, Japan, and Hong Kong. The country has limited natural resources (coal, tungsten, graphite, and lead), but significant hydroelectric power potential.

FISCAL FLASHPOINT

One of the most often-heard clichés is that, thanks to advances in technology and communications, the world is steadily getting smaller. Actually, though, in terms of economics, the world is getting *bigger— much bigger!* According to the National Intelligence Council, the global economy is projected to be about 80 percent larger in 2020 than it was in 2000, and average per-capita income is expected to be roughly 50 percent higher.

Changing Hemispheres and Heading South—To Brazil

Brazil's growth rate ranks only third among the BRIC nations—but it's fourth in the entire world at roughly 3.9 percent. According to the U.S. Department of State's survey of South American economies, GDP was estimated at $1.85 trillion in 2007, or $8,400 per capita. With large and well-established manufacturing, mining, agricultural, and service sectors, the Brazilian economy doubles the numbers generated by its nearest South American neighbors.

The country has a strong industrial base, with textiles, shoes, chemicals, cement, lumber, iron ore and tin mining, steel, aircraft, motor vehicles, and parts the leading industries. Although unemployment topped 10 percent in early 2009, the overall economy was supported by the country's strong export position in agricultural products (led by coffee, soybeans, wheat, and citrus products) and natural resources, particularly iron ore, tin, manganese, nickel, uranium—and gold and platinum. Other leading exports include footwear and transportation equipment, while machinery, chemical products, and oil are the leading imports. Despite that last import item, Brazil is actually among the most oil-frugal countries in the world, deriving just 8.3 percent of its electrical energy from fossil fuels while generating 82.7 percent by hydroelectric operations. Leading trade partners are the United States, Germany, China, Argentina, Nigeria, and the Netherlands.

Brazil is a top choice for future investment opportunities because, regardless of what happens around the world and in the developed nations, it will remain the dominant economic force in South America.

India Also Tops the Growth Charts

Although India ranks second behind China in overall GDP growth, having hit 7.0 percent in 2008 (down from 8.5 percent in 2006 and 2007), I don't rate it as high on the opportunity scale for several reasons. Chief among them are the large schism between urban and rural economies, incomes, and education levels (three-fifths of the work force is still engaged in agriculture) and the fact that more than half of India's economic output is based on services.

The country's potential also suffers because of its continued adherence to the caste system, in which millions of people are held down or excluded from any semblance of an economic future simply by virtue of their birth. The roster of disadvantaged includes 167 million Dalits (16 percent of the population), people outside the caste system entirely, who are subject to discrimination in virtually every aspect of Indian life.

On the plus side, the past decade has seen India significantly liberalize its financial sector and open up to capital flows from abroad. The stock markets have become more sophisticated and increasingly liquid, thanks in part to a major influx of foreign funds. However,

India's overall financial "depth"—the strength of its financial system relative to the size of its economy—is still low by global standards.

Several other systemic weaknesses also remain that could hinder overall growth and prevent India from creating large numbers of new jobs. For example, the government bond market is small and fairly illiquid, and Indian banks have the lowest ratio of lending to national GDP of any of the emerging-market nations (though the default rate is tiny, too). This situation is partly the result of restrictive banking rules and the government's use of banks, especially state-owned ones, as a source of deficit financing. In other words, rather than letting the banks lend to foster business growth, they're forcing them to buy government bonds.

In spite of these drawbacks, India's GDP topped $2.96 trillion in 2008, based on strong performance from software and software support industries, as well as textiles, chemicals, food processing, steel, cement, mining, and transportation equipment. The country also has a large class of craftsmen, contributing to substantial exports of gold ornaments, jewelry, and gems. Agricultural production was led by rice, wheat, cotton, oilseed, tea, and farmed fish, with leather byproducts from the raising of sheep, goats, and water buffalo being a major export item. Oil is India's leading import product and 81.7 percent of the country's power is generated by fossil fuels. Major trading partners include the United States, the United Kingdom, Hong Kong, China, Germany, and the United Arab Emirates.

With improving education, more government support for business and industry and a loosening of bank purse strings for financing, the potential offered by India's labor force of 496 million—many of whom will also be rapidly joining the consumer ranks, bolstering domestic consumption and economic demand—the country obviously offers substantial future investment potential. It's just not my top choice at this time.

Russia's Open—But Do We Want to Go There?

I talked a little about Russia back in Chapter 7, concluding that you likely won't find any superlative opportunities there at present. I stand by that analysis, though Russia is interesting enough to merit a little more discussion.

The country is 19 years into its transition from central planning to a free-market economy, and it still presents a conflicting picture. On the free-market side, *Forbes* ranks it second in the number of billionaires after the United States. At the same time, the structure of its economy continues to bear a strong imprint from its Soviet past. In an October 2008 report, the Brookings Institution described it thusly:

> The production structure—the type and size of factories and the location of entire cities—is highly unnatural from a market standpoint. Its management model is also distinct: a combination of companies operated by private owners but under the watchful eye of the closed inner circle of the country's political leadership. The description of the Russian economy as "Russia, Inc.," is apt.

The other problem at the moment is that Russia's recent downswing is worse than most other nations—for both political and economic reasons. For the first eight years of the new century, Russia benefited from the global commodities boom as did few other countries in the world. It became the source of choice for European energy needs (especially natural gas), and careful handling of the resulting oil and gas windfall led to large fiscal and financial surpluses. Both the overall welfare of citizens and the level of private wealth rose accordingly. That also turned Russia into a major market for consumer and investment goods provided by the rest of the world.

FISCAL FLASHPOINT

The surplus generated by Russia's energy exports was one of the largest in the world, and that could be a major factor in how well it is positioned as the global economy emerges from its current troubles. As Figure 11.2 clearly shows, countries that had surpluses or minimal deficits going into the crisis—notably Russia, China, and South Korea—should have much healthier fiscal balances than countries that entered the crisis with large deficits.

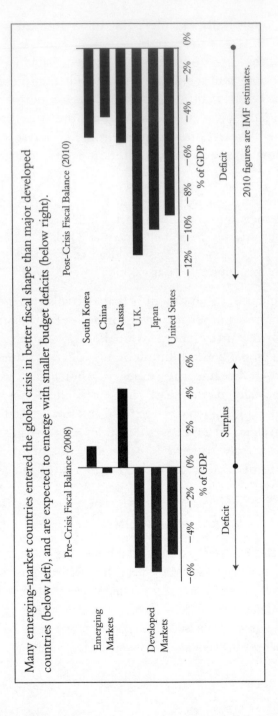

Many emerging-market countries entered the global crisis in better fiscal shape than major developed countries (below left), and are expected to emerge with smaller budget deficits (below right).

FIGURE 11.2 Countries with the Least Debt Will Emerge from the Crisis with the Mildest Fiscal Hangover

Sources: International Monetary Fund; FMRCo (MARE).

238

However, the outlook for Russia dimmed considerably in late 2008 and early 2009. Oil and gas output slowed, and then actually declined. This slammed the Russian stock market, which was also hit hard by the worldwide credit crunch. Russia's invasion of neighboring Georgia in August 2008 also ramped up political tensions, leading to calls from the West that Russia be excluded from the global economy and hit with assorted sanctions.

All these developments were almost certain to end Russia's eight-year run of 7-plus percent annual growth in GDP and threaten the country's potential future contributions to the global economy. Yet, with more than 140 million consumers—a multitude of desires still unfulfilled after 70 years of the severe form of communism—Russia has to be viewed as one of the world's most attractive markets. So, while I wouldn't go looking to invest *IN* Russia right now, when the economic upturn starts to gain steam, I'd take a very close look at the industries and companies that will be catering *TO* Russia and its consumers. That kind of growth potential can't help but translate into profits, even if the ride is a rocky one in the meantime. That will prove particularly so if Russian strongman Vladimir Putin remains involved in the country's continued evolution. Once criticized for his KGB-like tendencies, I believe Putin now understands the importance of an outward-facing vision, as illustrated by his comments encouraging Russian companies to be more like the Chinese in regard to their externally focused growth. His protégé and now President Dmitry Medvedev seems to send out the same message, and that's especially encouraging from an investment standpoint.

One Country from Off the Charts

Although it doesn't even show up on the chart of growth rates shown in Figure 11.1, there's one other country that should be worth a look in the very near future—Indonesia.

Indonesia is the world's third-largest democracy—behind India and the United States—and it is the largest Muslim country. And, though growth was negative in 2008, Indonesia has done surprisingly well despite the global economic turmoil and some internal terrorist activity. The country is rich in natural resources—minerals, metals, oil, and natural gas—and, being a nation of islands and beaches, it has a rapidly expanding tourist industry.

As opposed to being export-based, its expansion before 2008 was fueled by internal development and growing consumerism among a youthful, increasingly educated population and a growing middle class. Those same factors—coupled with low interest rates—are expected to reignite growth, which has been forecast to return to the 8 percent annual mark by 2011. The government is also working to promote prosperity, cutting government debt as a percentage of GDP by half since 2003, instituting policies to cut annual inflation to 5 percent, and actively soliciting private investment, which has grown 20 percent over the past five years.

Because of declining oil reserves, Indonesia formally opted out of OPEC in 2008, but it ranks second in the world in liquefied natural gas exports, a huge percentage of which is going to China (which is financing new production and transport facilities). It also ranks third in world coal reserves, first in tin production, and has significant gold, silver, copper, and nickel deposits. Agricultural exports include rubber, coffee, cocoa, tea, palm oil, wood, tobacco, spices, and shrimp.

The Jakarta Stock Exchange is also well run, with adequate liquidity and a good regulatory structure, and individual stock valuations are reasonable relative to India and other South Asian markets. Many of Indonesia's leading companies are also resource-driven, meaning their stocks will get a major boost from an uptick in commodity prices, particularly gold, silver, copper, nickel, and natural gas.

All in all, Indonesia is definitely worth putting on your "watch" list.

ECONOMIC SECTORS AND INDUSTRIES PRIMED FOR GROWTH

Obviously, there are numerous other countries with sufficient potential to be worth a look, but they are further down the list and will still need a few more positive developments to move up. Besides,

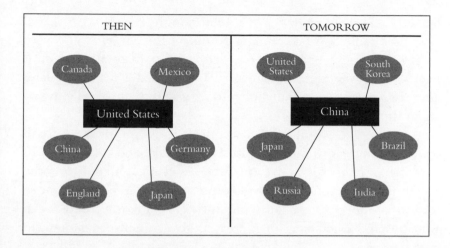

FIGURE 11.3 Then and Tomorrow—China Will Move to the Center of the New Global Economy

Source: Fitz-Gerald Research Publications, LLC.

unless you have much more analytical time on your hands than I do, the nations just listed should be plenty to get started with.

Actually, that could probably apply to China alone—which, as Figure 11.3 indicates, I believe is rapidly moving to the center of the new global economy. Whereas the United States, Europe, and Japan dominated in the past, China and its emerging compatriots will almost certainly assume the lead in the generation ahead.

Having said that, you still need to know where to look for the best opportunities within the top emerging countries—as well as anywhere else you may want to invest—so here are some guidelines regarding which sectors and industries will lead the ongoing recovery.

Start with Natural Resources

The aforementioned possible (I'd actually say *guaranteed*) uptick in commodity prices is one reason that natural resources leads the roster of market sectors you should examine in your search for the best global investment opportunities. With the world's population expected to grow by more than 1.5 billion in the next 20 years—and a growing middle class becoming a dominant force in virtually every emerging economy—demand for every type of natural resource is almost certain to increase. And, as a rule, increased demand translates to increased prices—especially for resources that might also be dwindling in supply.

Industries and companies that deal in commodities of all kinds—from precious metals, industrial metals, and oil and gas to construction materials and foodstuffs—will all benefit from the population explosion, which will bring not only an increased need for basic products, but a growing insistence on improved social conditions and a mandate for increased government investment in infrastructure.

That's one reason that, in spite of the sharpest global economic pullback since the Great Depression, prices for nearly all commodities— oil, copper, gold, soybeans, to name a few—bottomed in 2009 at their highest "recession levels" of all time. David Rosenberg, chief economist and strategist for Gluskin Sheff, a leading wealth-management firm based in Canada, says that was due in large part to the already reviving economies of Asia in general, and China in particular. In fact, the need for natural resources—or finding substitutes for them— is at the root of four of the five unstoppable trends you'll want to target with your global investment strategy. These five trends are:

1. Expanding consumerism throughout the developing world.
2. Infrastructure enhancement in those same regions.
3. Pollution control and resource management (components of the so-called Green Movement).
4. Development of alternative and renewable energy sources.
5. Medicine, technology, and improved health care, particularly with reference to the aging of the larger world population and extended life spans (a particular concern in the United States as Baby Boomers reach their 70s).

With respect to all these trends, you will also want to look for inflation resistance among the individual companies you select.

FISCAL FLASHPOINT

Just in case you think I might be exaggerating the potential for finding companies outside the United States worth investing in, I decided to throw in a little supporting data (supplied by MSCI and RIMES Technologies). Believe it or not, if you look in foreign markets, you will find:

- Nine of the world's 10 largest metals and mining companies.
- Eight of the world's 10 largest electronic equipment and instruments companies.
- Seven of the world's 10 largest automobile companies.
- Seven of the world's 10 largest manufacturers of household durable goods.
- Seven of the world's 10 largest telecommunications companies.

A Closer Look at Consumerism and Infrastructure

Right now, my primary trend focus is on consumerism and infrastructure enhancement, simply because both are such obvious sources of opportunity in China, our primary investment target. Also, with the middle class growing at such a dramatic rate, the two tend to feed off of one another.

With respect to consumerism, I've already mentioned the emergence of the *Chuppies*—China's equivalent of America's yuppies—but a couple of the statistics are worth repeating, especially since they will likely serve as a preview for similar consumption growth in other emerging economies such as India, Brazil, Indonesia, and the like.

In spite of the global disruptions, the Chuppies have been consuming with very little restraint. According to China's National Bureau of Statistics, Chinese retail sales were up 21.8 percent in 2008 (to $1.59 trillion, or 10 trillion RMB), and that was expected to increase even more in 2009, thanks to a 14.5 percent rise in annual per-capita urban incomes to 15,781 RMB and a 15.0 percent rise in rural incomes to 4,761 RMB. The spending covers the gamut of consumer goods, from household items like washers and dryers and kitchen appliances to electronics gear and designer fashions. Autos are also hot items, with 2009 car sales expected to grow by 10 percent compared to a decline of at least 8 percent worldwide. (Not to brag, but I suggested a few years ago that China would overtake the United States as the world's largest car market. Now China's done it not once, but for each of the first three months of 2009, with sales reaching a record 1.1 million vehicles.)

The growing needs (and, dare I say, demands) of the growing middle class—in China and elsewhere—are also driving much of the growing infrastructure spending by both government and private industry. A research report by Merrill Lynch & Co. analysts projected that emerging-market nations will spend $22 trillion over the next 10 years on infrastructure projects, with a huge percentage of that coming from China, which budgeted $725 billion for infrastructure from 2007 to 2010 alone. Here's a look at just some of the projects approved or already underway—a clear guide to the types of industries and companies that will generate your biggest opportunities for future wealth creation:

- *Roads:* China was on course to construct 300,000 kilometers in new rural roads from 2006 to 2010, an increase of nearly 50 percent. On my last trip to China, construction of new urban expressways and highways was also evident in every city I visited (as were additional projects like schools, sports stadiums, and other public facilities).
- *Railways:* China's railways carry 25 percent of the world's rail traffic on just 6 percent of the world's track, but the country is undergoing the biggest expansion of railway capacity by any country since the nineteenth century. Between 2006 and 2010, China was expected to invest $200 billion in new tracks, terminals, and freight-handling facilities, four times more than in the preceding five years.
- *Air travel:* Chinese air passenger traffic increased 2,542 percent from 1985 to 2007 (from 7 million passengers to more than

185 million). China's government plans to build 97 airports by 2020, adding to the 142 in operation at the end of 2006. Airports with an annual handling capacity over 30 million passengers will grow from three to 13.

FISCAL FLASHPOINT

Lest you think infrastructure spending is limited to China—or even Asia—take note of the situation in Dubai, where investment in new construction is so staggering that the small but rich Middle Eastern nation is currently said to be home to 25 percent of the world's supply of cranes—the kind used in building, not the birds.

PICKING STOCKS THAT WILL RIDE THE TRENDS

As I've said repeatedly, the recent economic collapse and continuing recession is clearly setting the stage for a new Golden Age of Wealth Creation, led by China, India, South Korea, Brazil, and other developing nations—not unlike the world of 1900, when the American industrial powerhouse was shifting into high gear. I firmly believe that untold fortunes will be made in this new Golden Age.

Leading the way in wealth creation for the next 10 years will be *real* businesses, locked into *unstoppable* global trends and *immune* to financial crises, government deficits, credit crunches, oil depletion, and the other maladies of the modern economic age. These are what I call *vanguard* companies—companies rich in natural resources or engaged in industries fueled by infrastructure improvement, companies in electrical power production . . . the manufacture of construction machinery and other heavy equipment . . . shipping . . . pipeline operations. (The latter two are perfect examples of "defensive" industries. Even if gas or oil prices drop to rock-bottom levels, product will still have to be *moved*—and shipping companies and pipelines will collect a dividend for doing it.)

From your standpoint, the key to future success will be to identify the companies in the best position to take advantage of the unstoppable trends before other investors do—and while their stocks are still cheap. Again, the best place to begin your search is within industries in countries that are rapidly redeploying their assets into infrastructure. It's an almost ironclad rule: Where there's infrastructure improvement, *there's value—and money to be made.*

Why? Because every growing economy must pave its roads and power its people—in other words, take care of the basics—before it can pave the way to improved business and greater wealth creation. Thus, you really can *follow the money* by tracking a country's spending on infrastructure.

FISCAL FLASHPOINT

A good way to identify top growth candidates is to look for companies whose stocks are trading at or below their actual cash value. With the current recession and economic uncertainty, there are a lot of them out there, many of which are still doing great business. Be aware, however, that when you're buying value, the near-term outlook often sucks.

Some Parameters for Selecting Individual Stocks

Once you've singled out industries or market segments in which the money is flowing, there are some key parameters to look for in selecting individual companies that will offer you the best current value and the greatest opportunity for future growth. They are:

- *Revenue certainty*—This can be established through a proven history of stable demand, a long-term record of market leadership, a monopolistic position (thanks to either government controls or supply exclusivity), or products that are price regulated or indexed for inflation.
- *Profitability*—This should be demonstrated by real revenues, high operating margins, the use of sustainable leverage, and a cost structure appropriate to the industry and specific business.

- *Longevity*—Regardless of where its revenues come from—for example, foreign suppliers to China—the company should be located in a country with a stable political system, a firm economic foundation, well-regulated markets, and an equitable legal system.

The following is a list of companies I've uncovered that I feel meet most of these requirements and also offer substantial potential for future growth. I've included brief descriptions—but, because they could be substantially different by the time you read this, I've excluded specific price, revenue, or earnings data. Also, for those of you who want to get your global diversification strategy underway without spending a lot of time on research, I've included some recommendations for funds and other alternate investments. (Note: Included stock symbols are for trading on U.S. markets.)

Gold, Oil, and Natural Resource Stocks

Resource stocks include mining operations—for both metals and other essential elements like coal—and oil and gas exploration companies and firms engaged in the delivery of these vital products.

- *Gold Fields Ltd. (GFI)*—Based in South Africa, this is the world's fourth-biggest gold producer, with about 90 million ounces in reserve from its operations in Africa, South America, and Australia.
- *Yamana Gold Inc. (AUY)*—Canadian-based Yamana boosted its bottom line in 2008 by increasing its production to take advantage of higher gold prices. It's also expected to double its gold production to 2.2 million ounces per year by 2012, primarily from its mining operations in Brazil and Argentina. It passed a chunk of those profits on to investors, boosting its annual dividend by 300 percent at the end of its 2008 fiscal year.
- *Barrick Gold Corp. (ABX)*—Also based in Canada, Barrick has been on a spending spree, buying stakes in a half-dozen mines in 2008, multiplying its reserves and production capacities to capture record gold prices. Barrick now owns 27 mines on five continents, and produces over 8 million ounces of gold per

year, making it the world's largest gold miner. The stock also pays a healthy dividend, which it raised 33 percent in 2008.

- *Yanzhou Coal Mining Company Ltd. (YZC)*—China needs lots of energy, and Yanzhou is the largest producer in eastern China, operating six mines with about 2 billion tons in proved and probable reserves.
- *CNOOC Ltd. ADRs (CEO)*—A subsidiary of China National Offshore Oil Corp., CNOOC conducts upstream activities, including exploration, development, and production in offshore China of crude, natural gas, and other petroleum products for the wholesale and refining markets.
- *PetroChina Company Ltd. ADRs (PTR)*—A fully integrated oil and gas company operating within China, PTR's operations include multiple levels of development, production, refining, marketing, and distribution. PetroChina operates an extensive natural gas and oil pipeline system, as well as a distribution network that includes a variety of petrochemical and petrochemical derivatives.
- *Core Laboratories (CLB)*—Operating in more than 50 countries, Core Laboratories offers up- and midstream oil and gas development and production support, including quality analysis and life-of-well studies.
- *Diamond Offshore Drilling (DO)*—Operating in waters off six continents, Diamond conducts midstream operations (including production and transport) of raw oil and natural gas from third-party reserves. The company specializes in deep-water and harsh-environment operations, with drilling platforms and submersibles capable of working at depths of 10,000 feet. It works with 50 different oil companies, but Petrobras is its major customer.
- *China Petroleum and Chemical Corp. (SNP)*—Also called Sinopec Corp., the company manages fully integrated oil and natural gas operations, including acquisition and development, refining, storage, marketing, and distribution of a variety of refined petroleum and petrochemical derivative products.
- *Transocean Ltd. (RIG)*—Transocean conducts up- and midstream operations for third-party holdings, including oil exploration, development, and production, operating in Brazil, Canada, the

Middle East, Asia, and India. The company specializes in deep-sea and harsh-environment production, with 136 offshore drilling units, including 67 semi-submersibles.

- *EOG Resources, Inc. (EOG)*—An independent offspring of once-powerful Enron, EOG has reserves of 7.3 trillion cubic feet of natural gas and 225 million barrels of crude oil. Based in Houston, the company operates in Canada, offshore Trinidad, the North Sea, and in China's Sichuan basin.

- *Total SA ADRs (TOT)*—Based in France, but operating in more than 130 countries, TOT has interests in 25 refineries and about 16,500 gas stations in Europe, Africa, and Asia. The company also has interests in liquid natural gas (LNG) production, coal mining, and power generation.

- *Murphy Oil (MUR)*—Based in Arkansas, Murphy Oil explores for and produces oil in the United States, Canada, and Malaysia, owns pipelines, two refineries, and more than 1,000 gas stations—almost all of them located in Wal-Mart parking lots in the United States and Britain.

- *Hess Corp. (HES)*—Hess Corp.'s multinational operations include all levels of natural gas and oil production, including exploration, refining, marketing, and distribution. It has operations in Azerbaijan, Brazil, Indonesia, Malaysia, Russia, Thailand, and 15 other countries. It also operates 1,370 gas stations, mostly in the eastern United States and provides electricity to customers in the Northeast and Mid-Atlantic states.

- *EnCana Corp. (ECA)*—Based in Calgary, Alberta, EnCana is an integrated oil and gas company with proven reserves of 13.7 trillion cubic feet of gas and 1 billion barrels of oil. Operating in five major North American regions, ECA is the continent's largest natural gas producer, having provided 1.4 trillion cubic feet in 2008.

- *ENI S.p.A. ADRs (E)*—Headquartered in Rome, ENI is one of Italy's largest companies, with divisions in oil and natural gas, petrochemicals, oil field services, and power generation. It has 6.6 billion barrels of proven oil equivalents in Italy and Africa, with additional operations in Kazakhstan and Pakistan.

- *Energy Transfer Partners (ETP)*—A distribution company for U.S. natural gas and propane, ETP operates 14,600 miles of interstate gas pipelines, 2,700 miles of gathering pipelines, and numerous storage facilities. Headquartered in Dallas.
- *YPF Sociedad Anonima (YPF)*—This Argentine subsidiary of Repsol YPF, Spain's largest oil company, produces, refines, and markets oil, natural gas, and petrochemicals throughout South America. It has three refineries and more than 1,690 service stations.
- *Petroleo Brasileiro SA ADRs (PBR)*—More popularly known as Petrobras, this is Brazil's largest industrial company. It has production and refining facilities, 14,200 wells, 21,140 kilometers of pipelines, and more than 5,970 gas stations—but the Brazilian government owns 32 percent of the company and 56 percent if its voting stock.
- *Petro-Canada (PCZ)*—A major integrated oil and gas company, PCZ operates in western Canada, Europe, North Africa, and the Caribbean. It also operates 1,320 gas stations in Canada and owns refineries, a Montreal chemicals plant, and a lubricant plant.

Consumerism Plays

Stocks with a consumer-driven income stream include durable goods manufacturers—including those for autos and household appliances—suppliers to those companies and firms in such sectors as food, retailing, and consumer services.

- *Bunge Limited Pfd. (BG)*—A Bermuda conglomerate headquartered in New York, with substantial global agribusiness and food production and distribution operations, including soy products, which are critical to many of the world's fastest-growing food markets.
- *Geely Automobile Holdings, Ltd. (HKG:0175)*—Traded on the Hong Kong Exchange, Geely (or Hong Qi, as it is referred to in China) is one of China's leading manufacturers of non-luxury autos and auto parts.

- *BYD Company Limited (HKG:1211)*—Another top China automaker traded in Hong Kong, BYD is noteworthy because Warren Buffett took a major stake in the company in September 2008 and cashed in a $1.02 billion profit in July 2009.
- *General Steel Holdings (GSI)*—GSI has four production facilities in China and Mongolia capable of producing 4.8 million tons of steel products per year. Primary customers include Chinese consumer appliance and machine manufacturers, and construction companies. This small, but highly innovative company is one of the few in China in any industry that understands the advantage of a Western-style holding company structure.

Infrastructure Leaders

Think roads, rails, airports, and power companies, as well as facilities such as sports arenas, parks, and other public facilities, and you're thinking infrastructure companies.

- *Huaneng Power International, Inc. (HNP)*—China's largest independent power producer, with 16 operating power plants in 12 provinces and partial or controlling stakes in 18 power companies. Most of its facilities are coal-fired, but it has new cleaner plants under construction and is also growing through acquisitions.
- *Kinder Morgan Energy Partners (KMP)*—A major energy distribution company based in Houston, Texas, KMP owns part or all of 26,000 miles of natural gas pipelines, and owns 170 bulk terminals and rail facilities handling more than 87 million tons of coal and related products per year. The company has major consulting contracts in numerous developing countries, including China, providing expertise for pipeline and power distribution projects.
- *Navios Maritime Holdings (NM)*—A Greek shipping company with more than 40 vessels for hauling dry bulk products such as coal, grain, and iron ore. It also operates port facilities in South America and has long-term contracts with commodity

producers to deliver to customers around the world, including in China and other areas of Asia. China is also using this shipper to import bulk materials needed for earthquake recovery efforts in hard-hit Sichuan province.

- *Yingli Green Energy ADRs (YGE)*—China's only totally "green" power company, Yingli makes photovoltaic (PV) power cells and modules, which it incorporates into solar energy systems. Though based in China, Yingli gets the bulk of its sales in Europe, mostly from Germany and Spain.
- *ABB Limited (ABB)*—A Swiss conglomerate that provides power production, transmission, and automation technologies to utility and industrial customers in 100 countries around the world, including China and other developing markets. A solid earnings foundation comes from Europe, where ABB gets about half its total sales.
- *POSCO (PKX)*—A South Korean conglomerate that makes hot- and cold-rolled steel products for the auto and shipbuilding industries. Producing more than 30 million tons per year, it is the world's Number 3-ranked steelmaker.

Global Titans

Global titans are large companies with extensive international markets, stable or growing earnings, and stock prices that have weathered the recent market troubles well. All have proven market positions and pay worthwhile dividends. Some of the better ones are:

- *The Coca-Cola Co. (KO)*—Based in the United States, the world's largest soft drink producer.
- *PepsiCo Inc. (PEP)*—Major U.S.-based soft drink producer.
- *Diageo PLC (DEO)*—The world's largest producer of premium distilled spirits and beers, with eight of the world's top 20 brands. Based in Britain, but labels include Guinness Stout, Johnnie Walker, Jose Cuervo, Tanqueray Gin, and Smirnoff Vodka. (If your other investments go bad, you may be able to drown your sorrows at a shareholder discount.)

- *Yum! Brands Inc. (YUM)*—The world's largest fast-food opera- tor in terms of stores, with more than 36,000 outlets in 110 countries. Brands include KFC, Pizza Hut, Taco Bell, Long John Silver's, and A&W Root Beer. YUM! is opening more than one new restaurant per day in China—and could for years without saturating the markets.
- *McDonald's Corp. (MCD)*—The world's largest fast-food opera- tor in terms of sales.

Select Funds and Alternate Investments

For those who like to balance their individual stock selections with investments in funds and other alternative vehicles, here are some potential selections in those areas:

- *SPDR Gold Trust (GLD)*—For investors who want to buy gold without the worry of storing it or keeping it at home, the SPDR Gold Trust is an ETF that trades like a stock, but has a value that directly tracks the price of gold bullion (historically within plus-or-minus 2 percent).
- *EverBank Select Metals Account*—EverBank offers two types of gold accounts. One, in which your gold is pooled with that of other investors, eliminating storage and maintenance costs, requires a minimum deposit of $5,000. The other, in which you directly own the gold you purchase and it's held in your own private account, has a minimum deposit of $7,500. Both types of accounts can be set up online (www.everbank .com) or by phone at 866-326-6241. Be sure to tell them that you're reading *Fiscal Hangover* when you do. (Note: I do not receive compensation for any of these recommendations. I just like what they do and the products they offer!)
- *Market Vectors Russia SBI (RSX)*—An ETF that invests in shares of Russian companies with an emphasis on the energy, steel, and telecom industries.
- *iShare MSCI Brazil Fund (EWZ)*—A diversified ETF investing in a basket of stocks to mirror Brazil's leading market index.

- *RYDEX Series FDS, Inverse S&P 500 Fund (RYURX)*—A non-correlated ETF structured to move opposite to the movements in the Standard & Poor's 500 Index. A hedging choice for U.S.-heavy portfolios.
- *PowerShares Int'l. Dividend Achiever (PID)*—An ETF with a global income portfolio designed to help you spread risk internationally while also earning income.
- *Alpine Dynamic Dividend Fund (ADVDX)*—A specialized income-oriented ETF that uses a "dividend-harvest strategy" to enhance yields.
- *Chinese Renminbi Deposit Account at Everbank*—This account, denominated in Chinese renminbi (which many analysts feel is undervalued by as much as 60 percent) provides protection against currency risk in other Chinese investments, as well as offering the potential for exchange-rate gains. Requires a minimum deposit of $10,000 and is FDIC-insured against bank insolvency.

HOW YOU CAN ACTUALLY BUY AND SELL FOREIGN STOCKS

Now that I've given you some tips on finding and evaluating foreign stocks, there's one other issue that needs to be addressed. What should you do if you've done some diligent research into international companies and identified the stock opportunity of a lifetime—only to have your broker say he can't (or won't) buy it for you?

If you think that's a far-fetched notion, then you obviously haven't *truly* invested internationally yet. Otherwise, you'd know that most regular retail brokers in the United States aren't equipped to deal in stocks listed on foreign exchanges—*nor have they historically wanted to.* That applies to TD Ameritrade, Scottrade, and many other online discount brokers as well.

For far too long, if U.S. investors asked their local broker or financial adviser about buying a foreign stock, they were instantly warned about loose financial controls, political turmoil, economic uncertainty, and currency risks—a whole laundry list of reasons to avoid those securities. I want to assure you, however, that *those warnings are increasingly bogus in a truly global marketplace.*

Despite the misinformation often put forth discrediting foreign securities regulations, many of the best-performing foreign exchanges—Singapore, Thailand, South Korea, Australia, and the like—have first-class accounting standards, rigorous transparency, and histories of strong governance and oversight. In the wake of scandal after scandal, can the same be said about the NYSE and NASDAQ?

Besides, there are just too many opportunities overseas to pass up. In his book, *A Bull In China,* legendary investor Jim Rogers gave more than 140 stock ideas—but more than 100 of those are *not* listed on any U.S. exchange. The list I gave you isn't as exclusionary, but there are many other stocks I could have included that *can't* be traded in the United States. Fortunately, that's really *NOT* a problem—*IF* you're willing to slightly expand your brokerage horizons.

That's because success in trading foreign stocks really is *all about the broker.*

Finding the Right Broker

If your current broker can't talk you out of buying a foreign stock, she may finally give in and agree to do it after all. But be skeptical of this sudden reversal. U.S. brokers will sometimes attempt to purchase foreign securities for you through domestic market makers in the over-the-counter (OTC) market (sometimes known as the *pink sheets*). In the process, these brokers virtually guarantee that their clients will pay more for the stock than those buying it directly in the foreign market where it trades. These "middlemen" typically pocket up to 10 percent of the value of each trade in the very "thin" domestic OTC markets. Most investors aren't even aware of *how much* of their money winds up in the pockets of the intermediaries.

To efficiently purchase foreign stocks that aren't traded on U.S. markets as American Depositary Receipts (ADRs) requires a relationship with traders who deal in the targeted foreign markets. By executing orders directly on foreign exchanges, U.S. brokers can cut out the market maker—and capture the value otherwise lost to the middleman.

What Brokers *Not* to Use

Unfortunately, most U.S brokerage firms do not fall into this category. They don't provide direct access to foreign stocks, or they limit access to only a few securities, or grant it only through domestic OTC market makers. So, you have to shop around.

The first inclination when doing so is to check with the major international firms. Since they have offices all over the world, it would seem they'd be best positioned to trade directly on foreign exchanges. Surprisingly, this may not be the case. All too often, full-service brokerage firms aren't set up to handle foreign stock orders of small or even average size. SEC regulations regarding unregistered securities, related custody issues, and redundant stock symbols make foreign trading a cumbersome business for firms not specially set up to do it. As a result, some of the big houses either won't take a small order or will take them and fill them as market makers at high markups (which they're not required to disclose) or rotten exchange rates (that are also often hidden).

As noted earlier, most of the online brokers—especially the discounters—don't offer direct foreign stock-trading services, either. These brokers will usually steer you toward ADRs, exchange-traded funds, or closed-end country-specific mutual funds. If an online broker does offer trading in foreign stocks, it's usually a very small part of their business and entails special restrictions or minimum-wealth requirements.

Can Your Current Broker Get the Job Done?

Still, before you go running off in search of a broker to buy foreign stocks, definitely check with your existing broker to see if he can handle the business. Remember, though, that they don't want to *lose* your business, so they may tell you, "Sure, no problem," when in fact the broker has no real concept of whether the trades can be effectively carried out or not.

Although more and more firms have started offering foreign stock services, they might require high minimum investments, deal only with limited markets, require security access, and have high commissions or additional fees and costs. All of these can make for a bad trade—and the best way to avoid one of those is to keep it from happening in the first place, which you can do by asking five simple questions to see whether your broker knows what she's talking about and what capabilities the firm actually has. The key questions are:

1. What exchange rate do I get? Currency conversion should cost you no more than 10 to 15 basis points (a basis point is 0.01 percent), but many firms charge 1 to 3 percent. That's a big difference—and, unless you ask, you may never know you paid it.
2. Can I be certain my order will be executed directly on the local foreign exchange, and not by a market maker in the United States using the pink sheets?
3. Can I place "limit orders"—those restricting execution to a specified price or better—in the foreign currency?
4. Can I choose to receive dividends and proceeds from sales directly in a foreign currency?
5. Are there minimum-transaction amounts, special fees for overseas orders, or other hidden costs and miscellaneous fees? Will you provide a list of all charges?

Once you receive satisfactory answers to these questions, you're in business. If you receive unsatisfactory answers, it's time to go elsewhere. Fortunately, if you need help finding a competent, trustworthy broker who specializes in foreign stocks, I've got some good suggestions. And be assured, I have absolutely no financial interest in any of these firms—I'm providing their names only as a service to future wealth builders like you.

Full-Service Brokers

With full-service brokers, you get more than simple trade execution. Access to research reports, help in portfolio management, and access to a wide variety of markets are included (along with a little hand-holding if needed), but commissions are higher, too.

• *Euro-Pacific Capital*—Founded in 1980 and headquartered in Darien, Connecticut, Euro-Pacific is a full service, NASD-registered broker/dealer recognized for its expertise in foreign markets and securities. Peter Schiff—author of *Crash Proof 2.0: How to Profit from the Economic Collapse* and a pioneer in the field of global investing for individuals—is the firm's president. Euro-Pacific purchases foreign securities in local markets in the local currency, and focuses on helping clients select a portfolio of relatively conservative, high-dividend paying foreign equities. Such stocks provide three potential sources of protection:

1. They pay good dividends, many of which qualify for the lower dividend tax.
2. These dividends are paid in currencies other than the U.S. dollar, meaning their value will rise as the dollar falls, as will the principal value of the underlying shares.
3. The investments provide the potential for true capital gains, as the shares themselves may appreciate in terms of their local currencies.

Although Euro-Pacific specializes in international securities, it also offers access to all U.S. stocks and bonds, and provides a full array of other financial services, including retirement and trust accounts, financial planning, checking accounts, life insurance, and annuities.

> *Contact:*
> Euro-Pacific Capital
> Peter Schiff, President
> 10 Corbin Drive, Suite B
> Darien, CT 06820
> Phone: 203-662-9700 or 800-727-7922 toll free
> Fax: 203-662-9771
> Web site: www.europac.net

• *International Assets Advisory, LLC*—This firm has championed the cause of globally diversifying portfolios for nearly three decades. It does its own independent analysis and works to develop proper asset-allocation strategies that enhance returns and lower portfolio risk. The IAA team has direct access to an array of international markets and the stocks and bonds traded there, but not on U.S. exchanges. The firm also offers full-service brokerage accounts and expertise in the domestic markets, with financial, retirement, and estate planning services.

> *Contact:*
> International Assets Advisory, LLC
> Jeff Winn, Managing Partner
> 300 South Orange Ave., Suite 1100
> Orlando, FL 32801
> Phone: 407-254-1500 or 800-432-0000 toll free
> Fax: 407-254-1505
> E-mail: jwinn@iaac.com
> Web site: www.iaac.com

Discount Brokers

If you do your own research and make your own decisions, discount brokers can provide execution of your orders at a minimum cost.

- *Interactive Brokers*—Interactive says it provides "direct-access trading worldwide at lower trading costs," and they follow through on that claim, offering direct access to options, futures, forex, stocks, and bonds in over 70 market centers worldwide from a single Universal Account. Commissions are clearly stated for each type of trade and market. The firm provides straightforward stock trades, but offers experienced investors plenty of sophisticated trading strategies as well.

> *Contact:*
> Interactive Brokers
> Phone: 877-442-2757 toll free
> Web site: www.interactivebrokers.com.

- *Charles Schwab Global Investing Service*—Schwab's international service offers access to more than 40 foreign markets and expertise in handling the complexities of trading non-U.S. instruments. However, only orders of $5,000 or more will be done directly on a foreign exchange.

Contact:
Schwab Global Investing Service
Phone: 800-992-4685 toll free
Web site: www.schwab.com (although it's difficult to navigate to the global service through this broad portal)

- *E★Trade*—Now offers online trading in six global markets—Canada, France, Germany, Hong Kong, Japan, and the United Kingdom—while allowing customers to diversify among five currencies so they can manage exchange-rate risk and hedge their U.S. dollar exposure.

Contact:
E★Trade Global Investing
Phone: 800-ETRADE-1 or 800-387-2331 toll free
Web site: www.etrade.com

U.S. Banks

Most domestic U.S. banks offer limited investment services for their regular clients, but a few offer more. Here's one.

- *EverBank*—EverBank is an innovator in electronic global banking, providing clients with opportunities for capital appreciation across an array of financial markets. It provides all the personal deposit accounts (checking, money market, and CDs) you'd expect from a normal bank, but also offers a wide range of investment services in foreign currencies. It does everything from executing your stock trades on foreign exchanges and providing access to high-quality foreign bonds to letting you speculate on currencies and metals. EverBank's World Currency Accounts also offer a simple way to diversify your portfolio out of the U.S. dollar. You can open a Single-Currency CD in one of more than 15 foreign currencies and earn an interest at local rates, or select a Multi-Currency CD structured with a variety of currencies, each strategically designed to focus on a specific regional strength or area of geopolitical or economic development. EverBank also recently introduced a new currency investment product—DollarBull CDs, for those who think the dollar is ready to get stronger.

> *Contact:*
> EverBank
> Phone: 888-882-EVER toll free
> Fax: 888-882-6977
> E-mail: service@everbank.com
> Web site: www.everbank.com

Foreign Banks

There is always the option of opening up a foreign bank account directly. This will involve some extra effort on your part, but the added privacy and security benefits may be important enough to justify the effort. The following offshore banks have access to multiple foreign stock markets, as well as offering conventional banking services.

> *Jyske Bank (Denmark)*
> *Contact:*
> Thomas Fischer
> Jyske Bank Private Banking
> Vesterbrogade 9, DK-1780
> Copenhagen V, DENMARK
> Phone: (45-3) 378-7812; Fax: (45-3) 378-7833
> E-mail: Fischer@Jyskebank.dk.
> Minimum Investment: US$25,000

> *Weber Hartmann Vrijhof & Partners (Switzerland)*
>
> *Contacts:*
> Robert Vrijhof or Rene Schatt
> Weber, Hartmann, Vrijhof & Partners Ltd.
> Zurichstrasse 110B, CH-8134
> Adliswil-Zurich, Switzerland
> Phone: (41-1) 709-1115; Fax: (41-1) 709-1113
> Account Minimum: US$100,000

Bank Julius Baer

Contact:
Martin Bucher
Bank Julius Baer
Bahnofstrasse 36, CH–8010
Zurich, Switzerland
Phone: (41-1) 228-5111; Fax: (41-1) 211-2560
Web site: www.juliusbaer.com
Account Minimum: US$1,000,000

MOVING ON TO THE STRATEGIES

I've now given you a solid overview of the types of investments on which you should focus in your search for hangover relief, as well as the global regions, specific countries, and most-promising market sectors and industries to explore. You also have in hand a fairly lengthy list of starting-point stocks—those that I believe have top prospects and are either based in the aforementioned countries or derive a major portion of their revenues from operations in those markets.

All you need now are some specific strategies for actually getting those investments into your portfolio in the proper proportions and profitably managing them once you do—and that's what you'll find in Chapter 12. So, turn the page and begin taking the final steps needed to launch your personal economic recovery and light the fuse to ignite your own future wealth-building boom.

CHAPTER 12

———

NEVER GET FOOLED AGAIN

The Pyramid Strategies

Becoming wealthy is not a matter of how much you earn, who your parents are, or what you do. . . . It is a matter of managing your money properly.

—Noel Whittaker, Australian author and financial adviser

I've now given you repeated reassurances that, as bad as things were and as uncertain as they may still seem, both the economy and the stock markets will recover—eventually. Always have, always will.

But I've also shown you that those recoveries alone aren't enough. To regain what you've lost and build even greater future wealth, you must adopt an international perspective, looking outside the United States to the developing economies in general—and China in particular. I've even pointed you toward some specific industries and companies you'll likely want to target.

However, I wouldn't have done my job if all this book concluded with was a few stock picks. What you really need to succeed is *a complete strategy,* with elements ranging from portfolio structure and market analysis to methods for future stock selections and some tips on the best ways to implement your strategy. And that's what this final chapter provides.

I show you how to build a simple, internationally concentrated portfolio with built-in safety brakes that you can maintain with minimal time and effort—and maximum results. It features a combination of stable, income-producing investments that assure long-term asset growth, along with just enough speculative flavor to spice up your quest for new wealth without adding in more risk than you can handle. By the end of this chapter, you'll be fully prepared to successfully manage your own portfolio using a simple, consistent process that ramps up your returns, tightly controls your risks and enables you to outperform most of your fellow investors.

WHERE MOST INVESTORS GO WRONG

Studies show that most investors lose money over time because they don't—or can't—stick to a well-defined set of rules. For some, this is driven by reckless personal behavior in search of profits. For others, it's the constant shift between bad decisions and bad advice that creates whopping errors and poor performance.

Most of the time, however, investors incur these losses simply because they don't grasp the concept of *Gambler's Ruin.* You may not be familiar with Gambler's Ruin, but you need to understand it for two simple reasons—especially given current market conditions. First, Gambler's Ruin can represent the difference between long-term financial success and outright failure. Second, the negative outcome it produces is a foregone conclusion from a mathematical standpoint.

THE INSIDIOUS COURSE OF GAMBLER'S RUIN

Gambler's Ruin is a mathematical principle that deals with the preservation of assets—or, more accurately, the probability that you'll lose them over time. Here's how it works:

Imagine that Player One and Player Two each have a finite number of pennies, which they flip one at a time, calling heads or tails. The player who calls the flip correctly gets to keep the penny.

Since a penny has only two sides, it would seem on the surface that each player has a 50 percent probability of winning—and that's indeed the case for each individual flip. But, if the process is repeated indefinitely, the probability that one of the two players will eventually lose *all* of his pennies must be 100 percent. In mathematical terms, the chances that Player One and Player Two (P1 and P2, respectively) will be rendered penniless are expressed as:

$$P1 = n2 / (n1 + n2)$$
$$P2 = n1 / (n1 + n2)$$

In English, what this says is that, if you are one of the players, your chance of going bankrupt is equal to the ratio of pennies your opponent starts out with to the total number of pennies. While there are wrinkles in the theory, the basic concept is that the player starting with the *smaller* number of pennies has *the greater chance of going bankrupt*.

Most people who've been to Las Vegas understand this at some level, and also recognize that, the longer you stay at the tables, the greater the probability that you will lose. What most people miss, however, is that the same principle holds true when it comes to investing. Since Wall Street casinos (aka investment houses, hedge funds, mutual funds, and the like) have more pennies than their individual patrons (retail investors), they can play the game longer—and, more often than not, that means they come out ahead because the smaller players get wiped out (or give up).

Unless you have some means of protecting your assets—whether you're at the gaming tables or in the investment markets—the principle of Gambler's Ruin mandates that you will eventually give them up. It may be through losses or the attrition of accumulated commissions and fees, but if you do not change your behavior, it *will* happen. If you start with lots of money, it may take several generations, but the fact that it takes extra time doesn't invalidate the math.

INTRODUCING THE 50-40-10 PYRAMID STRATEGIES

So, what's the secret? How do you beat Gambler's Ruin? The easiest approach is the most obvious—just don't play the game. But longer term, that's simply not realistic when it comes to investing.

A more practical approach is to establish a properly *concentrated* portfolio that will help level the playing field by both increasing your returns and reducing your risk—a portfolio based on the 50-40-10 Pyramid structure I developed many years ago and that I regularly advocate in my *Money Morning* articles and to audiences around the world.

I'm going to explain that structure to you in just a second, but before I do, I want to make one thing perfectly clear—when I talk about a Pyramid strategy, I'm *NOT* talking about pyramid "schemes" of the Bernie Madoff ilk. What I'm talking about is a time-tested and battle-proven principle of portfolio structure, one that's far different from the conventional models foisted on the investing public by traditional Wall Street types—one that ensures I have both minimum risks and a "positive expectancy" in my investments.

If you're not familiar with the term, *positive expectancy* relates to how much money an investor can expect to make for every dollar placed at risk. This is far different from the concept of *how often you win*, which is what most retail investors are programmed to think about in their investing. They are more concerned about winning a certain percentage of the time when what really matters is that you win more money than you lose *over time*—no matter *how many times* you lose.

FISCAL FLASHPOINT

I'm vehemently opposed to the way Wall Street presents the concept of diversification, which has led most investors to believe that a well-rounded portfolio means a lot of stocks, a few bonds, some real estate, a little gold, and some cash. All that really amounts to is spreading around the pennies in the Gambler's Ruin equation. What really matters is how you *concentrate* your money—aimed first at ensuring the security of your returns and second at maximizing your profits relative to the risks you do take.

If you've never thought about investing in this way, you may be shocked to learn that most of the best traders and investors are right only *40 percent of the time,* yet they still rack up consistent profits over time. That's because they only do trades with a positive expectancy— trades that give them *huge gains* when they win and only *small losses* when they're wrong.

In other words, consistent risk management is more important than profits over long periods of time. My take is simple . . . *if you properly manage the risks above all else, the returns will come.*

Another way to think about this is that having the appropriate portfolio structure is a lot like having good DNA. It helps ensure that you have a good, long life, but is constructed without reference to short-term gyrations. In money terms, that means *having the right portfolio structure at all times* is more important than making good individual stock picks—although *those certainly do help!*

Now back to the 50-40-10 Pyramid. When properly structured, it will ensure that you *always* have the correct mix of conservative positions and aggressive holdings—regardless of practically anything the market is trying to throw your way. To explain the name, the 50 refers to what I call *base-builder investments,* the 40 is the percentage of the portfolio devoted to *global growth and income positions* and the 10 consists of speculative plays—what I call the *rocket riders.*

Base–Builder Investments: 50 Percent

Base–builder investments make up the safety-and-balance portion of the portfolio—conservative (actually defensive) positions that will hold the bulk of their value better than other choices in practically any situation, thus protecting you from severe economic declines like the "perfect financial storm" we've recently experienced. (An example of a good base-building selection is the Vanguard Wellington Fund, which is discussed later in this chapter.) That's not to say they won't feel the heat when the going gets tough, it's just that they will take less punishment and be far less volatile than other sections of the portfolio during the bad times. This speaks volumes—not only to the don't-lose-it-in-the-first-place argument, but also, and more importantly, to the notion of having a stabilizing influence in your portfolio *at all times, NOT* just when it's convenient.

Global Growth and Income Positions: 40 Percent

The global growth and income portion of the portfolio consists of stocks and funds with an international focus—either based abroad or deriving much of their earnings from foreign sales or assets—and a strong emphasis on dividends. They provide a stream of cold, hard cash—even in range-bound markets (which is what studies show we have roughly 85 percent of the time)—as well as a thick layer of financial armor to protect against any domestic market or economic disruptions.

The key here is that most investors simply don't understand that the combination of growth *and* dividends can offer as much as a 22-to-1 advantage over pure growth stocks when it comes to investment returns over time. (And Wall Street hasn't helped matters by foisting the myth of growth-stock superiority on millions of investors for more than 40 years.) As a result, growth and income stocks are significantly under-weighted in most investors' portfolios—even though, as my grandmother Mimi used to say, they're *not* just for little old gray-haired ladies (and she *was* one).

Rocket Riders: 10 Percent

The rocket rider plays—often involving aggressive stocks in special situations or made using options or other more speculative vehicles—offer spectacular upside potential and can lift overall performance well above market averages during good times, even though they constitute just 10 percent of the portfolio's holdings, at most.

Many people are reluctant to put *any* of their money into speculative, rocket rider–type plays. What they don't understand is that, if you have the bulk of your money in the safety and balance section, as well as a properly assembled collection of growth and income choices, *you have the freedom to screw up.* You can comfortably take the occasional potshot without having to worry about ruining your entire financial future.

Many other people are just the opposite. They love the rocket riders and came into the current crisis with far too many of them—and hardly any income stocks. They also viewed each investment as an individual entity, with virtually nonexistent consideration given to overall balance. That's why they were hurt so badly. Instead of getting pushed gently around—as those following the 50-40-10

(VERY IMPORTANT) FISCAL FLASHPOINT

It is not necessary—or even prudent—to invest 100 percent of your capital in search of a 10 percent gain when *the same result can be achieved by investing 10 percent for a 100 percent gain*. Still, the first approach is exactly the one most people take—even those whose goal is high income. Because the risk is proportional to the reward, it can be an acceptable strategy in stable, prosperous times—but that is unlikely to be the case in the next decade. If the current economic disruption continues as long as I expect, this standard approach to portfolio returns will most likely produce *substandard results*—and it won't give you a hedge against the unexpected either.

portfolio structure did—investors with an excessive percentage of rocket riders got hit with a hammer . . . right between the eyes. Then they fell backward into the ditch they conveniently dug for themselves over the course of the past few years.

Get Added Protection by Using Protective Stops

I also augment the defensive aspects of the 50-40-10 Pyramid strategy by *always* using *protective stops* to help maximize (and preserve) profits and prevent small losses from becoming catastrophic ones.

If you're not familiar with the concept, a protective stop is simply a standing, or good-till-canceled (GTC), order telling the brokerage to sell your long position should the stock's price fall to a specified level—or buy back a short holding if its price rises to a given level. Once the market price reaches the designated level, the stop order is automatically converted to a market order, which will be filled at the next available price. (Be aware, however, that in fast-moving markets, the actual execution price may be different from the specified stop price.)

No matter how you "feel" about the prospects for a particular company or the outlook for the market in general, protective stops are an essential money-management tool—and not just in bear markets. One of my favorite Wall Street adages tells us, "You can never go broke taking profits." Applying stops in bull markets on stocks in which you already have substantial gains ensures that your profits will *stay* substantial—and that you *will* take them. By moving the level of your stop higher (or lower for short positions) as a stock moves in your favor (a so-called trailing stop), you lock in an ever-increasing portion of your profits and take the emotion out of deciding to sell should the stock (or market) turn against you.

Many people are reluctant to use protective stops because they believe stops force them to sell stocks that appear to be trading cheaply, that have good prospects, or represent a company that's a household name. They tell me they just don't "feel good" about cutting loose a company that well known or that's believed to be too big

---

FISCAL FLASHPOINT

One absolute rule regarding the use of protective stops: While adjusting stops regularly as prices move in your favor is an essential strategy, you should *NEVER* move your stops when prices move *against* you—in other words, down on a long position, or up on a short position. That *reduces* your level of protection and negates the purpose of using stops in the first place.

While your risk tolerances may vary, I suggest starting with a 25 percent stop on every investment. In other words, if you buy a $20 stock, place your initial stop at $15. This gives your position room to move—reducing the chances of missing out on a big profit by being stopped out just before a major advance—while also preventing a small early loss from becoming a catastrophic one. If you're tempted to dismiss this logic, just ask yourself how much money you could have saved had you been stopped out a long time ago, just as this crisis was getting started.

---

to fail. In answer to that, I have just two words: General Motors! Or, Lehman Brothers . . . but that's four.

Besides, in down markets, dumping your losers while the losses are still manageable is precisely what you *want* to do. You don't want them to become major disasters—no matter how familiar the name. And believe me, history—especially recent history—is full of such names. In addition to GM and Lehman Brothers, there's Countrywide, Citigroup, Bear Stearns, AIG, Home Savings and, further back, Pan-American World Airways, Eastern Airlines, Enron, MCI WorldCom, Montgomery Ward . . . the list's too long for a book this size (and this is a pretty good-sized book).

So, *always* use protective stops. They're a key element of effective money management and risk control, the two primary factors—not, as many people think, astute stock picking—that will determine whether you're among the losers or the winners when the economy recovers and that next stock market turnabout comes.

FISCAL FLASHPOINT

One of the problems that plagues most investment advisers—and virtually all investors—is that knowing *when to sell* is far harder than knowing when to buy. Protective stops, placed on both your losing and winning positions, remove the pressure of having to make that decision. They also facilitate calm, predetermined action in lieu of out-of-control, knee-jerk reactions—and lower the ol' "ulcer index," too.

HOW DO YOU FILL THE PORTFOLIO SEGMENTS?

With respect to actually filling each of the 50-40-10 portfolio segments, I gave you some insights into some countries and industries I favor, and even mentioned a few companies that might be appropriate. However, since you'll be doing most of the work on your own, I thought I'd best provide some additional details on how I make my selections.

Whenever I'm ready to make a new investment (meaning I have some cash in my pocket, usually from profits just taken), I begin with a broad market assessment. This involves a simple five-step process that helps me group information and make timely decisions. It's a combination of top-down (which is what most pros use) and bottom-up analysis, in which I review:

1. *The present world outlook*—Is the global economy currently booming, trending higher, chugging along in neutral, sliding back, or collapsing—and how long is that condition likely to last?
2. *Trends and money flows*—Which regions and countries are gaining ground, which are losing, and what factors or trends are responsible for the movement of wealth from one to the other? How strong are those trends, and are they likely to continue? Remember the list in Chapter 11.

FISCAL FLASHPOINT

We all like to see things going well, but just because they aren't is no reason *not* to buy. In fact, many of the best buys I've ever made have come during the worst of times. That's because high levels of uncertainty are frequently accompanied by low prices. By the time uncertainty is resolved, prices will most likely have risen. So, a good strategy—assuming all of your other criteria are met—is to buy when markets are *at their worst,* even if you're ahead of time. Not only do you get value at a discount price, but you get a bigger margin of safety in times of uncertainty. If things are already bad when you buy a good stock, odds are they'll get better rather than worse. There are no guarantees, of course, but most of the time it's better to be early to the party than the last guy there before the lights are turned out.

One added point: In answering these questions, don't make the mistake of *thinking too small.* For example, invention of a new medical device is *a micro trend,* while development of a new fertilizer to be used in 30 countries based on exclusive government permissions is a *macro trend.* Inflation, clean water, energy transitions . . . these are all worldwide trends that will cause money to move—*and you want to move with it.* We discussed that in Chapters 10 and 11.

3. *Stock screens*—These help me step down from the big picture to more specific companies or regional funds that are benefiting from the trends and overall economic situation—or, even better, ready to benefit in the future. I have more on specific values I like to use as part of this process in just a minute.
4. *Technical indicators*—These provide me with guidance on when and at what price levels to buy, as well as helping me decide where to put initial protective stops when I do. This doesn't have to be complicated, and I discuss my favorite indicators in a couple of pages.

274 DR. FITZ-GERALD'S AMAZING HOME REMEDY

5. *Risk assessment*—This is merely a gut analysis of the likelihood I might be wrong on any of the first four measures, which helps me decide how much of my available portfolio assets I should concentrate in a given section of the 50-40-10 Pyramid or any particular investment within those segments. If I'm losing sleep over any position I've taken, I've bitten off more than I can chew. So it's time to lighten up.

FISCAL FLASHPOINT

With respect to Step Number 2, you should always strive to have *as many trends as possible* working in your favor when making any specific investment. The more trends a company is riding, the greater the odds that your investment in its stock will be a success—and the lower your risk of an unexpected setback. Trends—especially the globally unstoppable ones like China's growth or the others I outline later—simply don't reverse overnight. Besides, the current ones also have trillions of dollars behind them, which only adds to the wind in their sails.

Procedures 1, 2, and 5 are based primarily on experience and observation, with only a few quantifiable measures, most of which are specific to the occasion. As such, I won't discuss those in greater depth. But I will offer some added tips on using stock screens and technical indicators.

Some Basic Guidelines for Using Stock Screens

I'm far from alone in using stock-screening programs to identify new opportunities, but there is one thing you need to recognize from the outset: Screens are useless unless you know exactly *what* you are looking for—*and why.* So, what should you be looking for now? Here are five questions you'll want the screen to answer:

1. *Does the stock line up with one or more of the unstoppable global trends?* These include:

- The economic growth and expansion of consumerism in China, India, Brazil, Eastern Europe, and so on.
- The huge expansion in spending on infrastructure enhancements in those same regions.
- The weak U.S. dollar, its translation into domestic inflation and the continued decoupling of the U.S. economy from those of the developing nations.
- Rising interest rates likely to come in 2010 and beyond.
- A global resource crisis due to increased consumption and depletion.
- Growing fundamentalism and the potential for war, terrorism, and increasing ugliness.

2. *Does the stock maintain the proper balance between risk and reward?* Without even realizing it, most investors take too much risk relative to the potential reward. They think they're investing when what they're really doing is speculating. As a means of doing a "gut check," ask yourself whether you could live without the money you've just invested should the stock, option, or whatever go to zero. If the answer is no, chances are you're speculating when you think you're investing.

3. *Does the stock have superior fundamentals and growing earnings?* Look for a history of high margins, steady cash flow, and earnings surprises (a pattern of beating expectations).

4. *Is the stock fairly priced?* Buying below the "fair price line" increases your chances of winning. Be aware, however, that an ideal reading on Number 3 often leads to high valuations as well. A hidden benefit with respect to valuation may be a lack of investor understanding of what the company actually does or "research obscurity," meaning few analysts have examined the company, so the amount of public information on it is thin.

5. *Can you reduce or eliminate risk?* Unsystematic risk can be reduced by diversification. Systematic risk results from movement of the market as a whole and cannot be diversified away. Evaluate standard deviation and beta (or variance from the market) with respect to the stock's historical price movements.

Finding stocks about which you can answer yes to all five of these considerations will:

- Greatly increase your odds of winning bigger—and more often.
- Let you take advantage of the market's normal behavior.

My favorite stock screen identifies real business and a history of real annual growth, defined as follows:

Revenue Growth Year to Date (YTD) Versus Year-Ago YTD	> = 20%
Earnings Per Share (EPS) Growth Rate, Year Versus Year	> = 20%
Percentage of Recent Quarterly Earnings Surprises	> = 5%
Annual Growth Rate in EPS over a 5-Year Period	> = 20%
Next Year Projected Growth Rate	> = 0%
Price-to-Earnings Growth Factor (PEG)	<1

As far as locating a good preprogrammed stock screener that will let you find what you want with ease of use, I suggest you begin with the MSN Deluxe Stock Screener. It's *FREE* and a great place to start.

FISCAL FLASHPOINT

One of the primary reasons for using stock screens is that, even when the market is doing its worst, there are some individual stocks that are *doing their best.* Finding a potential winner while all around you are languishing in bearish gloom can be a source of joy—and a great launching pad in your quest for greater wealth once things improve.

Make Sensible Use of Technical Indicators

A lot of market technicians *live* technical analysis, eating, drinking, and breathing every little indicator—and taking pride in identifying obscure new ones. Me, I just *use* some of the most reliable and time-tested indicators to improve my timing and my sense of accuracy in the selection of stocks that are *ready to move*.

I feel that putting in more effort than that is essentially a waste of time because the true goal of technical analysis is to identify and get on board trends, yet history has shown that the markets (and most individual stocks) are range-bound roughly 85 percent of the time—meaning the trends technicians are looking for are really in force only 15 percent of the time. As such, I try to ignore the *noise* and work with the market, using only those indicators that typically signal bottoms, tops, or reversal points. The key indicators I follow, all of which can be found in the technical section of most stock screeners, are:

- *The state of the markets*—Are conditions relatively stable, or are they plagued with uncertainty and excess volatility?
- *Volume*—Are there more sellers than buyers? Is volume rising or falling?
- *The 200-day moving average*—Is it flat, moving higher, or on a downward slope?
- *The 21-period EMA (exponential moving average)*—I've spent literally thousands of hours of computing time analyzing different time frames, and what I've found is that a 21-period EMA best represents the market's natural rhythm over most of them. It's also highly correlated to the Fibonacci Cycle and Sequence, and is a key factor in determining the market's direction. Sometimes, the market is a little *tighter* (meaning fewer than 21 periods might be more appropriate), or *looser* (meaning more than 21 could be better)—but, in general, a periodicity of 21 seems to be most acceptable.
- *R-squared*—R-squared values range from 0 to 100; values over 80 typically signal pending reversals. This is a *predictive* indicator.
- *Relative Strength Indicator (RSI)*—This is a momentum indicator that compares the magnitude of recent gains to recent losses in an attempt to determine overbought and oversold conditions of an asset. Over 70 equals expensive; under 30 equals cheap.

Most preset screens set the RSI at 14 trading periods, but I've found better results using shorter periods, with a setting of 4 being my favorite for picking out trading entries—especially when it comes to eliminating daily noise.

Based on these indicators, I look for the following criteria when considering entry to a *long position:*

- 200-day moving average is heading up, or it is flat and rolling over.
- 21-period EMA is headed up.
- Volume has spiked in the last five days.
- R-square has topped 80 and is rolling over.
- The 4-period RSI is under 30 and rising.

And these are the criteria I hope to see when considering entry to a *short position:*

- 200-day moving average is heading down, or it is flat and rolling over.
- 21-period EMA is headed down.
- Volume is drifting, with no real pattern, up or down.
- R-square has topped 80 and is rolling over.
- The 4-period RSI is above 70 and falling.

I'm not going to spend any more time talking to you about theoretical use of these indicators. Just go online, search out the MSN Deluxe Stock Screener or one of the numerous other free screeners, plug in these values, and see what you come up with. Then experiment and see if you can improve on my recommendations.

FINDING QUALITY DIVIDEND PAYERS

One item that I didn't include in the preceding section on stock screeners was dividend payouts—which, as you should realize by now, I consider *an essential component* of any sensible wealth-building plan, as well as a strong defensive element in the lower 90 percent of your Pyramid portfolio. All of the screeners I know about give you the option to specify dividend payout levels and yields, and you should always do so when running an initial screen. I didn't mention it earlier just because I want to talk more about how to find quality dividend payers here.

AN INVESTMENT YOU CAN TAKE TO A DESERT ISLAND

While dividends can and should be a part of the base-builder portion of your portfolio—the 50 percent segment—the real point of concentration there is on *keeping risk low*. Remember, as I've noted several times, what you earn is not nearly as important as *what you keep*.

An example of a holding that I've considered to be an ideal anchor for my Pyramid portfolio for many years is the Vanguard Wellington Fund (VWELX). This no-load fund invests 60 to 70 percent of its assets in dividend-paying common stocks of large and medium-sized companies that have well-established leadership positions in key industries, including energy and communications. Many of the companies it holds also have significant international exposure.

Although the Wellington Fund, like everyone else, lost ground in 2008, it preserved investor value better than most other domestic income funds, maintaining a five-year growth rate of 14.92 percent, helped by its dividend yield, which stood at 3.85 percent in mid-2009. It also paced the 2009 summer recovery, posting a 20.78 percent return through July 31, 2009.

The Wellington Fund has been a hero throughout its history, serving as a key safety valve in both flat and down markets for those following my Pyramid strategy. In fact, because of its unmatched record for predictability and its potential for compound growth over the years, I refer to it as my Desert Island Fund—the one I'd choose to own if I were forced to live on a desert island and rely on just one investment for the rest of my life. (Minimum initial investment is $10,000.)

Though many day traders and short-term-oriented "active" investors scoff when asked about it, *income investing* has never gone out of style—*and it never will.*

Indeed, some studies show that dividend-paying stocks have accounted for 60 percent of total stock market returns since 1870—and reinvestment of dividends might have pushed that figure up to as much as 97 percent, depending on the time frames analyzed! What's more, dividend stocks have not only outperformed the markets in broad terms, but they have done so at *less risk.*

Most people dramatically underestimate how powerful this is—but I'm not about to let you make this mistake. That's why I want to provide some added advice on how to stock the 40 percent portion of your Pyramid portfolio with high-dividend-paying shares.

First though, a couple of current events headlines. In the second quarter of 2009, a record-setting 367 U.S. companies decreased their dividends, leaving many income investors shell-shocked. Yet, at the same time, 283 companies authorized *increased* payouts—and, according to Standard & Poor's, an even larger group held their payouts in line.

Not surprisingly—at least not to me anyway—the companies raising their dividends were predominantly *international* in nature. Virtually all of them also project explosive growth potential in the emerging markets.

How explosive? Consider this. While the TV gurus were talking about how much trouble China was having because of the U.S. woes, the Shenzhen 100 Index quietly climbed *110.10 percent* in the first six months of 2009. By comparison, the S&P 500—despite the strongest month of July since 2002—was up just 5.98 percent in seven months. Yet, even with such a stunning run-up in the first half of 2009, most Chinese companies were still compelling buys, with some priced for just pennies on the dollar relative to their underlying value. Add in solid dividend payouts, and many were even more attractive.

The story was much the same in other parts of the world, too. Not with equal clarity, mind you, but with every bit of the potential—especially as it relates to dividends. At the end of the second quarter of 2009, for example, there were at least 115 international income funds with yields *greater than 6 percent.*

Here are some things to look for when seeking stocks or funds—both domestic and foreign—with the same kind of potential:

- *International Sales*—It's becoming clearer by the day that developing countries like China and India will almost certainly leave the Western world in the dust. As such, it makes sense to begin the hunt for the world's best dividend payers with those that offer significant exposure to emerging markets. My favorites include companies that derive 40 percent or more of their sales from the Pacific Rim—and specifically from China.

- *Payout Ratios*—One way of gauging the relative security of your investment in any given company is the dividend payout ratio. In case you're not familiar with the term, the *payout ratio* is the percentage of a company's profit that it pays out to shareholders in the form of dividends. While there are exceptions, if the payout ratio approaches 100 percent (and the choice I'm considering is *not* a Canadian trust or limited partnership created expressly for dividend-payout purposes), that's a red flag in my mind. The reason is, if business conditions stink or management doesn't have as good a handle on cash flow as it thinks it does, any decrease in earnings will obviously affect dividend-payout plans. On the other hand, if the payout is around 50 percent, for example, history suggests that is a sustainable level and management is unlikely to severely decrease the dividend payment—barring catastrophic earnings, of course.

- *Distribution Source*—Thanks to all manner of accounting tricks—politely called *adjustments* in financial jargon—it's harder than ever to determine where a company's income is coming from. For example, some investments, particularly Canadian income trusts and shipping partnerships, like to pay from available cash flow rather than from more traditional sources like bottom-line earnings. Not only does this make the payout ratio higher, but it can be misleading as to the sustainability of future dividend payments.

Generally speaking, dividends come from earnings, and they're usually predictable. Sometimes, however, special distributions come from short- or long-term capital gains, the one-time sale of assets or accounting transactions. While it's nice to get these bonus payouts, don't confuse them with the cash you can expect to get from ongoing operations. Be wary of return-on-capital events as well. These are also nice gifts for investors, but they're not regular either, resulting instead from such items as tax savings, depreciation, or write-ups in the value of company assets.

FISCAL FLASHPOINT

Return-of-capital transactions are a danger sign in my book because the firm may be trying to give back your original investment, and that's a strategy often pursued when a dividend cut is imminent, but not yet announced. Which, of course, is one thing you never want to see, especially in uncertain times like these.

Another reason for my emphasis on dividend-paying stocks is that they tend to be more stable than their nondividend-paying brethren. Because of their income streams, investors are apt to treat them better when markets get rocky—hanging on rather than selling and driving prices down. As a rule, dividend payers outperform nondividend stocks by even more in down markets than in rallies. That downdraft resistance helps portfolios with higher yields last longer when the withdrawal process starts—a very important consideration for investors nearing or already in retirement.

Investors who consistently reinvest dividends also substantially expand their asset base in down markets, because the dividends buy more shares—and that puts those investors way ahead of the game when the markets eventually recover and stock prices rebound.

SITTING ON THE SIDELINES IS *NOT* A VIABLE OPTION—OR IS IT?

Even when they're receiving a healthy stream of dividend income, many investors feel uncomfortable staying in the markets during uncertain times. They'd rather sit on the sidelines. That may appear safe, but a couple of studies have found it really isn't.

For example, after looking at S&P 500 returns between 1993 and 2007, Davis Advisors Funds found that investors who remained invested and didn't try to "time" the market made an average annualized return of 10.5 percent. But investors who missed just the 30 *best* trading days over this stretch saw that return drop all the way down to 2.2 percent. And, the more strong days an investor missed, the worse the returns got— actually turning into a 7.4 percent loss if the *90 best days* were missed.

Those results were seemingly confirmed by a study conducted by Birinyi Associates and published in *Barron's*. That research, which covered the period from 1966 through October 2001, found that a $1,000 investment in the S&P 500, held for the duration of the period, would have grown to $11,710, a compounded annual return of 6.86 percent. But, had an investor missed the *five best days* each year, the $1,000 would have *shrunk* to just $150.

That seems like a fairly convincing argument for staying in the market—which is why Wall Street hammers on it as justification that investors should be fully invested at all times. But, and you knew this was coming by now, *there's a flip side to the coin*.

Being an optimist in a skeptical world, I decided to run my own study. Examining the S&P 500 from January 1950 to December 2007, I discovered something interesting. First, $1,000 invested in the S&P in 1950 would have grown to $613,013 by December 2007. But, had you tried to time the market and missed the 30 best months in that period, the value of the initial $1,000 would have risen to just $35,404.

Now for the truly surprising—in fact, I'd say amazing—part. Had you tried to time the market and missed the 30 *worst* months, your $1,000

(continued)

would have grown to *$9,509,094!* Yes, you read that right—*more than $9.5 million!!*

So, which do you think is more important now? Being in there for the gains—or protecting yourself in bad markets?

You see, getting the optimum returns is not about market timing at all, nor is it about the risk of missing the *best* market days. It's about being there *for the best* days while *missing the worst* days. And that speaks volumes about always having the appropriate portfolio structure in place and using protective stops at all times.

WHEN HEDGING, GO FOR THE GOLD

Another key element of the Pyramid portfolio is hedging—the allocation of a relatively small amount of capital to insure the rest of your assets, thus reinforcing that prime rule of investing: "Keep what you have." Sadly, far too many investors learn the principle of hedging only after it's too late to apply it.

The best hedges are investments that move counter to the general market or economic trends—an example being the inverse S&P 500 ETFs I discussed earlier. The other widely used hedges are investments that will take advantage of future risk factors, such as inflation. And that, of course, means gold.

But, it *doesn't* mean gold as everyone traditionally thinks of it—as full-time protection against inflation. In fact, despite widespread marketing propaganda to the contrary, gold has *never* been a statistically viable anti-inflation investment. However, it *IS* a great crisis hedge and also has a direct link to bond interest rates—which, of course, are directly affected by inflation. Therefore, you want to own it.

Studies have shown that the inverse correlation between gold and interest rates—and therefore bonds—is roughly 10 to 1. This essentially means that, to hedge the bonds in your portfolio, you should hold $100 worth of gold for every $900 worth of bonds you own.

In other words, a portfolio containing *both bonds and gold* is safer than one holding either bonds or gold in isolation.

> **FISCAL FLASHPOINT**
>
> When buying bonds for your Pyramid portfolio, stick to maturities shorter than 10 years. Studies show you can capture 70 percent (or more) of the returns of longer-term bonds, but with substantially less volatility. How much less? Try 35 percent or more, depending on what you buy. Longer-term bonds are also more volatile when it comes to interest-rate changes. Therefore, they're likely to be among the most violent offenders when rates are on the rise. You thus want to take steps to capture the returns they offer while minimizing this form of volatility risk.
>
> In general, interest rates—and, by proxy, bonds—can also help predict movements in the stock market. If interest rates decline and bonds rally, smart stock investors buy. But, if bond prices fall and interest rates rise, you'd better pull out the umbrella because it's probably going to rain on your Wall Street parade.

TWO OTHER TRICKS FOR TRADING STOCKS

I have one other absolute rule of investing that I don't think I've mentioned yet: When buying stocks, *never* pay full price for anything—*ever!*

In most cases, this simply means I work really hard to ferret out undervalued issues. However, even if a stock I want *isn't* undervalued, I use a technique that allows me to buy it at a below-market price—and get paid for waiting until I do.

How is that possible? Actually, it's quite easy—*if* you know how to employ one of the fundamental strategies using listed stock options. It's called *selling cash-secured puts* (or, if you're a little more risqué—and willing to take a bit more risk—you can also sell *naked puts*).

For those unfamiliar with them, an option is a derivative instrument—*not* one of the really bad or complex ones like credit-default swaps—in which the seller grants the buyer the "right" (but not the obligation) to buy or sell a specific underlying stock (or other instrument, such as a currency or a futures contract) at a given price for a given period of time. In exchange for granting that right, the seller receives a modest fee from the buyer, called a *premium*. There are two basic kinds of options—*calls*, which give the owner the right to *BUY* 100 shares of the underlying stock at a specified price (called the *striking price*, or *exercise price*), and *puts*, which give the owner the right to *SELL* 100 shares of the stock at the stated exercise price.

Okay, I know, at first reading, it *sounds* complicated, but it's really not—as I show you in just a second.

Listed options, which trade on an exchange and have standard features and uniform exercise prices, have been around for a little more than three decades (though options themselves have been around for centuries). And, not surprisingly, they share one major characteristic with foreign stocks—traditional Wall Street brokers regularly advise *against* trading them. "Too risky," "Only for sophisticated investors," and "You can lose all of your money in just weeks" are only a few of the admonitions thrown around about them.

FISCAL FLASHPOINT

Seventy-five percent of American investors need to undergo a paradigm shift in the way they think about options. I employ them in several different strategies to get better prices on the stocks I want to buy, protect profits on those I already own, and increase the revenue stream and yield on my overall portfolio. And, if you want to be a truly successful wealth builder, you need to learn to use these strategies, too.

But, when used properly, that's not the case. In fact, options are among the most versatile of investment vehicles, capable of being used in dozens of strategies—ranging from outright speculation to income production to guaranteed risk control. In fact, that's why most Wall Street firms actually have their own carefully designed options programs in place to help them manage the house money.

But, that's neither here nor there. What's important is that options, when used properly, really can be used to buy stocks at bargain prices. Here's how:

Assume you've decided China is truly committed to cleaning up its pollution problems and you want to jump aboard this growing trend in both alternative resources and infrastructure improvement. You like the outlook for Yingli Green Energy Corp., China's only totally *green* power company, which trades in the United States as an ADR under the symbol YGE. However, given the timeline for major revenue increases from new solar projects, you think it may be a bit overvalued at its current price of $13.93 a share. (Note: I'm using *actual* stock and option prices from late July 2009.) You think $12.50 a share might be a more accurate valuation—but how do you get that price?

Since you were planning to buy 1,000 shares, we'll assume you have at least $12,500 in available cash. So, rather than using that to buy YGE stock, you post it as security for the sale of 10 YGE December put options with a striking price of $12.50 a share. (Remember, each option represents 100 shares of the underlying stock, so 10 puts would equate to 1,000 shares.) As the seller of 10 December $12.50 YGE puts, you give the buyer the right to *sell to you* 1,000 shares of Yingli Green Energy stock at a price of $12.50 per share any time up until the expiration date, which in this case would be the third Friday of December 2009. In exchange for selling this right, you receive a premium from the option buyer of $3.50 per share (or $3,500), which can be either taken out or used to reduce the $12,500 security deposit on the transaction—called a *cash-secured put sale*.

Now what happens? For you, there are three possible outcomes:

1. If YGE's stock price rises before December, the puts you sold expire worthless and you get to keep both your $12,500

and the $3,500 premium you received. You don't get the shares, but you've made a 28 percent return on your money in just over five months *without* owning the stock (excluding commissions). Plus, you can repeat the put sale in December, using options that expire in March or June of 2010.

2. If YGE's stock price stays flat—or falls slightly, but remains above $12.50 a share—the puts you sold expire worthless and you still get to keep both your $12,500 and the $3,500 premium you received. You don't get the shares, but you've still made a 28 percent return on your money in just over five months. And, again, you can repeat the strategy. (I think you're starting to see the point here.)

3. If YGE's stock falls below $12.50 a share—say to $12.00— the person who bought the options can *put* 1,000 shares of YGE to you at a $12.50 per share, or $12,500 total. The money to pay for the stock is the $12,500 you put up to secure the original sale. Since the price is now $12.00 a share, you have an immediate loss of 50 cents per share, or $500—but, remember, you still have the $3,500 premium you received. So, you're actually $3,000 ahead (a 24 percent return on your money)—and you got the stock at the bargain price you originally wanted. *What a deal!*

This strategy can be employed to buy any stock on which listed options are traded. The only real drawback is that, if the stock rises sharply, you'll miss out on the gain because you didn't buy the actual shares. But, you'll still have the premium you received to ease the pain—and you can continue selling puts on the stock every five or six months until its price *does* fall back and you finally get to buy it. Plus, if you decide at some point, you no longer want to buy it, just *stop selling puts.*

But what if the stock falls sharply? So what? In YGE's case, you'll be buying the stock at a 10 percent *discount* to where it was trading on the day you sold your puts. You wouldn't go to a 10 percent *more* sale, would you? I didn't think so.

TWO ALTERNATE OPTION STRATEGIES

If you're willing to accept a bit more risk, you can greatly compound your returns on the strategy discussed in the main text by selling *naked puts.* This simply means you *don't* put up the entire amount of cash it would take to actually buy the underlying stock if the puts were exercised. Rather, you would put up only a *margin deposit*—typically 20 to 25 percent of the exercise value of the underlying stock—which would have to remain in your margin account (this trade can't be done in regular accounts), along with the premium received, until the expiration date. There may also be other adjustments, depending on the position of the stock's price relative to the exercise price (in other words, whether the option being sold is *in the money* or *out of the money*).

In the YGE situation, you would have had to put up $2,500 in margin to secure the naked put sale (20 percent of the $12,500 exercise value) and leave the $3,500 premium in the account as well. But, if the puts expired worthless, you'd keep both, giving you a 140 percent return (less commissions and margin interest, of course). And, if the puts were exercised, you'd again have to buy the stock—at the bargain price you originally wanted.

The increased risk factor arises if you have only the $2,500 margin deposit and not the full $12,500—which you'd have to come up with instantly if the puts were exercised.

Another option strategy you can use once you've actually purchased the stock is called *covered call writing.* In this strategy, you simply sell one *out-of-the-money* call option—in other words, one with a striking price *higher* than the actual current stock price—for every 100 shares you own. If the stock's price rises to a level above the exercise price before its expiration, you have to sell your stock—at a profit. You also keep the premium you originally received for selling the call. If the stock's price stays flat or falls, the call option expires worthless and you get to keep both the stock and the premium you received, which can either add to your income yield or offset losses on stock declines.

TWO STRATEGIES FOR REBUILDING LOST VALUE

If you're like most investors, your portfolio lost ground in the 2007–2008 market collapse—and, in spite of the summer 2009 rally, you've still got some losses to recover. One easy, yet relatively painless strategy you can use to make up those losses is called *value averaging*. Value averaging is a combination of its better-known cousin, dollar-cost averaging, and a process known as *portfolio rebalancing*.

In case you're not familiar with it, *dollar-cost averaging* is a means of accumulating investment assets by buying the same dollar amount of shares on a regular schedule, regardless of the price at that time. For example, a neighbor of mine invests $100 a month—like clock-work—in his favorite mutual fund. By definition, this means that he buys *more* shares when the prices are *lower,* and *fewer* shares when the prices are *higher.* Over the long run, his cost is likely to be lower than it would be had he bought an equivalent number of shares in a single transaction. In essence, he is "averaging" his purchase price over time, thus reducing the risk of buying once at the "wrong" (that is, very high) price. Hence the name *dollar-cost averaging.*

Value averaging is a little different. Whereas my neighbor invests his $100 every month, I prefer to *grow* my portfolio by a fixed amount every month. As an example, let's assume that I want to make my portfolio grow by $100 a month—every month. In some months, I would invest $100 just like my neighbor. However, if the $100 that I contributed last month lost a bit of ground and is now worth only $90, I'll contribute $110 this month to make up the difference. On the other hand, in months during which I made more than my target, I might not contribute anything at all because the portfolio value had grown by $100 (or more) on its own.

This simple twist, devised by former NASDAQ chief economist and Harvard Business School Professor Michael E. Edleson, has been shown to produce better results over time than the old dollar-cost-averaging method, thanks to one simple twist. By considering a portfolio's expected rate of return—something that the

HOW YOU CAN OWN STOCKS—FOR FREE!

Another tactic I regularly use helps build my portfolio by letting me own stocks for free. How do I do that? Well, any time one of the stocks I own makes a 100 percent gain—in other words, doubles in value—*I sell half*. This lets me return valuable trading capital to my account for other investments, while still hanging on to a hot stock for the potential of still more gains ahead. Here's an example:

Assume you owned 1,000 shares of Yingli Green Energy (YGE) that you'd bought at $12.50 when the puts you sold were exercised. Now assume the company received a huge contract to provide solar heating systems for a new Beijing government facility, and the stock price shot up to $25.40 per share on the news. What you should immediately do is sell half of your holdings—or 500 shares. At the new price of $25.40, that would bring in $12,700—enough to completely recover your original cost for the 1,000-share position (with some added change to offset commissions).

The end result: You now have $12,500 to put to work in new investment opportunities—and you still own 500 shares of YGE, worth $12,700, at a cost of . . . *ZERO!*

Again, what a deal—*owning stocks for free!*

dollar-cost-averaging method neglects—the value-averaging method helps identify periods of over- and underperformance.

When the portfolio is underperforming, share prices are likely to be low—so, you'll invest more to make up for that underperformance. When the portfolio is outperforming your target rate of growth, share prices are likely to be high. That means it's not a good time to buy—and *you wouldn't*. In fact, you could even *sell* a portion of the assets for a profit—so long as you held onto the first $100 to maintain your required average growth rate.

Value averaging is a nice way to ensure you follow one of the best-known investment mandates: Buy low and sell high. The method is particularly valuable during times of high volatility because it helps ensure that you maintain your discipline in investing.

For more experienced investors, there's also a risk-management technique known as *fixed-fractional sizing*. It can help increase returns and minimize risk by varying position sizes based on the risk associated with each trade. The simplest explanation here is that fixed-fractional position sizing increases investment size and return potential when the market—or individual stock—is on a winning streak, while reducing it accordingly when conditions aren't so great. If you want to know more, a complete discussion of the concept can be found online at www.tradingrecipes.com/files/pw.pdf.

THAT'S ALL, FOLKS!

I won't say I've now told you everything I think or given you everything I know—but you've received a good portion of both. Of key importance is the knowledge I've imparted about the 50-40-10 Pyramid structure, essential in keeping what you already have safe and providing opportunities for future growth without taking on excess risk. This two-pronged approach is more effective in building wealth than any other process I've seen.

Also vital is the information you've learned about options and other strategies you can use to protect your holdings, buy stocks at bargain prices, generate added income from your portfolio, and even own shares for free. Consider these techniques strong medicine to help speed your personal recovery from the fiscal hangover we're now suffering through. I do have a couple of final jewels of financial wisdom to share with you—as well as a tiny bit of motivational blather to further incite you to put what you've learned to work—but I've saved those for the conclusion. Don't neglect to turn the page just one more time and check them out.

CONCLUSION

---

10 MORE RULES FOR SUCCESSFUL INVESTING

The most terrifying words in the English language are: I'm from the government and I'm here to help.

—Ronald Reagan (while running for President)

I originally wrote a conclusion that featured a detailed and fairly lengthy recap of everything I've covered in this book. You know, the standard ending to the old "Tell 'em what you're gonna tell 'em, tell 'em, then tell 'em what you told 'em" routine. I then closed with some serious motivational urgings and a call to immediate action: "You can do it! Start today! Be successful! Get rich! Rah! Rah! Rah!"

The only problem was, the recap had nothing new in it, so it bored even me—and the only thing the motivational stuff did was motivate me to *not* give it to you.

So, I decided to take a different tack—recounting a couple of my latest insights and then sharing some rules that have served me exceedingly well through my financial career, my hope being that they would

293

provide enough astute advice to be motivational in their own right. First the insights.

One thing I did say several times in the book that's worth repeating here is this: "No nation in recorded history has *ever* hauled itself out of recession by doing what we are doing now. *Ever!*"

That's why—even though things picked up economically in mid-2009, the stock market managed to rally nicely from its March lows and a couple of government ideas appeared to be working, most notably the Cash for Clunkers program—my greatest concern is that Congress or the Obama administration will do something stupid at *precisely the wrong moment,* like engage in a protectionist rant when it comes to China.

Hence the quote at the beginning.

Don't misunderstand me—I'm *not* being political. I use Obama's name only because he is the sitting President of the United States. The financial crisis itself is *not* partisan. It makes no difference who's in the White House or which party is running the show at the moment. The biggest risk is that "we" do something idiotic—something that will make the "fiscal hangover" we're all experiencing much worse instead of helping to relieve it.

Neither our congressional leaders nor many of Obama's top advisers are particularly sophisticated in economic terms—and they're stunningly ignorant on most *international* financial issues. Obviously, however, they're *not* stupid people. The problem is that they mirror their constituencies, so regardless of political affiliation, they're unlikely to do anything that hurts anybody—which might result in them getting fired or voted out of office.

In that sense, populism is hampering the recovery as much as any of the other issues I address in this book.

The government needs to focus on fixing problems instead of just throwing money at things. I'm talking about job creation, a shifting of the American attitude from one of excess consumption to increased exports and, most importantly, a further reforming of our financial systems to restrain companies from taking on risks that threaten the capital structure of the entire country.

Sadly, I fear that Turbo Tim and his pals at Treasury, the boys at the Fed, and the leaders in Congress will respond to the tough choices ahead by doing what politicians almost always do—side-step the really difficult decisions and merely *print more money.* This stinks from a personal standpoint because the inflationary and recessionary implications of these actions will hit all Americans squarely in the wallet. However, from an investment perspective, it's actually *great* because it puts trillions of dollars behind the global trends you and I are now following—giving us the opportunity to enhance the already solid returns available in foreign markets.

Only time will tell whether the lessons our leaders—and Americans as a group—*failed* to learn from past crises will sink in this time around.

I also want to make one point regarding the lighter tone I tried to take in most of this book. Obviously, everyone in the world feels that the subject of his or her money and what to do with it is *a serious one*—and I agree. I assure you, I *do* take investing and wealth-building *very* seriously—and I'd never want to offend you by discussing them in a humorous manner.

However, I'm also an optimist by nature and I try to encourage my clients and my readers to adopt this same attitude, simply because taking yourself and your money *too seriously* can lead to over-analysis, missed opportunities, post-trade remorse and severe headaches—the ultimate symptom of a prolonged fiscal hangover. Besides, the way things have been going recently, it's difficult to resist cracking a joke now and then. As Will Rogers said more than 80 years ago, "It's easy being a humorist when you've got the whole government working for you."

Now for those additional rules of investing I promised you— several of which I touched on at least tangentially in earlier chapters. Most of these guidelines are based not on classes in Investment Finance or MBA programs, but on common sense—and decades of observing both the markets and the people who play in them. As I said earlier, I hope you will find them instructional, inspiring—and, ultimately, *highly profitable.*

OH, MY GOSH—STILL MORE RULES!

Rule Number 1: Growth is illusory. Unlike the objects reflected in your side-view mirror, investment returns are generally *smaller,* not larger than they appear. As such, rather than investing for capital gains, you should aim for the highest possible yields and the most certainty you can find. The real secret to wealth-building is compounding small gains over long periods of time. In fact, studies show that compound returns can outperform so-called growth stocks by as much as *22 to 1.* Furthermore, *dividends account for a huge percentage of total returns*—varying studies have claimed anywhere from 60 percent all the way up to 97 percent over time. So, *don't ignore them!*

The glorification of growth stocks is the single biggest hoax foisted on the investing public over the last 200 years. Of course, this is *not* to say that growth is impossible—only that it's *a lot harder to achieve* consistently than Wall Street would have you believe.

Rule Number 2: Think like a plumber. Big losses—like six inches of water in the living room—are expensive and can set you back years. Professional traders—and I'm *not* including the risk-junkie cowboys who drove the derivatives mess to heck in a handbasket—know this. And, because they do, they focus the majority of their efforts on *avoiding losses* rather than capturing gains. It's counter-intuitive, but it really makes a difference . . . not to mention the fact that preventing those portfolio pipes from bursting prevents assets from dripping away so you can sleep better at night.

Rule Number 3: Valuations matter. Buying when the underlying value is "right" can mean the difference between market-beating returns and pathetic single digits. It's hard to make money when valuations—as reflected by price-earnings ratios—are over 20. More normal valuations sit in the 12 to 14 range. However, to *really* make money, you need to buy when valuations have been beaten down into the single digits—assuming, of course, that the company's underlying value is *real*. Doing so puts the odds strongly in your favor and can dramatically boost returns.

Rule Number 4: Invest on the right side of major economic trends. Don't fight the Fed. Rising interest-rate environments make meaningful gains difficult to sustain—unless you know what to look for! Far too many investors got it wrong from 2000–2003 and in 2008–2009 by betting on growth stocks in a recessionary economy—and they're still getting it wrong. They're likely to get burned again should the economy slow further in spite of the government bailout and stimulus efforts. Analyze all of the other major global trends as well—and ride the ones that are truly unstoppable. You'll know 'em when you see 'em because they'll have trillions of dollars behind them—infrastructure, inflation, energy, food, and water (both supply and purity) are great examples. Sadly, war and terrorism are also growth industries at the moment.

Rule Number 5: Start early and leave your money alone for as long as possible. Note that this is *not* the same thing as "buy-and-hold." Buy-and-hold is not an investing strategy, it's a marketing gimmick—and, these days, it's more like "hope and pray" anyway. The world's most successful investors—think Rogers, Templeton, and Buffett, to name a few—*don't* buy and hold, and I don't believe you should either. They buy and "manage," picking only stocks and using only strategies that meet their specific objectives. Given that one of our critical objectives is to have our money *working hard for us* rather than *us working hard for it,* the point is that you want to *start as early in your life as possible* and *never miss an opportunity to invest.* The longer you have your money in play, the better you will be paid when you're ready to cash in!

Rule Number 6: Sell your winners. This may seem counterintuitive—but, if you want to succeed, you *must* sell your winners. Rule Number 2—thinking like a plumber to prevent losses—is only part of the success equation. To be really effective, *you have to take profits,* too. That way, you get more capital that you can put to work. Think of it this way—Safeway regularly replenishes the inventory in its Produce Department to keep it fresh. You should do the same with the "inventory" in your Pyramid portfolio because, if you let your stocks sit on the shelf too long, *they'll eventually go bad*—just like fruit that's past its expiration date.

Rule Number 7: Always sit in an exit row. This rule goes hand in hand with Rule 6. One of the most common problems investors have is not knowing *when to sell.* Sometimes, they'll let a big loss get out of control (which violates Rule Number 2)—or, worse, they'll sit on a big gain so long that it sneakily turns into a loss. The bottom line is that, up or down, you should *always* have *planned exit points* when you initiate a position—and enforce them with *protective stops,* adjusting them as prices move in your favor (but *never* when they go against you).

Rule Number 8: Retirement is a lifestyle issue, not a monetary one. When most people think about retirement, they think about safety. Big mistake. The single biggest problem facing us today is running out of money before we run out of life. If you've followed Rule Number 5, this shouldn't be a problem. However, if you've thought about safety and have not invested *enough,* what you're really doing is crippling your ability to earn future income—income you're going to need to eat, keep a roof over your head, and provide long-life health care. Oh yeah, and *have some fun!*

Rule Number 9: Your broker is a salesman. So, unless you know you want to buy what he has, don't go shopping today! Wall Street is *not* a service business. Brokers exist for one reason and one reason only— to sell you stuff and make money . . . from your money. And, the more of your money you give to them, *the less you have to make more for yourself.* So, buy only what you want and what fits your goals and objectives—not the "stock of the day" the broker is pushing to meet his weekly quota.

Rule Number 10: All investments contain risks—but not all investments contain the same risks! Despite all my talk about avoiding losses, the simple truth is this: If you want to grow your wealth, you *have* to take on risk. *It's unavoidable!*

Every investment involves risk—the only questions are *how much* and *under what circumstances.* Remember, as I've said before, success is not about how much money you can make, but about *how much money you KEEP!* As such, the true secret of wealth-building is *taking risk properly.* George Patton once said, "There is nothing wrong with taking risks." Then he added, "That's quite different from being rash." And I agree.

It's a fact of life that, if you want to be successful in *anything,* you have to take a certain amount of risk every day. Yet, most folks are unwilling to do so—or they spread themselves too thin, over-diversifying under the guise of "protecting" themselves. But, in doing so, they set themselves up for failure.

No, not because they take *too much* risk, but because they don't *concentrate* the risks they do take in the right places! *The places that provide the potential rewards to justify their risk.*

MIMI WAS DEFINITELY RIGHT

On that note, I *will* conclude—with an affirmation of what my Grandmother Mimi told me 30 years ago. The world definitely *is* bigger than our own backyard—and, if you climb over the fence and explore the opportunities it presents, recovering your past losses and building your future fortune will be *easier than you ever imagined.*

Oh, yes, I do also want to end with *just one* of those rah-rah motivational statements:

"Go China, *GO!*"

APPENDIX

THE $300 TRILLION RECOVERY ALMOST NOBODY'S TALKING ABOUT

As I write this, everyone from Wall Street to Main Street is using the word *recover* in every other sentence. But what does a recovery actually look like and why should you care?

And, perhaps more importantly, how can you make back what you've lost in the meltdown? How long will it take? How can you speed up the process? Which sectors and business segments will lead the way?

It's tough to admit, but the U.S. economy may take years to recover—if it ever does.

Just look at Japan as an example. Its economy has still not yet recovered from the bubble they experienced nearly 20 years ago. If our government is taking many of the same actions theirs did, why would we think things are going to be different for us?

Remember, Japan is not some backwoods marketplace in the boonies—it's the second-largest economy in the world, which means you can't dismiss what happened there in light of what's happening here and now. Especially when you consider Japan was an export-based economy to begin with. The United States presently derives less than 15 percent of its GDP from exports and fully 70 percent from consumer spending.

That places tremendous pressure on a group of people who are not only tapped out, but are licking their collective wounds after a 24-month financial meltdown.

Simply put, things will never be the same again.

SUVs no longer grow on trees, home-equity lines do not constitute a personal piggy bank, and derivatives are now destined for the financial trash heap.

Looking ahead, you can bet anybody who wants to buy a house will face tougher lending requirements. Credit-card debt will come home to roost and many companies that once existed on the margin will be forced to come to terms with their tricky accounting.

No siree, Bob. We believe that things will be radically different from now on. The rules of money truly have changed.

While this sounds scary, there's a flip side—new rules mean new opportunities. You just need to know where to look to find them.

HOW CAN A $300 TRILLION RECOVERY HIDE IN PLAIN SIGHT?

There is no question that the financial crisis has reshaped the world in ways the average investor is only just beginning to understand. But inasmuch as that's hard to stomach, don't forget that every crisis has produced legendary wealth for those savvy enough to capitalize on the changes it brings.

Using history as our guide, we think the current financial crisis could produce some of the largest gains ever recorded and generate as much as $300 trillion in new investment in the next few years alone.

Unfortunately, we believe that most investors, led by traditional economists, misinformed pundits, and gonzo journalists, will miss it.

Instead of looking at what's actually happening, they'll have their heads in the sand. Not only will they fail to see the new reality that's unfolding right in front of their very eyes, but they'll never set foot in the places where much of this growth is happening.

In other words, they'll apply the same old tired theories to markets that demand different results. And that's hardly a good or profitable mix.

What they should be doing is looking for profits where they're being made *right now!*

THE BIGGEST ECONOMIC SHIFT IN 200 YEARS

It's ironic . . . at a time when economists in the United States and Europe are looking for signs that things are getting better, there's a legion of folks in other parts of the world who are too busy managing real growth to pay attention to our problems.

They are not only watching the beginnings of this $300 trillion recovery, but actively taking steps to capitalize on it right now. They know that 60 percent or more of the growth they're chasing will come from new global markets that most people can't even pronounce yet.

That's double the projected growth from established markets like the United States and Japan.

You'll be tempted to dismiss this, and I wouldn't blame you. This isn't for everybody . . . just those who understand that events thousands of miles from our own borders will set the pace for decades.

Indeed, the move has already begun and foreign stock markets, once regarded as fringe investments, are already outperforming our own— and have been throughout the entire financial crisis (see Figure A.1).

Imagine what happens when things really get better!

Most investors have yet to understand that much of this growth is driven by China. There is not an industry or business segment on the planet that it won't completely dominate or substantially influence in the years ahead.

Here too, in Figure A.2, the move is already under way.

Name	3 MO	12 MO	3 YR	5 YR
MSCI Brazil USD	39.21	−5.14	11.89	30.04
MSCI Indonesia USD	52.92	−26.67	11.29	22.24
MSCI EM Latin America USD	36.99	−37.40	7.90	22.87
BSE SENSEX LCL India	49.29	7.67	10.96	24.7
MSCI Argentina USD	31.69	−3.72	−0.4	58.99
MSCI Turkey USD	53.16	−17.21	0.8	11.998
MSCI World/Metals & Mining USD	28.35	−50.07	−3.72	12.06
MSCI Mexico USD	34.65	−34.67	−1.10	12.94
MSCI EM GR USD	34.84	n/a	3.27	15.09
MSCI Chile USD	32.27	1.27	13.15	17.32
S&P 500	**14.59**	**−22.04**	**−23.02**	**−10.89**

FIGURE A.1   Annualized Average Returns (in US$) Ended July 31, 2009
Source: Index Universe.

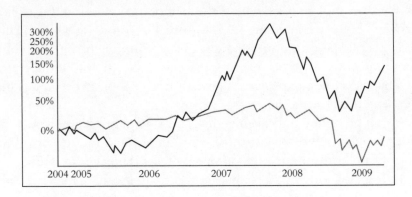

FIGURE A.2   Shanghai Versus S&P 500 Last Five Years

Even with the massive sell-off in the Chinese markets that began in late 2007, investors who placed their bets there have dramatically outperformed those who thought they were getting a better deal with the S&P 500.

And if that's not enough, consider how radically the share that each country contributes to the world's GDP has changed in five short years.

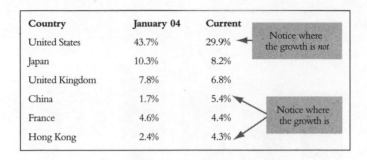

Country	January 04	Current	
United States	43.7%	29.9%	Notice where the growth is *not*
Japan	10.3%	8.2%	
United Kingdom	7.8%	6.8%	
China	1.7%	5.4%	Notice where the growth is
France	4.6%	4.4%	
Hong Kong	2.4%	4.3%	

FIGURE A.3 Contribution to the GDP by Country

The United States has seen its contribution drop by 31.57 percent while China and Hong Kong have increased their contributions by 217.65 percent and 79.17 percent, respectively (see Figure A.3).

ELECTRICITY AS A MEASURE OF GROWTH

One of the simplest yet most overlooked indicators of all reinforces this message: electricity demand. In a nutshell, where electricity demand is growing, GDP follows.

Figure A.4, from the Department of Energy's Energy Information Administration, says it all. . . .

Electricity demand in the Far East is projected to exceed North American demand by 2020—a short 10 years from now. But we believe this is conservative and that it may actually pass North American demand by 2015—a full five years *earlier*—which gives us even more reason to pay attention.

ARE THE CHINESE KILLING OFF THE U.S. DOLLAR?

The U.S. dollar has been the world's reserve currency for the last 60 years. Many people find it inconceivable that this will change.

But it already has.

In 2009 alone, China initiated over $200 billion worth of swap agreements that allow their trading partners to pay for Chinese goods and services *directly*, without converting into dollars or having to

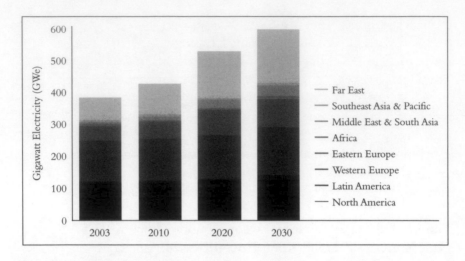

FIGURE A.4   Electricity and GDP Growth
Source: Department of Energy.

trade their currency openly. We think the odds are good that the actual (and closely guarded) figures may be more than double that.

So far, most of these agreements have been with smaller economies in Asia and South America, but we don't think it will be long before Western or European countries jump on board.

The point is that while the United States struggles, China and her trading partners are taking matters into their own hands and creating a new global marketplace for currency trading that's outside the traditional currency exchanges used by the West. It's an end run of epic proportions and *one more sign the world's economic center of gravity is shifting away from the West . . . permanently.*

THE SECOND COMING OF CHINA

While most people think the financial crisis is about the fall of Western financial markets, history will view it as critical to the *second chapter* of China's remarkable rise to world economic dominance.

Ninety-nine percent of all Westerners don't understand that while we're busy dealing with the fallout, China views what has happened as the mother of all opportunities . . . *for them*. In keeping with the Confucian concept of yin and yang, China understands that where there is darkness, there is also light. So they're doing everything they can to expand while the competition lacks the resources to act.

Considering that China has the world's largest stockpile of cash reserves—over $2.3 trillion by some estimates—they could create the single largest liquidity event in recorded history. Bigger than the Internet, housing bubble, and gold *combined!*

THE BIGGEST BUYING OPPORTUNITY OF *MANY* LIFETIMES

We think this represents a buying opportunity of unprecedented magnitude.

History clearly shows that the greatest fortunes are made by those savvy enough to recognize when the rules have changed and invest accordingly. Which is why we want to begin investing now, when everybody is too busy looking at the right hand to notice what's going on with the left.

It's also critically important to understand that China (and many of the emerging markets) remains underdeveloped by Western standards. Which, in and of itself, represents another king-sized opportunity in fundamental industries like power, water, and transportation systems that we take for granted.

We've already explored a bunch of these in *Fiscal Hangover*, but there's more out there—and the list of potential investments is growing by the hour.

Which is why we invite you to grab your fair share by visiting us at www.fiscalhangover.com.

We think you'll be glad you did.

BIBLIOGRAPHY

BOOKS

Adam, Thomas. *Germany and the Americas: Culture, Politics, and History.* ABC–CLIO, 2005.

Barber, Benjamin. *Jihad vs. McWorld: How Globalism and Tribalism Are Reshaping the World.* New York: Crown Publishing, 1995.

Bellamy, Edward. *Looking Backward: 2000–1887.* New York: Signet, 1960.

Bordo, Michael D., and Barry Eichengreen. *A Retrospective on the Bretton Woods System: Lessons for International Monetary Reform.* Chicago: University of Chicago Press, 1993.

Bradford, William. *Of Plymouth Plantation.* New York: Capricorn Books, 1962.

Burstein, Daniel, and Arne de Keijzer. *Big Dragon.* New York: Simon and Schuster, 1998.

Coxe, Tench. *A View of the United States of America.* Philadelphia: Oxford University Press, 1794.

Day, R. H., and Ping Chen. *Nonlinear Dynamics and Evolutionary Economics.* New York: Oxford University Press, 1993.

Edleson, Michael. *Value Averaging: The Safe and Easy Investment Strategy.* Chicago: International Publishing Corp., 1991.

El-Erian, Mohamed. *When Markets Collide.* New York: McGraw-Hill, 2008.

Ferguson, Niall. *The Ascent of Money: A Financial History of the World*. London: Allen Lane, 2008.

Fraser, Steve. *Wall Street: A Cultural History*. London: Faber and Faber, 2005.

Friedman, Milton, and Anna Jacobson Schwartz. *A Monetary History of the United States, 1867–1960*. Princeton, NJ: Princeton University Press, for the National Bureau of Economic Research, 1963.

Frum, David. *How We Got Here: The '70s*. New York: Basic Books, 2000.

Galbraith, John Kenneth. *The New Industrial State*. Boston: Houghton Mifflin, 1967.

Griffin, G. Edward. *The Creature from Jekyll Island: A Second Look at the Federal Reserve*. Tarrytown, NY: American Media, 1998.

Jaeger, Robert A. *All About Hedge Funds: The Easy Way to Get Started*. New York: McGraw-Hill, 2002.

James, Harold. *International Monetary Cooperation Since Bretton Woods*. New York: Oxford University Press, 1996.

Kagen, Robert. *The Return of History and the End of Dreams*. New York: Random House, 2008.

King, Ronald R.; Vernon L. Smith, Arlington W. Williams, and Mark V. van Boening. *The Robustness of Bubbles and Crashes in Experimental Stock Markets*. New York: Oxford University Press, 1993.

Kotlikoff, Laurence, and Scott Burns. *The Coming Generational Storm: What You Need to Know About America's Economic Future*. Cambridge, MA: MIT Press, 2005.

Lardy, Nicholas R. *China's Unfinished Economic Revolution*. Washington, DC: Brookings Institution, 1998.

Lewin, Leonard. *Report from Iron Mountain*. New York: Free Press, 1996.

Mandebrot, Benoit, and Richard L. Hudson. *The (Mis)Behavior of Markets: A Fractal View of Risk, Ruin and Reward*. New York: Basic Books, 2004.

Mullins, Eustace. *Secrets of the Federal Reserve, The London Connection. (orig. Mullins on the Federal Reserve)*. New York: Kasper and Horton, 1983.

North, Douglass C., and Robert Paul Thomas, eds. *The Growth of the American Economy to 1860*. University of South Carolina Press, 1968.

Palmer, R. R. *The Age of Democratic Revolution*. Princeton, NJ: Princeton University Press, 1969.

Peiss, Kathy L. *American Women and the Making of Modern Consumer Culture—A Lecture Based on Hope in a Jar: The Making of America's Beauty Culture*. New York: Metropolitan Books/Henry Holt, 1998.

Peterson, Peter G. *Running on Empty: How the Democratic and Republican Parties Are Bankrupting Our Future and What Americans Can Do About It*. New York: Farrar, Straus and Giroux, 2004.

Polanyi, Karl. *The Great Transformation: The Political and Economic Origins of Our Time*. Boston: Beacon Press, by arrangement with Rinehart and Company, Inc., 1944, 1957.

Prigogine, Ilva. *Order Out of Chaos.* New York: Bantam Books, 1988.

Rogers, Jim. *A Bull in China.* New York: Simon and Shuster, 2008.

Shiller, Robert J. *Irrational Exuberance.* Princeton, NJ: Princeton University Press, 2001.

Smith, Adam. *An Inquiry into the Nature and Causes of the Wealth of Nations.* New York: Random House Modern Library, 1937.

Sornette, Didier. *Why Stock Markets Crash.* Princeton, NJ: Princeton University Press, 2003.

Soros, George. *The New Paradigm for Financial Markets: The Credit Crisis of 2008 and What It Means.* New York: PublicAffairs, 2008.

Taylor, Alan M. *International Capital Mobility in History: The Saving-Investment Relationship.* Cambridge, MA: National Bureau of Economic Research, 1996.

Veblen, Thorstein. *The Theory of the Leisure Class.* 1899. http://xroads.virginia .edu/~HYPER/VEBLEN/veblenhp.html (accessed May 2009.)

Weber, Max. *Die Protestantische Ethik und der "Geist" Des Kapitalismus (The Protestant Ethic and the Spirit of Capitalism).* Germany, 1905; Talcott Parsons, trans., 1930; reprint New York: Scribner's Press, 1958.

Yergin, Daniel H. *The Prize: The Epic Quest for Oil, Money and Power.* New York: Simon and Schuster, 2008.

ARTICLES

BBC News. "Chinese Job Losses Prompt Exodus." http://news.bbc.co.uk/2/hi/ asia-pacific/ (accessed July 2009).

Buchanan, Patrick J. "China's Path to World Power," *Human Events.* www .humanevents.com (accessed June 2009).

Chodorov, Frank. "The Divide Between Society and State," *Ludwig von Mises Institute.* http://mises.org/story/3403 (accessed May 2009).

Das, Krista. *The Great Debate: Decoupling, Contrarian Profits.* www.contrarianprofits .com/articles/the-great-debate-decoupling/617 (accessed June 2009).

Dismal Scientist, Global and Asia/Pacific News and Statistics. www.economy .com/dismal/ (accessed June and July 2009).

Economichistory.net: *Economic History of Pre-Modern China, 221 B.C. to A.D. 1800.* http://eh.net/encyclopedia/article/deng.china (accessed June 2009).

Fallows, James. "China's Way Forward," *The Atlantic,* April 2009. www.theatlantic .com/doc/200904/chinese-innovation (accessed July 2009).

Lebow, Victor. "Price Competition in 1955," *Journal of Retailing,* Spring 1955.

Lundestad, Geir. "Empire by Invitation? The United States and Western Europe, 1945–1952," *Journal of Peace Research* 23 (3), September 1986, Sage Publications, Ltd. www.jstor.org/stable/.

MacLeod, Calum, and Paul Wiseman. "Economy Rocks China Factories," *USA Today,* October 21, 2008. www.usatoday.com/money/world/2008-10-21-wred-dragon-china-factories-economy_N.htm?loc=interstitialskip (accessed June 2009).

Maloney, C. J. "1819: America's First Housing Bubble," *Ludwig von Mises Institute.* http://mises.org/story/3395 (accessed May 2009).

Navsarjan Organisation. "Who Are Dalits?" www.navsarjan.org/navsarjan/dalits/whoaredalits (accessed July 2009).

The Plunge Protection Team Blog. http://plungeprotectionteam.com (accessed June 2009).

RIMES Technologies, Global Economic Data. www.rimes.com/ (accessed July 2009).

Rockwell, Llewellyn H. "The Dollar Crisis." www.lewrockwell.com/rockwell/reading-dollar-crisis.html (accessed July 2009).

Russiaprofile.org. "Who's Who?" www.russiaprofile.org/resources/whoiswho/alphabet/m/medvedev.wbp (accessed July 2009).

Sabin, Greg. "Nightmare on Wall Street: 4 Other Times Our Economy Tanked." *Mental Floss* magazine, January/February, 2009. http://mentalfloss.com (accessed June 2009).

Scheuttinger, Robert L., and Eamonn F. Butler. "Wage and Price Controls in the Ancient World," *Ludwig von Mises Institute.* http://mises.org/story/3346 (accessed May 2009).

Siegel, Jeremy. "The Future for Investors: Why the Tried and True Triumph Over the Bold and New," Cocktail Hour Paper, 2005. bear.cba.ufl.edu/karceski/FIN7447/ch%20papers/Brian%20Wika%20paper%20JeremySiegal.pdf (accessed May 2009).

Swanson, Tim. "Long on China, Short on the United States," *Ludwig von Mises Institute.* http://mises.org/story/3293 (accessed June 2009).

Tradingrecipes.com. "How Fixed-Fractional Sizing Works." www.tradingrecipes.com/files/pw.pdf (accessed June 2009).

Yahoo.com. "China Challenges U.S. Global Financial Leadership"; "China Monthly Auto Sales Climb"; and "China Sees Signs of Economic Recovery." http://finance.yahoo.com/news/ (accessed June-July 2009).

GOVERNMENT SOURCES

Bureau of Economic Analysis, U.S. Department of Commerce: www.bea.gov.
Bureau of Labor Statistics, U.S. Department of Labor: www.bls.gov.
Central Intelligence Agency: www.cia.gov.
Congressional Budget Office: www.cbo.gov.
Energy Information Administration, U.S. Department of Energy: www.eia.doe.gov/.
European Commission, Committee on Economic and Financial Affairs: http://ec.europa.eu/economy_finance/index_en.htm.

Federal Deposit Insurance Corporation (FDIC): www.fdic.gov.

Federal Reserve: www.federalreserve.gov.

Federal Open Market Committee, Board of Governors of the Federal Reserve System: www.federalreserve.gov/monetarypolicy/fomc.htm.

House Financial Services Committee, U.S. House of Representatives: http://financialservices.house.gov.

International Trade Administration, U.S. Department of Commerce: www.ita.doc.gov.

National Bureau of Statistics—China: www.stats.gov.cn/enGliSH.

National Intelligence, Office of the Director: www.dni.gov/.

National Intelligence Council (NIC): www.dni.gov/nic/NIC_home.html.

North Atlantic Treaty Organization (NATO): www.nato.int/cps/en/natolive/index.htm.

Senate Committee on Banking, Housing and Urban Affairs, U.S. Senate: http://banking.senate.gov.

U.S. Census Bureau: www.census.gov.

U.S. China Economic and Security Review Commission: www.uscc.gov.

U.S. Department of State: www.state.gov.

U.S. Department of the Treasury: www.ustreas.gov.

U.S. International Trade Commission: www.usitc.gov.

U.S. Trade Representative, Office of the: www.ustr.gov.

White House Office of Management and Budget (OMB), *Budget of the United States Government*, FY2008, Historical Tables, GDP Growth, 1940–2005, 192–194.

World Bank: http://worldbank.org.

World Economic Forum (under the supervision of the Swiss Federal Government): www.weforum.org.

ORGANIZATIONS, FOUNDATIONS, UNIVERSITY, AND THINK TANK SOURCES

ABAcUS, China Economic Statistics from Official Sources. http://chinese-school.netfirms.com/China-economic-statistics-2.html (accessed June-July 2009).

The Brookings Institute: www.brookings.edu.

Council on Foreign Relations: www.cfr.org.

Depository Trust and Clearing Corporation: http://dtcc.com.

Economic History Services (in conjunction with the Economic History Association, the Business History Conference, the Cliometric Society, the Economic History Society, and the History of Economics Society): http://eh.net.

Economic Policy Institute: www.epi.org.

Encyclopaedia Britannica: www.britannica.com.

The Heritage Foundation: www.heritage.org.

The History of Economic Thought, Department of Economics of the New School of Social Research: http://homepage.newschool.edu/het.

The Hoover Institution, Stanford University: www.hoover.org/research/factsonpolicy/facts/41184372.html.

Institute for Policy Initiative: www.ipi.org.

International Economics Study Center, George Washington University: http://internationalecon.com.

International Swaps and Derivatives Association, Inc.: www.isda.org.

National Bureau of Economic Research: www.nber.org.

National Retail Federation: www.nrf.com.

Organization for Economic Co-Operation and Development (OECD): www.oecd.org.

Peterson Institute for International Economics: www.petersoninstitute.org.

Reason Foundation: http://reason.org/news/show/127595.html.

Recessionhistory.Com: http://recessionhistory.com/.

San Jose State University, Department of Economics: www.sjsu.edu.

Securities Industry and Financial Markets Association: http://sifma.org.

STRATFOR Global Intelligence: www.stratfor.com.

University of Sydney (Australia), Economic Statistics Library: www.library.usyd.edu.au/subjects/economics/statsinternet.html.

WEB SITES

Barron's: www.barrons.com.

The Big Picture (Barry L. Ritholtz blog): www.ritholtz.com/blog.

Bloomberg: www.bloomberg.com.

British Broadcasting Corporation (BBC): www.bbc.co.uk.

BusinessWeek: www.businessweek.com.

Cable News Network (CNN): www.cnn.com.

Central European Economics Watch (Michal Lehuta blog): http://ce-economics.blogspot.com.

Eastern Europe Economy Watch (Edward Hughes blog): http://easterneuropeeconomy.blogspot.com.

The Economist (China stories and statistics): www.economist.com/countries/china.

Financial Trend Forecaster: http://fintrend.com/ftf.

Financial Times: www.ft.com.

Financial Web Independent Financial Portal: www.finweb.com/.

A Fistful of Euros Webzine: fistfulofeuros.net.

Forbes: www.forbes.com.

Historyorb.com: www.historyorb.com/economic.

Huffington Post: www.huffingtonpost.com.

Ikeda Center: www.ikedacenter.org.

Inflationdata.com (part of Financial Trend Forecaster): http://inflationdata.com/
    Inflation/default.asp.

Investopedia.com (partner of AOL Money and Finance): www.investopedia.com.

Kabbalah Today: www.kabtoday.com

Mahalo, Asian and Chinese Economic Statistics. www.mahalo.com/china-economy
    (accessed June–July 2009).

Moody's Dismal Scientist: www.economy.com/dismal.

Microsoft/National Broadcasting Corporation (MSNBC): www.msnbc.com.

Mish's Global Economic Trend Analysis (Mike Shedlock blog): http://global
    economicanalysis.blogspot.com.

National Public Radio: www.npr.org.

New York magazine: http://nymag.com.

The New York Times: www.nytimes.com.

The New Yorker: www.newyorker.com.

Public Broadcasting System (PBS): www.pbs.org.

Stock Psychology: http://stockology.blogspot.com.

This American Life, Chicago Public Radio: www.thisamericanlife.org.

Time magazine: www.time.com.

U.S. Inflation Calculator: www.usinflationcalculator.com.

U.S. Misery Index: www.miseryindex.us/.

U.S. News & World Report: www.usnews.com.

Vanity Fair: www.vanityfair.com.

The Wall Street Journal: http://online.wsj.com.

Washington Post: www.washingtonpost.com.

The Zeleza Post: www.zeleza.com.

ABOUT THE AUTHOR

Regarded as one of the world's leading experts on global investing, Keith Fitz-Gerald is a seasoned market analyst known for his uncanny accuracy, perspective, and insight. As Investment Director of Money Map Press, Keith helps more than 500,000 subscribers a day in 30 countries successfully capture profits, generate income, and weather the ongoing financial storm despite extremely challenging market conditions.

A former professional trader and licensed CTA, Keith began his career at Wilshire Associates, one of the world's premier financial consulting firms. In the years since, he has provided investment analysis, commentary, and recommendations to institutions and qualified individual clients representing billions in assets.

Keith is a prominent and highly sought-after speaker at financial conferences around the world. A frequent traveler who believes there is no substitute for experience when it comes to identifying opportunities, Keith recently completed his latest investing tour of China, which forms the basis for many of the recommendations featured in this book.

Keith and his wife, Noriko, and their boys split their time between homes in the United States and Japan.

INDEX

consumer spending in, 140
country investment selection, 231
currency-exchange agreements, 46, 150, 152, 313
domestic consumption, 146
economic dominance, 143
economic growth, 128, 143
economic stimulus, 145
economy, 139–140
energy expansion, 146
exports, 137, 141
export strength, 141–142
foreign currency reserves, 148
global investing strategy, 212
growth in, 224
Haier Group, Inc., 146
impact of regional influences, 90
international swap agreements, 46, 150, 154
Internet usage, 146
labor costs, 144
leading recovery, 173
lending boom, 145
Lenovo Group, 146
luxury demand, 145
market capitalization, 226
mergers and acquisitions (M&A), 146
myths regarding, 138–142
national growth, 225
paper money, 148
People's Bank of China, 145
per-capita income growth, 231
pollution controls, 147
potential, 138–139, 155
railway investment, 244

regulatory controls, 140–141
reserve position, 152
resource investment strategy, 227
retail sales, 141
road investment, 244
savings rate, 144
Shenzhen 100 Index, 280
state investment cycles, 142
world currency, 147–155
Yingli Green Energy Corp., 286
yuan value, 127
yuan vs. U.S. dollar, 147
China Daily, 154
Chinese retail sales, 243
Chinese share values, 225
Chrysler, 85, 104
Chuppies, 141, 243
Circuit breakers, 104
Cisneros, Henry, 67
Citigroup, 271
Civilian Conservation Corps, 103
Civil War, 16–17, 96
Clinton, Bill, 29, 77
Cold War, 25, 27, 47
Colonial development, 13
Columbus, Christopher, 12
Commodity money, 46
Commodity prices, 182–184, 208, 220, 241
Communist government, 213
Community Reinvestment Act of 1977, 66
Company stock plans, 199
Concentration, 194–195
Concentration vs. diversification, 2
Congressional actions, 112, 121

If you agree with the position I lay out in this book, there's no better way to act than by using the advice in this report to help you recover what you've lost and get ahead in the new global economy. We feel so strongly about this that we're willing to throw in six investment opportunities of a lifetime—all of which could help double your net worth in the years ahead.

But, please act fast—this offer is limited to the first 2,000 readers who inquire. To grab your exclusive copy of this report, simply visit www.fiscalhangover.com.

Sincerely,

Keith Fitz-Gerald
Fiscal Hangover
www.fiscalhangover.com

P.S. Learn how to profit in the aftermath of the greatest financial crisis in generations—and get your free copy of "How to Play the $300 Trillion Recovery." Visit www.fiscalhangover.com now to get your copy—before it's gone!